BEING MUSLIM

Being Muslim

A Cultural History of
Women of Color in
American Islam

Sylvia Chan-Malik

NEW YORK UNIVERSITY PRESS
New York

NEW YORK UNIVERSITY PRESS
New York
www.nyupress.org

References to Internet websites (URLs) were accurate at the time of writing. Neither the author nor New York University Press is responsible for URLs that may have expired or changed since the manuscript was prepared.

Library of Congress Cataloging-in-Publication Data
Names: Chan-Malik, Sylvia, author.
Title: Being Muslim : a cultural history of women of color in American Islam /
Sylvia Chan-Malik.
Description: New York : New York University Press, 2018. |
Includes bibliographical references and index.
Identifiers: LCCN 2017044860| ISBN 9781479850600 (cl : alk. paper) |
ISBN 9781479823420 (pb : alk. paper)
Subjects: LCSH: Muslim women—United States. | African American women. |
Muslims, Black.
Classification: LCC HQ1170 .C486 2018 | DDC 305.48/697—dc23
LC record available at https://lccn.loc.gov/2017044860

New York University Press books are printed on acid-free paper, and their binding materials are chosen for strength and durability. We strive to use environmentally responsible suppliers and materials to the greatest extent possible in publishing our books.

Manufactured in the United States of America

10 9 8 7 6 5 4 3 2 1

Also available as an ebook

For my daughters and Badi

CONTENTS

Introduction

Being Muslim Women

This is a book about being Muslim. More precisely, this is a book about how women of color, primarily within, but not limited to, the United States, have crafted modes of Muslim being and practice that constitute critical histories of Islamic life and culture in the twentieth- and twenty-first-century United States. At the same time, this is a book about how women of color have continually shaped Islam's presence in the nation's racial and gendered imaginaries during this time and how women and issues of race and gender are essential to understanding Islam's cultural meanings in the United States. Stated another way, *Being Muslim* is an exploration of women—primarily Black, but also Asian, Arab, Latino, African diasporic, white, and multiracial—producing Muslimness as a way of racial, gendered, and religious being—for example, as both "American" and "global" subjects, as U.S. Muslims, and as part of the *ummah*, the global community of believers. This book is also an investigation of Islam's significant historical-cultural presence in the twentieth- and twenty-first-century United States as a religion, political ideology, and racial marker, with a focus on how this has been produced and signified by women.

A series of questions drives its inquiry: How do we tell a story of Islam in the United States that foregrounds the lives, labors, presence, and perspectives of women of color throughout the twentieth and twenty-first centuries? How does a focus on women of color produce alternative narratives of Muslim life and Islam's historical presence in the United States? How have Black women shaped histories of American Islam, and what are the legacies of their labors? What is the role of race in the formation of U.S. Muslim women's religious practices and cultural expression, and how have desires for agency and discourses of feminism influenced U.S. Muslim women's lives? How have Muslim women in the

1

United States engaged questions of social justice and struggles for free-dom through Islam? How do race and gender shape modes of religious practice and identity construction? Finally, is it possible—or for that matter, necessary—to articulate a collective experience of *being Muslim women* in America across time, space, and racial difference? If so, what does this experience tell us? And what is at stake in its telling?

In its response to these queries, *Being Muslim: A Cultural History of Women of Color in American Islam* presents a series of previously un-told or underexplored narratives that explore U.S. Muslim women's lives, subjectivities, representations, and voices during the last century. In the existing literature on American Islam, men's voices and perspec-tives dominate. Further, in the handful of texts addressing U.S. Muslim women's issues, there is generally a separation between the stories of Black American and non-Black American Muslim women, who are pri-marily Arab and South Asian American, although not at all exclusively.[1] As a result of such divisions, a number of texts on U.S. Muslim women, perhaps inadvertently, privilege the stories of non-Black Muslim women of Arab and South Asian backgrounds and relay U.S. Muslim subject formation as a process of immigrant Muslims "becoming American."[2] Such language enacts an erasure of the lives and representations of Black Muslim women (who are already American) and generally rel-egates their experiences to a separate chapter or section, as opposed to situating them as a central component of Islam's historical narrative in the United States. In addition, "becoming American" also marginalizes the experiences of many Latina and white female converts, who are also already American.

In *Being Muslim*, I instead place these varied narratives on a histori-cal continuum and argue that a desire for gender justice as expressed and conceived of by women of color has continually impelled and in-formed the construction of U.S. Muslim women's lives. While a num-ber of scholars have noted Islam's affiliations with movements of Black liberation, antiracism, and anti-imperialism in the United States,[3] few have contextualized Islam in relation to women's participation in these movements or through desires for gendered agency and freedom as ex-pressed by women of color. Indeed, if as Kimberlé Crenshaw has writ-ten, "the experiences of women of color are frequently the product of intersecting patterns of racism and sexism," and "these experiences tend not to be represented within the discourses of either feminism or antiracism," this book suggests that Muslim women in the United States have historically mobilized their engagements with Islam and articulated ways of being Muslim as simultaneous correctives to patterns of racism and sexism specifically directed at women of color.[4] *Being Muslim* seeks to demonstrate how women's ways of being Muslim and practicing Islam have continually functioned as a rejoinder and critique of the intersecting politics of race, gender, sexuality, class, and religion. By doing so, it reveals how "Black feminism," "womanism," and "woman of color feminism"—terms I explore more fully toward the close of this introduction—constitute integral components not only in approaching U.S. Muslim women's narratives and representations but also in fully narrating the twentieth- and twenty-first-century story of Islam in the United States. Their histories and meanings also gesture toward how organic forms of "Islamic feminism" and "Muslim feminism"—terms I explore at the close of this introduction and at length in chapter 5—are emerging in the contemporary United States.

Although a great deal of this book's focus is on the experiences and representations of Black American Muslim women, *Being Muslim* refuses balkanizing logics that might lead some to call this a book about only "Black American Muslim women," as opposed to "U.S. Muslim women." Indeed, I devote much of my focus here—the first three chapters, to be precise—to investigations of Black American Muslim women's lives owing to the realities of the historical record; prior to the 1960s, almost all U.S. Muslim women who appeared in the press or popular culture were African American. Thus, any historically accurate account of American Islam and U.S. culture must necessarily make central the lives and experiences of Black American Muslims—and in this case, Black American Muslim women—as their contributions have forcefully shaped the meanings and presence of Islam in the United Stated. Instead of stories of Muslims "becoming American," I suggest that narratives of being Muslim in America are far more flexible (and less exclusionary) in how they are applicable to approaching all U.S. Muslim women's subjectivities across racial and ethnic categories—and I detail the contexts and processes that women have historically and culturally configured their identities and practices as U.S. Muslims. Whether one is a third-generation Black American Muslim, a recent immigrant from Pakistan, a Mexican American convert, or a Syrian refugee, posing the question of how to be a Muslim woman in the United States offers insights, I suggest, into how Muslim-ness is produced and sustained against white, Christian social and cultural norms, as well as allowing us to see how Islamic identities and practices have evolved in relation to the shifting political exigencies of out times. As such, *Being Muslim* brings together a series of explorations of U.S. Muslim women's lives that begins with stories of Black American women and their engagements with Islam as a spiritually embodied practice of social protest. This book moves on a story of the encounter between "Islam" and "feminism" in the media during the late twentieth century, as signified through the bodies of "Middle Eastern," white, and Black American women, and it closes with a look into how women of color feminism and womanism shape expressions of "Islamic feminism" in the lives of contemporary U.S. Muslim women across racial, class, generational, and regional lines. Because I suggest that the legacies of early twentieth-century Muslim women, such as those featured in the first three chapters, shape present-day formations of being Muslim, the book proceeds chronologically, to show how being Muslim in the United States is an iterative and reiterative practice that arises out of racial and gendered structures of feelings within the domestic United States, as well as through the diverse transnational locales and diasporic cultural spaces that constitute U.S. American Islam.

Throughout the volume, I argue that a central component of Islam's presence in the United States is its enduring presence and significance as a Black protest religion and expression of Black cultural power.[5] Islam's legacy of Black protest, the book demonstrates, is critical to approaching the study of women, gender, and American Islam, as well as the collective subjectivities of U.S. Muslim women. This argument does not seek to marginalize or displace the experiences of non-Black Muslim women in the United States, nor does it ignore the transnational formation of U.S. Muslim women's subjectivities and the networks of culture, religious knowledge, economics, and labor that inform their lives. Indeed, blackness itself is always diasporic and cannot be viewed as merely "domestic"; it is also always part of larger Pan-African formations and consciousness. Instead, *Being Muslim* demonstrates how Islam's ideological and material presence as a minority religion in the United States is ineluctably linked to histories of blackness and Black people and culture in ways that did not simply disappear after the large-scale arrival of Muslim immigrants from South Asia and the Middle East to America after the passage of the Hart-Cellar Immigration Act in 1965 (which lifted restrictive immigration quotas) or because "Islam" has become conflated with foreign "terror" in contemporary political discourse. In addition, the last two decades have seen a sharp increase in the number of African Muslim immigrants in the United States, who have their own complex relationship with blackness and Black American Islam.[6] While I do not explore the nuances of Black American versus African immigrant Islamic practices in the United States, I am aware that this is a rich site of exploration, which deserves further investigation. Yet, as I consider in this volume, the nation overwhelmingly came to know, think about, and discuss "Islam" and "Muslims" in relation to, and in the context of, Black American people and culture for most of the twentieth century (and indeed, even long before then), a discourse that merged and overlapped with orientalized notions of Islam and the Middle East.

Thus I suggest that Islam's "blackness" in the United States—which dates back to earliest days of chattel slavery but which this book examines most closely from the early twentieth century to the present—continually informs the construction and evolution of contemporary U.S. Muslim identity, politics, and culture in both implicit and explicit ways, as well as in how Islam is discussed and how Muslims are racialized within the national imaginary.[7] For this reason, *Being Muslim* asserts that the lives of Black American Muslim women across the last century present paradigmatic experiences of U.S. Muslim life, insofar as they demonstrate how ways of being Muslim and practicing Islam have consistently been forged *against* commonsense notions of racial, gendered, and religious belonging and citizenship and require constant attention to, and cultivation of, embodied practices that are articulated *against* accepted social and cultural norms. Their experiences also reflect how the blackness of American Islam—that is, Islam's historical and cultural presence in the Unites States as emanating from Black American communities and culture—constitutes a set of racial, religious conditions with which non-Black Muslims must always engage and reckon with, even if this reckoning is characterized by disavowal. It is this continual *againstness*—which this book calls "affective insurgency"—at the scale of the body, one's community, the nation, and the *ummah* that I argue is a central hallmark of U.S. Muslim women's lives.

"WE ARE MUSLIM WOMEN"

In the early 1970s, the poet, activist, and intellectual Sonia Sanchez composed a series of Muslim poems. One of the leading voices of the Black Arts movement and certainly one of its most prominent female writers, Sanchez joined the Nation of Islam (NOI) in 1972 and remained a member through 1975. During these years, Sanchez, using the name Sister Sonia X Sanchez, wrote prolifically about her experiences of being a Black Muslim woman engaged in the organization's political, cultural, and spiritual project of Black nationalism and self-determination. When interviewed in 1989 for the documentary *Eyes on the Prize*, Sanchez said she was initially drawn to the Nation because it represented "this sense of what it meant to be an African American woman or man . . . this sense of support for Blackness." She continued on to say that "it [the NOI] was the strongest organization in America. . . . I had twin sons and I took them into the Nation, in a sense, I think, for probably protection. There was a real atmosphere of strength in the Nation." She also described its appeal for Black people who were just becoming "receptive" to their own blackness, to Black women who were coming into recognition of their own beauty and power. The NOI told Black women, Sanchez continued, "Yes, I respect your Blackness. I say you are a Black women, and you're beautiful and you're queen of the universe."[8]

It is important to note that Sanchez became a Muslim following the assassination of the NOI's most famous member, Malcolm X, in 1965—a man she had considered a friend and comrade—and in spite the controversy around the role of the NOI in Malcolm's death. The historian Ula Taylor has posed the question, Why anyone would join the NOI in the 1970s, following Malcolm's murder? In response, Taylor argues that "the religious nature of the Nation of Islam was not the major impetus for new membership" during that period, that it was instead the NOI's "secular programs, promising power and wealth, [which] were the key to its expansion."[9] In some regards, this was true for Sanchez. Her words demonstrate her attraction to the NOI's institutional structure and reveal how she saw the group as the strongest, most effective, and most

Figure I.1. Cover of the January 1974 issue of *Black World* magazine, featuring Sonia Sanchez.

viable group through which to achieve Black self-determination while also finding safety and protection for herself and her sons from the dangers of white supremacy.

Yet while such "secular" programs may have drawn Sanchez into the NOI, her poetry from those years is decidedly "religious" in content and tone, specifically in the how it employs Islamic terms and affirms God's centrality in the construction of Black NOI Muslim women's identities. In 1973, Sanchez published the poem "We Are Muslim Women," which first appeared in *Black World* magazine's January 1974 issue and was later published as part of Sanchez's poetry collection *A Blues Book for Blue Black Magical Women*, which she dedicated to her father, Wilson Driver, and her "spiritual father," NOI leader, the Honorable Elijah Muhammad.[10] Written the year after Sanchez joined the NOI, the poem is an unflinching declaration of Black Muslim womanhood, an avowal of black women's beauty and power, and an expression of devotion to God. In it, she interweaves being Muslim with women's self-determination and establishes "Islam" as a spiritual landscape and vehicle for Black women's liberation. The poem opens:

> WE ARE MUSLIM WOMEN
> wearing the garments of the righteous
> recipients of eternal wisdom
> followers of a Divine man and Message
> listen to us
> as we move thru the eye of time
> rustling with loveliness
> listen to our wisdom
> as we talk in the Temple of our Souls.

In this stanza, we immediately notice the embodied and metaphysical nature of Black Muslim womanhood. Muslim women wear specific "garments"—such as head coverings and modest robes—in order to express their spiritual devotion to "a Divine man and Message," the Honorable Elijah Muhammad and the message of Islam. Sanchez portrays "Muslim women" as righteous and wise and as key figures who transcend temporality, "mov[ing] thru the eye of time" in order to connect Black people to their future liberation. She also affirms their "loveliness" as Muslim women, gesturing toward the admiration Black women are supposedly due in Islam, and establishes women's knowledge and being as a space of worship, that is, a "Temple of our Souls."

Across the poem's five stanzas, Sanchez continually announces "WE ARE MUSLIM WOMEN" as a repeating refrain and intones "MUSLIM" as the signifier and expression of her—and other Black women's—embrace of blackness through Islam. To be a Muslim woman is to be exalted and to have a direct relationship with God, which is directly addressed in stanza 3:

> WE ARE MUSLIM WOMEN
> dwellers in light
> new women created from the limbs of Allah.
> We are the shining ones
> coming from dark ruins
> created from the eye of Allah:
> And we speak only what we know
> And we do not curse God
> And we keep our minds open to light
> And we do not curse God
> And we chant Alhamdullilah
> And we do not curse God
> WE ARE MUSLIM WOMEN

Here, Sanchez writes Black women into the creation myth. Infused with Islamic imagery, this section employs an anthropomorphization of Allah as a being with "limbs" and "eyes" to render "Muslim women" as the corporeal descendants of the divine—"created from the limbs of Allah"—a characterization that subverts Christian teachings that say women are made from Adam's rib. She names Islam as the state of being and political force in which Black people may "speak only what we know," as opposed to trumpeting what they now recognize as the lies and hypocrisies of white America, specifically in regard to Black inferiority. Full and shining Black female personhood emerges out of the poem's proclamation of Muslim-ness. This is not an individualized Muslim-ness: In her usage of the plural pronoun "WE," Sanchez emphasizes the collective nature of being Muslim as Black women, engaged together in a moral, cultural, political, and spiritual endeavor for which, she states at poem's end, "the earth sings our gladness."

In its collective expression of Muslim womanhood, Sanchez's poem ultimately articulates "Islam" as a set of racial, religious, and gendered *affective* practices of Black liberation for Black women. Such practices are expressed, not as solely political or secular acts, but as a set of unified moral practices ("we do not curse God"), religious rituals ("We chant Alhamdullilah"), and collective identity formation (the repetition of "WE ARE MUSLIM WOMEN"). The Muslim-ness the poem demonstrates—its feelings, its practices, its desires—is a type of being produced in the racial and gendered contexts and against which it is articulated. Spoken through poetry, Sanchez's proclamation of Muslim women's identity is legible because it announces Muslim-ness *against* the realities of physical and sexual violence directed at Black women; *against* notions of Black women as ugly, inferior, unwanted; *against* the sexism and misogyny of the church and patriarchal interpretations of biblical scripture; and *against* the degradation and subjection of blackness and Black people. Muslim-ness "shines" and Black Muslim women "dwell in light" because of the darkness of the racist and sexist logics against which Islam refracts itself through the bodies, voices, and actions of Black Muslim women. To put it another way, in Sanchez's poem, being Muslim is not only a set of proscribed religious practices but a state of *insurgent* being, in which the embodiment of Muslim womanhood itself is a form of unruly and rebellious expression against social, cultural, and political norms of race, gender, and religion. In the early 1970s, the proclamation of Muslim womanhood in Sanchez's poem announced itself against anti-Black racism, misogyny against Black women, and racist and sexist interpretations of Christian doctrine. Being Muslim, as expressed in "WE ARE MUSLIM WOMEN," is an insurgent ethical, political, and religious framework in which "Islam" facilitates holistic practices of Black women's liberation and spiritual awakening.

Sanchez was a member of the Nation of Islam for only three years. Although she would cite the group's patriarchal tendencies and the stifling of women's creativity as her reasons for leaving in 1975, Sanchez clearly and unequivocally declared her identity as a Muslim woman both in her poetry and public appearances (as seen in her photo on the cover of *Black World* magazine) during that time. Thus her words and presence indelibly shape the cultural history of women of color and American Islam and demonstrate how states of being Muslim—of being Muslim women, to be precise—in the United States arise at particular moments in history in response to and against specific racial and gendered iterations of Islam in U.S. culture. Such iterations do not disappear or dissolve in the face of shifting political contexts, I argue, but are negotiated and navigated through in future iterations of U.S. Muslim women's identities.

In 2015 Duke University student Nourhan Elsayed offered another expression of U.S. Muslim women's identity formation that reveals its affective nature and the continual racial and gendered insurgency that marks its formation. In an essay titled "Feeling Muslim," published in the *Chronicle* (Duke's student newspaper) on February 16, 2015, Elsayed describes her feelings walking across her college campus as a young, Egyptian American Muslim woman who wears the headscarf. "Before college," her essay begins, "I never felt Muslim." Once there, however, she becomes painfully aware of her Muslim-ness, especially in light of certain events that took place between 2013 and 2015. Of this awareness, she writes:

> When the Boston marathon bombings occurred—I felt Muslim. I felt what it meant to walk into a store and have 10 years of inaccurate media fueled hate projected on to my body by someone who knew nothing of me. When the *adhan* was going to be announced from the Chapel, I felt Muslim. When people's comments about my faith were wrought with a brand of animosity I still wish I didn't know existed so close to home, when people threatened to hurt Muslim students on this campus, I felt Muslim. . . . In post-9/11 mainstream America, to be Muslim is to be the bearer of evil.[11]

In referencing the Boston marathon bombings of 2013, the January 2015 controversy on the Duke campus regarding the calling of the *adhan* (Islamic call to prayer),[12] media coverage of Islam and Muslims, and threats to Muslim students at Duke and beyond, Elsayed articulates feeling Muslim as a type of fraught, ontological response, in which her sense of being is determined by a constant awareness of how her presence connotes distorted conceptions of Islam and Muslims.

This feeling is further heightened because Elsayed's essay was written as a response to the murders of three U.S. Muslim university students—Deah Barakat, Yusor Abu-Salah, and Razan Abu-Salah—the week prior. On February 10, 2015, at approximately 5:11 P.M., a forty-six-year-old white man named Craig Stephen Hicks murdered Deah, Yusor, and Razan execution style in their home in a condominium complex in Chapel Hill, North Carolina. Deah and his wife Yusor were dentistry graduate students at the University of North Carolina, and Razan, Yusor's younger sister, was a first-year student at North Carolina State University's College of Design. All were of Palestinian descent.[13] The two young women, Yusor and her younger sister Razan, like Elsayed, wore headscarves. Police reports later confirmed that all three—Deah at age 23, Yusor at 21, and Razan at 19—had died from gunshot wounds to the back of the head. Hicks, also a resident in the same complex, confessed to the murders, and news soon emerged that he was an unemployed gun enthusiast and atheist who had actively disdained religion on social media, particularly Islam. Many in the Muslim community in North Carolina viewed the murders as an anti-Muslim hate crime, and the killings sent shock waves through American Muslim communities as an example of an ever-rising tide of anti-Muslim sentiment across the country.[14]

Against these events and a tide of larger anti-Muslim sentiment in the United States and Europe, Elsayed closes the essay with the prayer that "feeling Muslim [doesn't] mean fearing for your life."[15] Beyond her religious practices or cultural affiliations, she has come to feel Muslim through the experience of knowing she is a trope of terrorism, of being aware that her body conjures notions of violent jihadists, suicide bombers, and oppressed women. Her essay reveals how feeling Muslim is to move through the world with the knowledge that both your body *and* your religious beliefs—the misperceptions of your internal and external states—rouse fear, loathing, and violence in others. Yet though she inspires fear, it is, in fact Elsayed, as a Muslim woman, who expresses fear that she is not safe, who fears she is vulnerable to attack, and who must always be on guard. Unlike the years before college, Elsayed may no longer forget that she is Muslim, that she wears a headscarf, that feeling Muslim means she is constantly fearful of threats to her safety and well-being. She is now ineluctably aware—and thus must carry in her body—what people think of her faith in constructing her own racial, gendered, and religious being in America. Some solace comes, however, as she stands "side by side in the crowd of over 5,000 people asking God to grant mercy" at a candlelight vigil for Yusor, Razan, and Deah—a space in which she finds temporary respite from her fears.[16]

In contrast to Sanchez's poem, Elsayed's essay articulates "Muslim-ness" against the ongoing logics of the War on Terror and its effects on U.S. racial politics. A decade and a half after President George W. Bush introduced the term to the U.S. public as formal set of state military and securitization strategies in response to the 9/11 attacks, "terror" has become a normalized presence in American life, which has sutured Islam and Muslims to notions of terrorist threat and anti-Americanism. Elsayed also voices her Muslim-ness against the demographic shifts of U.S. Muslim communities in the decades since the publication of San-chez's poem. Whereas in 1974 the majority of Muslims within the United States were still African American (whether part of the Nation of Islam or other Islamic organizations), by 2015 immigration from South Asia, the Middle East, and North Africa in the ensuing decades had trans-formed Islam's domestic presence, with Black Muslims by then making up approximately one-fourth to one-third of the U.S. Muslim com-munity, South Asians one-fourth, and those from the Middle East and North Africa one-third.[17] Alongside these demographic shifts, changing geopolitical and economic relations between the United States and the Middle East around issues of oil production and supply in the 1970s and 1980s, and then subsequent American wars in Iraq and Afghanistan, profoundly influenced cultural discourses around Islam and Muslims and normalized "Muslim" and "Arab" as interchangeable terms in the na-tional lexicon. As such, in the almost fifty years between the publication of Sanchez's poem and Elsayed's essay, the nature of being Muslim in the United States had been reshaped and recontextualized by the changing nature of domestic racial politics, racial and ethnic demographics of U.S. Muslim communities, and projects of U.S. militarism and empire in the Middle East.

Yet despite these shifts, Elsayed is engaged in Muslim-ness as a state of insurgent being against hegemonic norms of race, gender, and reli-gion in America. In 2015, Elsayed's experience of being Muslim is forged vis-à-vis orientalist constructions of Islam as a signifier of foreignness and terrorism, as well as against ongoing logics of white and Christian supremacy that produce U.S. Muslims as lesser citizens. Like Sister Sonia Sanchez before her, Elsayed incorporates the charged political nature of Islam and being Muslim in the nation's cultural imaginary into her processes of identity formation as a U.S. Muslim woman. Unlike being Muslim in Sanchez's poem, however, Elsayed's Muslim-ness in 2015 is not a pronouncement of political or spiritual empowerment, nor is it a means to reject the violence and dehumanization of racism; instead, it is a grappling with her existence as its constant projection. For Nourhan Elsayed, fifteen years after the start of the War on Terror, in the face of the demographic shifts within U.S. Muslim communities and in U.S.-Middle East relations, and following the horrific murder of three young U.S. Muslims in Chapel Hill, North Carolina, being Muslim is to feel profoundly unsafe because of one's Muslim-ness while seeking solace or refuge in her Islamic beliefs and practices. Thus, whereas Sonia Sanchez and other Black women embraced Islam as space of safety and sanctuary from anti-Black racism and sexual violence, young women like Elsayed struggle with whether to even express their Muslim identity in public spaces for fear of recrimination while navigating how to practice Islam as a faith while confronting "Islam" as a racialized and pathologized trope of terror. Yet in both instances—whether in the embrace of "Islam" and Muslim womanhood as an ethos of Black liberation and protection, or in the awareness of "Islam" and Muslim womanhood as signifiers of terrorism and thus catalysts for racial-religious hatred directed at Muslims—being a Muslim woman in the United States is always a deeply political and politicized process, in which women must continually create themselves as Muslims against the fraught intersections of race, gender, Islam, and the nation that circumscribe their lives.

In *Being Muslim*, I want to suggest that ways of being Muslim constructed by Black American Muslim women like Sister Sonia X Sanchez (and many others before her) operate as a historical index for the lives of women such as Nourhan Elsayed, who are part of a racially and ethnically heterogeneous generation of U.S. Muslim women made up not only of Black, Arab, and South Asian Americans but also of large numbers of Latino, white, and multiracial Muslims. Through the stories of women in the Nation of Islam, of Black women in the Ahmadiyya Movement in Islam, and of public figures like Betty Shabazz and the jazz singer Dakota Staton, I reveal ways of being Muslim in the United States that are steeped in the broader struggles of women of color in the United States while also intersecting with other domestic and transnational struggles of Muslim women worldwide. In linking their experiences, I seek to show how the "hate" directed at Muslims in the United States should be framed not only through logics of orientalism and xenophobia but also through the historical legacies and contemporary expressions of anti-blackness, misogyny, sexual violence, and the acknowledgment of the United States as an imperial settler colonial nation. At the same time, I want to show how women's ways of being Muslim in the United States, while seemingly partitioned by race and class, share common characteristics with how Islam signals a type of ontological response to notions of race and gender in the political realm. To understand anti-Muslim racism in the contemporary United States requires careful attention to the complex and multiple meanings Islam has historically held in our national imaginary, as well to the multifaceted ways race, gender, and class have produced Muslim-ness in the United States. As such, the stories of Black American Muslim women like Sanchez and others demonstrate how Islam has been historically mobilized by women of color to counteract the dehumanizing logics of racism and sexism and how being Muslim has been enacted and reenacted by women of color as a type of political, cultural, and spiritual ontology against white supremacy, gendered violence, and state terror.

American Islam as Lived Religion and Racial-Religious Form

To understand varied formations and expressions of being Muslim as expressed by women such as Sonia Sanchez, Nourhan Elsayed, and others, this book approaches Islam in the United States as a "lived religion" and "racial-religious form," paying careful attention to how gender informs understandings of each term, as well as how Islam has historically functioned at times as a signifier of political ideology. The encounter between Islam as lived religion and racial form in the United States, I argue, produces Muslim women's being as a continual process of "affective insurgency," a concept I have already mentioned. By "affective insurgency," I refer to the multiscalar, diffuse, and ever-shifting forms of againstness that this book argues are the hallmark of U.S. Muslim women's lives. As I will discuss, this againstness is not, nor has ever been, directed at a singular target; instead, it is a set of affective responses that emerge out of the ways Islam is consistently lived insurgently by women, responses that arise out of the ways U.S. Muslim women engage, navigate, and counter the ways Islam is imagined as an unruly and insurgent political presence at various moments in history.[18] In this section, I seek to bring together a set of terms from varying scholarly disciplines and discourses—namely, religious studies, ethnic studies, American studies, and women's and gender studies—to instigate a more robust conversation around U.S. Muslim women's lives and representations and to show how interdisciplinarity is always crucial to this endeavor. It is important to note that, as a scholar of race and gender in the United States—not a theologian, a scholar of Islamic studies, or even a scholar of religious studies—I do not attempt to address Islam through interpretations of its texts and teachings; instead, I focus on its presence and influence in people's lives and how this shapes the making of culture.

The concept of lived religion is drawn from the field of religious studies, where scholars such as Robert Orsi, David D. Hall, and Meredith McGuire have argued for an approach to the study of religious practices and impulses that is rooted in people's everyday lives.[19] As Orsi writes in his essay "Everyday Miracles," individuals "do not merely inherit religious idioms, nor is religion a fixed dimension of one's being, the permanent attainment of a stable self. People appropriate religious idioms as they need them, in response to particular circumstances. All religious ideas and impulses are of the moment, invented, taken, borrowed, and improvised at the intersections of life."[20] As this quote demonstrates, scholars of lived religion consider how religious meanings and actions are enacted and felt through the social environments of their practitioners' daily lives and acknowledge the presence of religion beyond holy texts and organized religious spaces and institutions. In the field of religious studies, lived religion has marked an attempt by scholars to abandon—or at least look more critically at—established categories of orthodoxy (correct belief) and orthopraxy (correct practice) and instead consider how religious beliefs and practices emerge through culture, lived experiences, and daily life, and not only in spaces of worship and religious institutions. Yet, as with the larger field of religious studies itself, there has been an absence of analysis in discussions of lived religion in regard to how race influences these everyday contexts in which religion takes place.[21]

In my considerations of U.S. American Islam as a lived religion, I engage closely with the existing scholarship on Muslim women in the United States and, in particular, research and writing on and by Black American Muslim women that closely examines intersections of race, gender, religion, and sexuality and acknowledges "Islam" not only as religious tradition or a set of religions practices but also as a signifier of political insurgency. The scholar Sherman Jackson forcefully situates "Blackamerican Islam" (as he calls it) within the "thoroughly American phenomenon of 'Black Religion,' essentially a pragmatic, folk-oriented, holy protest against anti-black racism"[22]—in other words, a form of U.S.-based liberation theology. In addition to Islam's "protest against anti-black racism," as described by Jackson and others, for many Black women, the religion also operated, as the Islamic studies scholar Amina Wadud writes, "an escape from the overwhelming phenomenon of double oppressions as an African-American woman," a spiritual tradition that seemingly offers "care, protection, financial support, and adoration for (Black) women."[23] Whereas Wadud goes on to say that many of these promises went unfulfilled, her words reflect how Black American Muslim women, in addition to a theology of racial liberation, also engaged Islam as protest against sexism and misogyny enacted upon Black women in the United States. As such, the experiences of Black American Muslim women reveal historical legacies of Islam in the United States as lived and practiced that directly contradict orientalist constructions of the religion as inherently oppressive to women and Muslim women as being forced to practice Islam. This is not say, however, that women of color *only* engaged Islam as politics. As I will demonstrate, women's reasons for being Muslim were, and are, always at once, political, cultural, moral, ethical, and deeply religious.[24]

The notion that Islam itself holds the potential for women's liberation has been central to women's ways of being Muslim in America, particularly for Black American Muslim women and, subsequently, other women of color. Although most of the Black American Muslim women I discuss here would not call themselves "feminists," they certainly implemented Islamic teachings and scriptures into their lives as potential sources of emancipation from racism and sexism, whether in the home, their communities, or in the public sphere. (I discuss the tensions produced by the term "feminism" in the next section, as well as in chapter 5.) The work of the anthropologist Carolyn Moxley Rouse is especially illuminating for understanding Islam's emancipatory significance in lives of Black American women. In her influential 2004 work on Black Sunni Muslim women in Los Angeles, *Engaged Surrender: African American Women and Islam*, Rouse argues that "African American Islam is a political stance of engaging the world, not only a way of escaping it."[25] Rouse's argument that Black American Muslim women "surrender" to Islam in a "way that engages their political consciousness and produces not only a spiritual but social epiphany" captures how lived religion operates as an organizing concept for the women and histories gathered here.

However, whereas Rouse's study focuses exclusively on Black American Muslim women in 1990s Los Angeles, *Being Muslim* extends her argument of Islam as means of lived political engagement to the last century and to non-Black Muslim women as well. This book considers—to paraphrase Orsi's citation above—how Islam has been appropriated as a religious idiom by both Muslims themselves and for the nation-at-large in ways that respond to the changing politics of race, gender, religion, and nation during the twentieth- and twenty-first-century United States. In the case of both Black and non-Black Muslim women in the United States, I argue that political consciousness and social epiphany are vital to understanding their engagements with Islam, especially as "Islam" has become increasingly enmeshed with the logics and optics of U.S. militarism, surveillance, and terrorism. As a result, being Muslim itself is, and has continually been, a type of religious *and* political ontology, an identity that is perceived and practiced in politicized contexts, especially in regard to Muslim women. Thus I argue that histories of Islam's political insurgency, its continual againstness to hegemonic racial, gendered, and religious norms, are always present in processes and expressions of being U.S. Muslim women. One history or experience does not subsume or replace the other, with such various iterations weaving and overlapping in complex and multifaceted ways.

In much of the existing scholarship on women and Islam in the West, the politicization of Muslim women's bodies has been contextualized through frameworks of European colonization and Western orientalism.[26] As such, Muslim women's agency and empowerment, including

articulations of feminism and Islam, are generally expressed in relation to postcolonial movements in Africa and Asia and oftentimes do
not consider the experiences of U.S. Muslim women. As stated above,
Being Muslim supplements such frameworks by examining how Muslim women in the United States have engaged questions of religious
agency and feminist practice, within and through American contexts of
race and gender. I point out that long before the War on Terror, Black
American Muslim women infused Islamic religious practices with social consciousness, which they carried out in different spaces than Black
men and which may not have been recognizable as "political," in practices such as prayer, fasting, dress, dietary restrictions, and so forth.
In the contemporary era, I contend that social consciousness continues
to motivate religious, cultural, and political ways of being for a new,
multiracial generation of young U.S. Muslim women who have come of
age in the decade and a half following 9/11 and, now, under a Donald J.
Trump presidency. *Being Muslim* demonstrates how the lives and labors
of Black Muslim women critically underwrite and inform ways of being
Muslims among a new generation of U.S. American Muslims, specifically in the ways that Islam has been at once lived as a religious identity,
a political stance, and an expression of racial and gendered agency in the
twenty-first century.

At the same time, in order to track how "Islam" has been produced
through racialized logics for much of the last century, this book engages
the notion of Islam as a racial-religious form, in which categories of
gender and sexuality are always constitutive. The term "racial-religious
form" builds on the concept of "racial form," borrowed from the work of
the literary scholar Colleen Lye in her *America's Asia: Racial Form and
American Literature, 1893–1945*, in which she considers how stereotypes
of "yellow peril" and "model minority" inform Asian racialization in the
United States, what she calls "the Asiatic racial form." Through material-
ist analysis of literary texts, Lye interrogates the putatively paradoxical
nature of the terms "yellow peril" and "model minority" and argues that
both are actually "two aspects of the same, long-running racial form,"
owing to how Asians in both are continually tied to "the trope of economic efficiency."[27] The Asiatic racial form, she argues, is the product of
shifting U.S.-Asia relations within contexts of globalization that produce
"the historical conditions, . . . social terrains, . . . and representational

material" of race making, that is, of ascribing meanings to certain groups of bodies on the basis of race.[28] To put it another way, changing economic, political, and social circumstances engender varying racial tropes or stereotypes of particular groups, which all coalesce into the racial form, in which meanings do not disappear but actually accrue to produce "mythic persistence into the present."[29]

In the case of Muslims in the United States, the idea of the racial form is useful, as "Islam" and "Muslim," while religious signifiers, have continually been characterized through racial terms. In addition, as the United States has increased its military presence in the Middle East and as Muslims from Southwest Asia have increasingly entered the U.S. economy as migrant workers and refugees from the latter decades of the twentieth century, it is important to acknowledge, as Junaid Rana does in his work on transnational Pakistani labor migrants in the wake of the War on Terror,[30] that "Muslims" have also accrued negative racial meanings in relation to capital, what Iyko Day has described as the type of "bad capital" that has been historically associated with Asian bodies in the United States.[31] Rana traces the historical construction of the Muslim through European and U.S.-based racial logics in his 2007 article, "The Story of Islamophobia," in which he writes, "Without a doubt, the diversity of the Islamic world in terms of nationality, language, ethnicity, culture, and other markers of difference, would negate popular notions of racism against Muslims as a singular racial group. Yet, current practices of racial profiling in the War on Terror perpetuate a logic that demands the ability to demand what a Muslim looks like from appearance to visual cues. This is not based purely on superficial cultural makers such as religious practice, clothing, language, and identification. A notion of race is at work in the profiling of Muslims."[32] Rana elaborates by identifying how Muslims were associated with indigenous peoples during the Reconquista, as they were the infidels and heathens who needed to be destroyed within Europe, while indigenous people in the United States were those who were to be conquered in the New World. This affiliation shifted with the forced arrival of African slaves to the Americas, many of whom were Muslim, an affiliation that continued with Black conversion to Islam during the early mid-twentieth century. At this time, Islam came to "represent a liberatory racial identification for African Americans" and became affiliated with blackness, specifically, the desire for

Black freedom—for many within Black communities—and Black rebellion—in the eyes of the state and the white cultural mainstream. Finally, Rana discusses how in the U.S. War on Terror, the Muslim has come to be conflated with Arabs and South Asians and "is incorporated into a racial formation that is adamantly anti-immigrant," that is, produced through anti-immigrant sentiment. Through his genealogy, Rana clearly shows how "the Muslim" has been iterated and reiterated through various racial logics and has taken numerous forms.

Yet Islam as merely a "racial" form is insufficient to capture the complexities of anti-Muslim sentiment that have become part and parcel of U.S. political discourse. As Sophia Rose Arjana argues in her 2015 study, *Muslims in the Western Imagination*, while negative constructions of Islam and Muslims have certainly been racial, they are also about "anxieties surrounding categories beyond race—in particular, those related to religion, gender, and sexuality."[33] Arjana articulates the intersection of these anxieties through the figure of the "Muslim monster" within the "West's *imaginaire* of Islam: the idea of the Muslim as a frightening adversary, an outside enemy that doesn't belong in modernity, who due to an intrinsic alterity, must be excluded from the American and European landscapes."[34] Working from the medieval period to the present, Arjana presents an array of Muslim monsters in the Western literary, cultural, and political imagination and charts the myriad ways that Muslims, in particular Muslim men, are rendered monstrous, "as interruptions that disturb normative humanity, civilization, and modernity"[35]—which she demonstrates long precedes the advent of orientalism as a field of study in the eighteenth century. In Arjana's analyses, it becomes apparent that Islam is monstrous because it exceeds race into the ideological. Its monstrosity arises because of Western beliefs that it is a pathological religious system, which marks Muslim bodies, as well as infecting their hearts and minds.[36] As Islam is a religion—not a race—with a set of foundational texts and practices (i.e., the Qur'an and hadith, the Five Pillars) in which all its practitioners engage, the West conceives of Muslims as following its "monstrous" ideology in lockstep; for example, if one Muslim is a terrorist, they all support terrorism, that "Islam" itself encourages terrorism. Thus, to name Islam as both a racial and religious form—a racial-religious form—in the United States is to note how not only Muslim bodies but also Islamic beliefs and practices are marked by abject monstrosity.

In addition to monstrosity, *Being Muslim* argues that within the United States during the course of the last century, Islam's racial-religious form has been signified through insurgency—the notion that Muslims are actively engaged in activities that rebel against and undermine Western "freedoms and democracy." Beyond orientalism, this form emerges through historical contexts of anti-blackness, U.S. foreign policy, and anti-immigrant sentiment. They have been primarily manifest in the tropes of the Radical Black Muslim and the foreign Islamic Terrorist (which I explore at length in chapters 2 and 4). Both are linked to notions of national threat, explicitly as threats to white, Christian, Anglo-Saxon norms and beliefs (as Rana details above), with the latter emerging as a ubiquitous, and menacing, figure in the post-9/11 United States. Yet in regard to the trope of the Radical Black Muslim, perhaps most famously represented through the figure of Malcolm X, it is critical to note that Islam's racial-religious form operates differently in the mainstream (white) and Black cultural imaginaries; whereas it functions as a symbol of threat and violence in the former, within Black cultural politics and discourses, as already discussed, Islam is oftentimes viewed as a religion of Black liberation, associated with representations of strong Black manhood and morality, antiracist struggle, revolutionary nationalism, and/or principled political protest, as exemplified by Malcolm X, as well as by the late boxer Muhammad Ali, by the basketball legend Kareem Abdul-Jabbar, and, for some, by the Nation of Islam leader Louis Farrakhan. Thus such racial difference fractures the racial-religious form of the Black Muslim radical in the U.S. cultural imaginary, as Islam holds divergent—and oftentimes contradictory—meanings, which are dependent upon racial affiliation as well as political ideology.

What is not divergent, however, is that all of these tropes are wholly gendered and almost always signify Muslim men. Yet, whether for the Radical Black Muslim or the foreign Islamic Terrorist, the female counterpart to such stereotypes is the figure of the Poor Muslim Woman, who is perceived to be oppressed by Islam and coerced into subjugation by Muslim men. Even in understandings of Islam as a religion or ideology of Black protest, Muslim women are portrayed—if they are represented at all—as silent supporters of Black men, relegated to domestic space. In their subjugation, Muslim women are understood to be tacitly supporting Islam's racial and religious insurgency. In *Being Muslim*, I identify the Islamic Terrorist, the Poor Muslim Woman, and the Radical Black Muslim as primary manifestations of Islam's racial-religious form in the United States, all of which are tied, I argue, to tropes of cultural insurgency and rebellion—racial, gendered, and religious—against white Anglo-Saxon Protestant norms. In the case of the Radical Black Muslim, I identify both the "positive" and "negative" aspects of Islam's racial meanings—that is, Islam as Black liberation, Islam as anti-white threat—and argue that both produce distorted images and understandings of Muslim women's lives. Throughout the book, I consider how U.S. Muslim women grapple and negotiate with Islam's unruly insurgent presence and how they themselves in turn work against such logics to produce their identities in affective and embodied ways.[37]

As stated above, this book understands being Muslim, or "Muslimness," as I call it at times, as emerging out of the engagement between Islam as lived religion and racial-religious form, which produces being Muslim as a continual process of affective insurgency, at times forged against Islam's own insurgent presence in the nation's cultural and political imaginaries. Islam is lived and practiced by U.S. Muslims as a nonwhite, non-Christian religion that is largely perceived in the last century as beyond the pale of Western values and liberalism, as well as an unruly, dangerous, and monstrous ideology, associated with blackness and Black people, as well as foreign terrorist threat. As such, Muslim-ness arises not only from enacting Islamic religious or cultural practices, but from the feelings and modes of embodiment that emerge in response to and against the ineluctable non-white and non-Christian presence of Islam in the United States. I argue that this process is always affective, enacted through the movements and negotiation of the body, how a body relates to the world around it, how a person feels in their own body and makes relationships with others, and perhaps most important, in the connections imagined and manifested between the self, heaven, and earth. As the influential work of the anthropologist Saba Mahmood demonstrates, the body as engaged in acts of religious and/or ethical formation is a vehicle of self-making, but one that takes place in "the technical and embodied armature" of a religion's moral-ethical frameworks and/or state power.[38] Thus, while the affective insurgency of U.S. Muslim women's bodies I identify here are undoubtedly agential—that is, it is produced through acts of agency on the part of women enacting them—they do not necessarily connote acts of resistance or subversion to hegemonic norms of race and gender. Indeed, at the same time that I seek to locate the social justice impulses of women of color within American Islam, I am also incredibly mindful of how the experiences and actions of many of the individuals documented here may reinforce "nonliberal" ideas (i.e., of heteronormative gendered and sexual relations, Victorian models of womanhood, polygamy, etc.). To characterize the actions and choices of U.S. Muslim women as insurgent is not advance their actions and modes of being as some sort of unified resistance to oppression or to advance Islam as an inherently counterhegmonic force against Western forms of racist, sexist, and imperial power. Instead, the recognition of processes of affective insurgency in U.S. Muslim women's lives is a means of making legible how religious identities and practices are animated in the "contact zones" between bodies and the social worlds around them—locations defined by the literary and cultural theorist and scholar Mary Louise Pratt as those "social spaces where cultures meet, clash, and grapple with each other, often in contexts of highly asymmetrical relations of power, such as colonialism, slavery, or their aftermaths as they are lived out in many parts of the world today."[39] Muslim identities and practices have always been expressed in such exceedingly uneven relations of power in the United States, with women's identities further circumscribed by hierarchies of gender and sexuality against which they meet, clash, and grapple.

Islam, Women of Color, and Feminism in the United States

Being Muslim situates "feminism" as critical to approaching women's ways of being Muslim in the United States during the past century, both in how Islam has constituted a religious framework of gendered agency for primarily women of color, and in how Muslim women have constantly negotiated their identities against Western feminist logics that categorize them as submissive, inferior, and unfree. In regard to the latter, in the United States and Europe, feminism and Islam are often posed as oppositional terms. As discussed in the previous section, the idea that Islam itself is somehow inherently oppressive and/or dangerous to women—and is thus antithetical to feminism—has become part of Islam's racial form in America. The Poor Muslim Woman is a static and essentialized trope that is deployed to justify U.S. military attacks and military occupation in the Middle East, the profiling and surveillance of Muslim communities in the United States, even the notion of "banning" Muslims altogether from the country.[40] To borrow the title of a 2013 book by the anthropologist Lila Abu-Lughod, the notion that Muslim women "need saving" by the West, or by Western feminist ideals, is a primary logic through which Muslim women are seen in the United States, while Islam is continually portrayed as an inherently misogynist religion that sanctions and promotes the oppression of women.[41] Such logics are rooted in the long history of what the scholar of religion and Islamic feminist Leila Ahmed calls "colonial feminism," a discourse that I discuss further in chapter 4, which, Ahmed argues, arose as late nineteenth-century European colonizers in the Middle East cited women's seemingly low status in the region to show the cultural inferiority of Islamic societies, which justified colonial occupation.[42] The "feminism" of the colonizing/occupying power—whether it be the British in nineteenth-century Egypt or the United States in 2002 Afghanistan—is thus prescribed as a tonic to Muslim women's oppression: an ideology Muslim women should and must subscribe to in order to throw off the sexist yoke of Islam (not to mention their veils).

In the United States, many Muslim women have avoided calling themselves "feminists" for a number of reasons. First, in recent decades, feminism has increasingly been deployed to shame Muslim women for their religiosity. As the novelist Mohja Kahf writes in her book *The Girl in the Tangerine Scarf*, which tells the story of a young Syrian American Muslim woman growing up in the in Midwest during the 1970s and 1980s, Muslim women may be subjected to "a broken feminist record" that tells them that religion is an instrument of male dominance, modesty and chastity are forms of patriarchal control over women's bodies, and thus religious women are stupid, brainwashed, or at the very least, victims of false consciousness.[43] Feminism, in contrast, is a "secular" orientation—a positioning that has led many Muslim scholars and clerics, mostly male, to characterize feminism as un-Islamic innovation that is unnecessary, and even dangerous, for Muslim women. Second, then, Muslim women distance themselves from feminism because it is considered to be harmful to one's *deen*, or faith, in particular in how it asserts *equality* between men and women as a goal, whereas Islam is said to promote *complimentarity* between the sexes, insofar that men and women are equal before God yet should not strive to perform the same tasks or occupy the same roles in society. Many scholars and Muslim women themselves feel that feminism demeans women's esteemed roles as wives and mothers in Islam, while emphasizing that Islam already grants women rights to own and hold property, to work outside the home, and control their own income. At the same time, though, because of such logics, men "are given the authority to manage the affairs of women and even punish women if they do not obey," writes the human rights activist and religious studies scholar Gwendolyn Zoharah Simmons, which "seriously erodes the rights given to women in Islam that Muslim are so quick to brag about."[44]

Third, and most important in regard to the narratives in this book, many U.S. Muslim women's adverse responses to "feminism" stem from the term's affiliations with a feminism that privileges the epistemologies and interests of white European and American women and thus disenfranchises and marginalizes the voices and subjectivities women of color. As Carolyn Rouse writes, such suspicion is particularly pronounced among Black American Muslim women because of how "Black women's distrust of 'feminism' can be said to be forged over centuries," from the open racism of white women in the suffrage movement to the second-wave feminists of the 1960s who "were rebelling against a particular 'Western' set of gender roles and ideas of femininity" that did not take into account the lived realities of Black women or other non-white women in the United States.[45] For example, Amina Wadud, author of *Qur'an and Woman*—the first gender-inclusive interpretation of Islam's holy book[46]—and a Black American convert to Islam who has been a longtime and, at times, controversial advocate for gender justice in Islam,[47] conscientiously does not call herself a feminist:

> I . . . describe my position as pro-faith, pro-feminist. Despite how others may categorize me, my work is certainly feminist, but I still refuse to self-designate as a feminist, even with "Muslim" put in front of it, because my emphasis on faith and the sacred prioritize my motivations in feminist methodologies. Besides, as an African-American, the original feminist paradigms were not intended to include me, as all the works on Womanism have soundly elucidated. In addition, socialist feminism has focused

clearly on the significance of class as it furthers problematizes the origins of feminism in the West. Finally, Third World feminisms have worked tediously to sensitize women and men to the complexities of relative global realities to resolving universally existing but specifically manifested problems in the areas like gender.[48]

In Wadud's words, we see how, even as she rejects the designation of "feminist," she gestures toward alternative feminist discourses beyond white feminism—namely womanism, socialist feminism, and Third World feminisms—"feminisms" with which she finds affinity and compatibility with her identity as a Muslim woman. Indeed, as stated earlier in the introduction, while many Black and other non-white Muslim women have sought gender justice through Islam, their wariness with whiteness-invested "feminism" and it attendant logics of racism, classism, U.S. exceptionalism, and now, anti-Muslim bias inhibits them from allying themselves with the term or the struggles that organize under its name.

With full acknowledgment of these trepidations regarding "feminism," however, *Being Muslim* argues that alternative feminist formations, such as the ones mentioned by Wadud, animate the history of Islam in the United States and have informed women's ways of being Muslim across the last century. As such, I contend that it is critical to understand the emergence of women's ways of being Muslim and practicing Islam in relation to such alternative "feminist" histories forged at the intersections of race, gender, class, sexuality, and religion in the United States. Specifically, I consider "Black feminism," "womanism," and "women of color feminism" as terms that have been used to denote women of color's desires for gendered agency and justice against hegemonic forces of racism, sexism, classism, and homophobia, as well as the critical social thought of women of color. While women of color have, of course, always been involved in antiracist struggles, as well as struggles for women's rights, Black feminism came to the fore forcefully in the 1970s and 1980s, when Black feminists sought to articulate the complexities of their identities and activism and refused the partitioning of their racial, gender, and sexual identities upon a political landscape that often demanded that they choose between their participation in struggles for women's liberation or Black freedom. As the authors of the

Combahee River Collective Statement—one of the key documents of contemporary Black feminism—wrote in 1978, "We believe that sexual politics under patriarchy is as pervasive in Black women's lives as are the politics of class and race. We also find it difficult to separate race from class from sex oppression because in our lives they are more often experienced simultaneously."[49] The Combahee Statement is largely acknowledged as the first major formulation of intersectional politics and intersectionality—the concept that would be formally coined by the legal scholar and critical race theorist Kimberlé Crenshaw in the 1980s to denote the interconnectedness of systems of oppression and domination. In 1990, the sociologist Patricia Hill Collins offered an expansive analysis of Black feminist thought as an intellectual legacy of critical social theory expressed through "African-American women's social location as a collectivity [that] has fostered distinctive albeit heterogeneous Black feminist intellectual traditions."[50]

Yet while the authors of the Combahee Statement and scholars like Collins defined themselves as Black "feminists," others rejected the term, opting instead to call themselves "womanists." The term "womanist" is most often attributed to the writer and poet Alice Walker, who first used the term in a 1979 short story, "Coming Apart," in which she wrote, "A womanist is a feminist, only more common."[51] She more explicitly defined the term in her 1983 volume *In Search of Our Mother's Gardens*, in which she stated that a "womanist" is "a black feminist or feminist of color [who] . . . loves other women, sexually or non-sexually" and "appreciates and prefers women's culture, women's emotional flexibility, and women's strength."[52] In the same spirit as the Combahee Collective, Walker also emphasized that a womanist does not partition her racial, gendered, and sexual identities; a womanist is "committed to the survival and wholeness of entire people, male *and* female."[53] Walker's definition famously ends, "Womanist is to feminist as purple is to lavender," essentially characterizing "feminism" as just one variant of womanism, which is understood as the broader and more encompassing concept.[54]

In its centering and privileging of the experiences of Black women, womanism appealed to those committed to Black nationalist and Black Power struggles and who did not wish to ally themselves with the perceived racism and hypocrisy of white feminists. As Collins noted, womanism "seemingly supplie[d] a way for black women to address gender oppression without attacking black men."[55] Womanism also offered, Collins continues, "a visionary meaning," in that Walker and other womanists saw it not just as a social movement or ideology (like feminism), but "as an ethical system" which was "continually evolv(ing) through its rejections of all forms of oppression and commitment to social justice."[56] In the academy, the womanist imperative to build relationships with Black men, as opposed to the seeming separatist gender ideologies of feminism, as well as its call for social justice, appealed to many Black Christian women, who were committed to enacting gender reform within religious frameworks. Womanist theology thus emerged through Black women's centering of their experiences in interpretations of biblical traditions, teachings, and scripture and offered Black female Christian theologians the opportunity to speak directly "to black women in the pews or on the prayer mats," as opposed to in academia or political rallies.[57] Thus, "womanist theology" came to be primarily articulated in the academy and theological seminaries as a collective religious ethos for Black Christian women who were "committed to the analysis of gender, race, and class . . . in order to deconstruct oppressions, sometimes recover lost meanings, and construct re-envisioned possibilities of being fully human."[58]

Whereas Black feminism and womanism primarily signified the critical social thought, intellectual labors, and activism of Black women, "women of color feminism"—or "U.S. Third World feminism," as it is also called—articulated a coalitional commitment to social justice by women of color in the United States, as well as making clear the transnational activist alliances between women of color (WOC) in the United States and the "Third World." The anthology *This Bridge Called My Back: Writings by Radical Women of Color*, edited by Cherríe L. Moraga and Gloria E. Anzaldúa, is often cited as a catalyst for WOC and Third World feminist theorizing and organizing in the United States. *This Bridge Called My Back* brought together the essays of Black, Latina, Native/indigenous, and Asian American women, as Moraga and Anzaldúa wrote in their introduction to the 1981 edition, to "reflect an uncompromised definition of feminism by women of color in the US" that was rooted in the ways "Third World women derive feminist political theory specifically from our racial/cultural background and experience."[59] Whereas much of the writing included in the collection is decidedly political in tone, it also consistently centers the feminist notion of the personal as political, including women's spiritual lives. At the start of the sixth section of the anthology, titled "El Mundo Zurdo: The Vision," Moraga and Anzaldúa specifically address the role of religion and spirituality in the lives of women of color, writing:

> We, the women here, take a trip back into the self, travel to the deep core of our roots to discover and reclaim our colored souls, our rituals, our religion. . . . The vision of our spirituality provides us with no trap door solution, no escape hatch tempting us to "transcend" our struggle. We must act in the everyday world. Words are not enough. We must perform visible and public acts that may make us more vulnerable to the very oppressions we are fighting against. But our vulnerability *can* be the source of our power—**if we use it**.[60]

The passage demonstrates how religion, as lived and practiced in "the everyday world" (i.e., as a lived religion), is a critical force in formations of women of color feminism, as a catalyst and/or vehicle for their "visible and public acts" of struggle. To put it another way, Moraga and Anzaldúa explain how religion and spirituality shape the lived experiences and, thus, affective insurgencies that make women of color "more vulnerable to the very oppressions we are fighting against," oppressions that are signified through racial, religious, and gendered forms and tropes that constrict women's lives. Yet in crafting identities that fully acknowledge the rituals and religion of women of color, the authors assert, women of color may also produce a sense of shared experience, of shared vulnerability, that "*can* be the source of our power."

Although the experiences of U.S. Muslim women may not be unproblematically mapped upon ideologies of Black feminism, womanism, and women of color feminism—for example, regarding LGBTQ communities and issues of sexuality, which many in U.S. Muslim communities continue to grapple with—I strongly contend that all three represent crucial systems of thought that have shaped the lives of U.S. Muslim women from the early twentieth century to the present. In particular, they are central to understanding the intersections of the personal and the political, the private and the public, and the religious and the secular in U.S. Muslim women's identity formations as well as to acknowledging how the experiences of Black American Muslim women and non-Black Muslim women in the United States are interconnected through histories of struggle. Perhaps most important, these alternative feminisms deeply inform how a multiracial and multiethnic generation of religiously observant, politically engaged Muslim women in the post-9/11, Trump-era United States are crafting relationships around race, gender, and faith to produce new modes of gender justice in Islam from which are emerging discourses of Islamic feminism and what I call U.S.-based "Muslim feminism," a term I use to situate the lives of the women discussed in this book into a larger history of Islam and feminism in the United States.

While I further elaborate upon Muslim feminism in chapter 5 in the specific contexts of U.S. racial politics, Islamic feminism, as Margot Badran writes, is "a term created and circulated by Muslims in far-flung corners of the global *umma*" which she notes began to have widespread purchase in the 1990s.[61] In her 2009 book, *Feminism in Islam: Secular and Religious Convergences*, Badran defines the term, stating, "What is Islamic feminism? Let me offer a concise definition: It is a feminist discourse and practice articulated within an Islamic paradigm. Islamic feminism, which derives its understanding and mandate from the *Qur'an*, seeks rights and justice for women, and for men, in the totality of their existence. Islamic feminism is both highly contested and firmly embraced."[62] Islamic feminism, Badran continues, is "being produced by Muslim women from both majority and minority communities in the African and Asia as well as from immigrant and convert communities in the West."[63] miriam cooke adds that Islamic feminist discourse operates as "multiple critique" that responds to the various forms of subjugation Muslim women encounter in transnational systems of power and is deployed as "a multilayered discourse that allows them to engage with and criticize the various individuals, institutions, and systems that limit and oppress them while making sure they are not caught in their own rhetoric."[64] It is of note—and, indeed, cooke cites the work of the Black feminist sociologist Deborah King on "multiple consciousness" in her essay—that multiple critique bears a strong resemblance to intersectionality theory. It is also significant that the world's best-known "Islamic feminist"—although, as stated above, she does not self-identify as such—is Amina Wadud, who writes frequently about the intersections of race, gender, and religious identity and references Black feminist, womanist, and WOC feminist paradigms in her advocacy of gender justice in Islam. Such connections indicate how, within the United States, expressions of Islamic feminism have consistently been—and will continue to be—shaped and influenced by discourses and ideologies of Black feminism, womanism, and WOC feminism.

A critical point of convergence between Black/WOC feminism and Islamic feminism occurs in the work of the U.S. Muslim scholar and theologian Debra Majeed, who advances a theory of "Muslim womanism" in her research on polygyny in Black American Muslim communities. She states that Muslim womanism is premised upon "the multiple and interlocking experiences of African American and other Muslim women of color" and constitutes "an epistemology, or way of knowing, that positions the experiences and wisdom of women at the forefront of any consideration of Muslim family life."[65] Muslim womanism, Majeed continues, overlaps with aspects of womanism (as espoused by Walker and others) and Black feminism (such as that expressed by the Combahee Collective), but it also "contains elements distinct from both, particularly in regard to its attentions to the varied conditions of black womanhood and diverse perceptions of justice as experienced by African American Muslims and the values of Islam they articulate."[66] In other words, Muslim womanism is grounded in the lived experiences of Black Muslim women, in ways of being Muslim and practicing Islam as enacted and embodied by Black women, an assertion of gendered power and agency that is, to return to Moraga and Anzaldúa's words in *This Bridge Called My Back*, "derive[d] specifically from our [in this case, Black women's] racial/cultural background and experience."[67] Furthermore, the Islamic and religious studies scholar studies scholar Jamillah Karim names the work of U.S. Muslim women in various racial and ethnic communities who are fighting issues of gender injustice "as embodying dimensions of Islamic feminist practice."[68] She identifies these issues in racially specific ways, citing how African American (Muslim) women might criticize some of the misogynistic attitudes and practices of African American men, whereas South Asian or Arab American Muslim women might decry cultural norms in their communities that prohibit women's participation in mosque spaces. "When women resist race, class, and gender inequalities and hold their ethnic Muslim communities to *ummah* ideals of justice and equality," asserts Karim, "they are certainly acting as Islamic feminists."[69]

As the works of Majeed and Karim demonstrate, forms of Islamic feminism are expressed and signified in the United States through the lived experiences of race and gender and against the realities of racism, sexism, and social inequality. Throughout this book, I identify and approach the stories and representations of the U.S. Muslim women gathered here as part of a broader tradition of Muslim women seeking forms of racial, gendered, and religious justice during the twentieth and twenty-first centuries, one that is rooted in the experiences of Black women but that has evolved in ways that inform the lives of all U.S. Muslim women, both Black and non-Black. Like Karim, I identify their desires and labors as part of the broader Islamic feminist tradition as well as being inexorably linked to histories of Black feminism, womanism, and WOC feminism in the United States, the intersections of which I argue produce a legacy of "U.S. Muslim feminism." In the stories of Black women in the Ahmadiyya Movement in the 1920s and 1930s, or of the women of Islam or of the Nation of Islam from the 1950s through the 1970s, or of Sisters Betty Shabazz and Dakota Staton, I highlight the complex matrices of power in and through which their desires for gender justice arose and manifested themselves in their relationship with Islam.

Finally, *Being Muslim* centers how issues of safety and security are critical to all discourses and ideologies of feminism and gender justice, and in particular for women of color, and thus to the examinations of U.S. Muslim women lives. To consider how Islam has functioned as a space of safety for women, as well as a source of violence directed toward women, a number of my chapters employ the concept of the safe harbor as defined by Toni Morrison in her 1973 novel *Sula*. Morrison uses the term to describe the relationship between the novel's two female protagonists, Nel Wright and Sula Peace, who realize, as young Black girls growing up in Medallion, Ohio, in 1922, "that they were neither white nor male, and that all freedom and triumph was forbidden to them," and thus they "set about creating something else to be."[70] "In the safe harbor of each other's company," Morrison writes, "they could afford to abandon the ways of other people and concentrate on their own perception of things."[71] In this space, at least momentarily, they do not fear bodily harm; they forget that they are targets of physical, emotional, and psychological violence. Yet while their safe harbor provides solace, it ultimately owes its existence to the dehumanizing forces of racism, sexism, poverty, and white supremacy: the very catalysts of the safe harbor's creation. Thus Nel and Sula's "safety" is premised on violence, a desire to create "something else" only because what already exists is fatal. Their safe harbor is ephemeral, shifting and evolving in response to external circumstances. Indeed, as those familiar with the novel know, Nel and Sula's adult relationship becomes marked by competition, disdain, jealousy, and ultimately, betrayal—emotions brought about by their struggles with the limits of race, gender, sexuality, and class that inform the trajectories of each of their lives.

Being Muslim argues that such safe harbors are integral to the lives and histories of U.S. Muslim women. They are spaces of respite; they may be cultural, political, and religious; they can be physical and ideological; they may span the space of a home, a *masjid*, a community, a classroom, a Facebook group, or an email Listserv. They are the spaces where Muslim women in the United States have been able to "abandon the ways of other people and concentrate on their own perception of things," where they need not explain away their bodies or the engagements of their bodies with Islam but simply focus on and proceed with relationships premised upon their worldviews as shaped by their understandings and lived practices of Islam. Yet U.S. Muslim women are never, truly *safe*, because safe harbors themselves are contingent upon the continual presence of racist, patriarchal, and imperial violence that necessitate their formation in the first place. As such, U.S. Muslim women, like the ones gathered here, know that it is precisely due to the ephermerality of such safe harbors that being Muslim enjoins practices of social justice, so they may work, worship, and live, insurgently, against that which endangers them.

* * *

As I stated earlier, the first three chapters of this book focus on the lives and representations of Black Muslim women. Chapter 1, "'Four American Moslem Ladies': Early U.S. Muslim Women in the Ahmadiyya Movement in Islam, 1920–1923," begins with an examination of the earliest known photograph of self-identified Muslim women in the

United States. Taken in 1922, the photo features four African American female converts to the Ahmadiyya Movement in Islam, a South Asia–based missionary movement that attracted significant numbers of Black women between the 1920 and 1960s. I offer a multilayered and, at times, circuitous account of the histories that produced the photograph, specifically the racial politics of 1920s Chicago, the race and gender politics of the Ahmadiyya missionary Dr. Mufti Muhammad Sadiq, and the desires for safety and spirituality that led Black American women to Islam.

In chapter 2, "Insurgent Domesticity: Race and Gender in Representations of NOI Muslim Women during the Cold War Era," I consider how the domestic spaces of Black Muslim women were portrayed in photography, media, and literature of the 1950s and 1960s and how the male gaze mediated these representations. In analyses of the 1959 CBS news documentary "The Hate That Hate Produced"; *The Messenger* magazine, the first official publication of the Nation of Islam, edited by Malcolm X in 1959; a 1963 photo essay in *Life* magazine, photographed by Gordon Parks; and James Baldwin's *The Fire Next Time*, the chapter characterizes images of the domesticity of Black Muslim women as "insurgent visions" of American Islam, oftentimes imagined by men yet enacted with women's consent and participation.

Chapter 3, "Garments for One Another: Islam and Marriage in the Lives of Betty Shabazz and Dakota Staton," examines the lives of two of the most prominent Muslim women in the United States in the 1950s and 1960s: the wife and later widow of Malcolm X, Betty Shabazz, and the jazz singer Dakota Staton. The Muslim-ness of both women was inexorably linked to, and oftentimes wholly predicated upon, their status as wives of Black American Muslim men. Through an exploration of how each woman approached Islam and marriage in their daily lives, I argue that Shabazz and Staton viewed their marriages and Muslim identities concurrently and through the racial and gendered contexts in which they approached marriage as an integral component of their practices of Islam.

In chapter 4, "Chadors, Feminists, Terror: Constructing a U.S. American Discourse of the Veil," I shift focus away from Muslim women in the United States to examines American media coverage of the Iranian women's revolution in March 1979. I look at how the major American television networks and print news media described Iranian Muslim women, covered the U.S. feminist Kate Millett's trip to Iran, and depicted the treatment of Iranian women in the feminist press. Crucial to my analysis is how post–civil rights era racial logics and the mainstreaming of second-wave feminist logics contributed to the construction of contemporary American "discourse of the veil," the term used by Leila Ahmed and others to describe the Western fetishization of the Islamic headscarf as a symbol of women's oppression.

Chapter 5, "A Third Language: Muslim Feminism in America," presents the voices of four U.S. Muslim women who actively incorporate social justice practices into their engagements with Islam and who articulate a clear relationship with gender justice and feminism in their lives. I explore how their work and perspectives refract the racial and gendered legacies of U.S. Muslim women across the last century, and I introduce the concept of Muslim feminism to link their experiences across racial, ethnic, and generational boundaries.

In the conclusion, "Soul Flower Farm," I visit a small urban farm in the East Bay Hills in California run by Maya Blow, a Muslim homeopath and herbalist. Through Blow's work, I consider the ways U.S. Muslim women, and Muslims more broadly, are engaging urban farming, environmentalism, and movements for food justice as "Muslim" issues in the twenty-first century by building upon existing legacies of women of color in American Islam.

Terminology

Before moving on, I want to briefly discuss and explain a number of the terms I use in the book. As this is a volume about Islam as a lived religion, about how women have produced ways of being Muslim against fraught political and cultural landscapes, I am mindful of the power of nomenclature. The terms we use matter, both in acts of self-signification and in how others identify us.

To refer to Muslims within the United States, I use the term "U.S. Muslims." I use this term, as opposed to "American Muslim" or "Muslim American" to clarify that my work does not engage with the diversity of Muslim life across the entirety of the Americas, which includes North, South, and Central America and the Caribbean islands. Furthermore, "U.S. Muslim" does not imply the necessity of formal citizenship or a notion of "claiming America" as a prerequisite for a U.S.-based Muslim identity. However, when speaking of Islam's historical presence in the nation, or referring broadly to Islamic practices in the United States, I employ the term "American Islam." This is due to the fact that there has already been a substantive body of work on Islam in the United States that uses this term, which I engage and build upon here.[72]

I use the term "Black American Muslim," or "Black Muslim," to refer to African American Muslims, regardless of the their sectarian or organizational affiliations, although at times I also use the term "African American Muslim." The idiom "Black Muslims" was once primarily used to describe members of the Nation of Islam and, as a result, was oftentimes rejected by African American Muslims who were not part of the group or who did not want to be affiliated with the NOI's black nationalist politics. My usage suggests that whether one was or is a member of the Nation of Islam, political insurgency has always marked being at once Black and Muslim in the United States and that it is critical to claim—not elide—this affiliation. As such, African American Muslims in the Ahmadiyya Movement in Islam or who follow Sunni Islam are also at times referred to as "Black Muslims" here. I use both the terms "Black American" and "African American" to refer to people of African descent in the Americas.

In the case of U.S. Muslims of other racial and ethnic backgrounds, I aim to be as specific as possible—for example, South Asian Muslim, Lebanese American Muslim, and so on. At times, when discussing interactions between Black Muslims and those of Asian, Arab, or African descent, I employ the terms "Black and non-Black Muslims." I prefer the latter term to "immigrant Muslim." Many non-Black Muslims in the United States are not immigrants. Some are second- or third-generation Americans, and others hail from families who have been in the United States for over a century. This terminology reflects the distinctive racial composition of U.S. Muslim communities, which, as stated earlier, is approximately one-third Black, one-third South Asian, and one-third Arab/Middle Eastern, although there are also significant and growing numbers of white and Latino converts to Islam.

Finally, I apply the term "Muslim" across sectarian differences in U.S. Muslim communities. As I am interested in the ways people have named and created themselves as U.S. Muslims, not in religious debates, I take an ecumenical approach to Muslim identity and do not engage discussions regarding the permissibility or authenticity of Muslim organizations. I strongly believe each and every group named here is integral to the fabric of U.S. American Islam. I also fully acknowledge that I do not adequately address Shiʻa Muslim women's experiences of race and gender in the United States, a critical strand of this history I hope to take up in the future and encourage other scholars to explore as well.

* * *

To close, I return to a question I posed at the start of this introduction: What is at stake in articulating a collective experience of being Muslim women? In writing a women- and race-centered narrative of American Islam, I have constructed this book against the rampant discourses of anti-Muslim racism, anti-blackness, sexism, and misogyny that pervade our present. *Being Muslim* reveals how religion inflects realities of race and gender in this country, how being Muslim is refracted through the lived experiences of race and gender and through the historical and ongoing precarity of Muslim life, which produces women's continual desire for safety and sanctuary. While my focus here is on Muslim women in the United States and Islam as lived religion and racial form within the nation, I also understand that transnational flows of knowledge and circuits of free-market capitalism produce the "new ethnicities"—to borrow a phrase from Stuart Hall—of a global Islam that defy and challenge national boundaries.[73] *Being Muslim* demarcates its inquiry on the United States, not to reify or celebrate the nation-state or the racial categories produced therein, but to examine Muslim-ness as formed within the specific contexts of what Toni Morrison has called the "wholly racialized society" of the United States.[74] Its aim is not to parochialize American Islam but to tell a story of U.S. Muslim women across time, space, and racial difference that allows for more expansive possibilities of affiliation and exchange among vulnerable populations both in the United States and worldwide.

1

"Four American Moslem Ladies"

Early U.S. Muslim Women in the Ahmadiyya Movement in Islam, 1920–1923

There is a photo. Because there is a photo, *this photo*, the story of U.S. Muslim women in the twentieth-century might begin with these women—four African American women in unadorned dresses, blouses, and skirts. Against a dark cloth backdrop, they face the camera wrapped in shawls and blankets fastened (with straight pins, or perhaps clothespins?) to conceal their shoulders, necks, mouths. The wraps appear to be large scarves, or maybe even bedsheets, although one woman is wrapped in a heavy woolen fabric with a carpet-like texture. Three wear church hats, the one who does not has wrapped her shawl around her head and pinned it above her mouth, exposing only her eyes and nose. The women are formal, stiff, and unsmiling, in a style typical of Victorian-era studio portraiture of the late nineteenth-century, although it is 1922. The photo's setting is simple: There are no ornaments, no frills; wherever the studio, it is modest and spare. Before the black drape, two women stand and the other two sit, one on a carved wooden stool a bit too tall, her feet dangling slightly off the ground, her right hand grasping an armrest. They appear middle-aged, ranging anywhere from their late twenties to their forties. Their eyes gaze in different directions; two of the women look directly at the camera, the two others stare off into the distance.

This is the first-known group photo of visibly identifiable Muslim women in the United States. It was originally published in the January 1923 edition of the *Moslem Sunrise*, the newsletter of the Ahmadiyya Movement in Islam (AMI) in the United States, a South Asia–based Islamic missionary movement that was one of the first major Muslim organizations in the United States. On the pages following the photo, there is a "Brief Report of the Work in America," a recurring feature in the

Figure 1.1. "Four American Moslem Ladies," from the *Moslem Sunrise*, January 1923. Image reproduction courtesy of the New York Public Library.

newsletter penned by the AMI's chief missionary, a man hailing from the Punjab region of India (now Pakistan) named Mufti Muhammad Sadiq, who led the organization's efforts in the United States from 1921 to 1923 and established the group's headquarters in the Bronzeville neighborhood of Chicago, where the photo was taken. In his report, Sadiq offers descriptions of his recent lectures on Islam and his other proselytization efforts,[1] but he includes no accompanying story or reference to the photo of the four women, making no mention of who they are and why the photo is included with this report, except for this short caption:

FOUR AMERICAN MOSLEM LADIES. Right to left: Mrs. Thomas (Sister Khairat), Mrs. Watts (Sister Zeineb), Mrs. Robinson (Sister Ahmadia), Mrs. Clark (Sister Ayesha)[2]

Such inclusion of the image alongside the omission of any information about the women themselves has also marked the photo's contemporary afterlife in the scholarship on Islam in the United States. In this corpus, the photo is generally contextualized through narratives of Black masculinity and nationalism, deployed to demonstrate the presence of Black women in Islamic movements such as the Moorish Science Temple, the AMI, and the Nation of Islam in relation to ideologies of Black nationalism and Marcus Garvey's Pan-Africanist movement.[3] Its placement within such narratives implicitly advances the notion that these Black American Ahmadi Muslim women "saw" Islam and the adoption of Islamic identities in the same ways that many Black American Muslim men did, for example, as intertwined with ideologies of racial separatism, Black uplift, and revolutionary political struggle.

While Islam's political significance—in particular, the understanding that it was a religious tradition that could foster African nationalism and develop Black racial pride and African civilization—certainly appealed to some Black women who joined early twentieth-century Islamic organizations, such politics were oftentimes not, this chapter suggests, the central or driving reasons that Black migrant women—and in particular, the Four American Moslem Ladies—chose to convert to Islam and adopt Muslim identities and practices in the rapidly industrializing, post–Great Migration North. Between 1921 and 1923, more than one thousand U.S. Americans converted to Islam through the AMI; anywhere from one-third to one-half of these new Muslims were women, and the vast majority of these women were Black. In what follows, I argue that, beyond the discourses and logics of Black nationalism, another set of at once deeply personal *and* unwaveringly political concerns animated Black American women's claiming of Ahmadiyya Islam during early decades of the twentieth century. These concerns were rooted in the desire for the safety and stability of themselves and their families and emerged in response to the particular struggles of newly arrived Black migrant women to Northern cities such as Chicago, Detroit, Philadelphia, and New York. Thus, although Black freedom—as expressed through Marcus Garvey's political oratories and the work of his United Negro Improvement Association or in calls for Pan-African solidarity and African liberation—may well have been on Black migrant women's minds, they also grappled with constant, pressing concerns in their daily lives. Those concerns included such matters as the sexual advances of their work supervisors or landlords, the dangers and stresses of raising children while working long hours, the lack of economic resources and supportive kinship networks, and the securing and maintenance of marital and familial relations in urban environments that were vastly different from what many newly arrived Black women—some former slaves or the children of slaves—had experienced in the South. In the face of such difficulties, "Islam" offered those such as the Four American Moslem Ladies a religious and political ethos that rejected the dehumanization of Black working-class women by white society and the Black bourgeoisie and presented expansive and productive conceptions of citizenship, belonging, and racial and gendered selfhood in a religious framework that was at once politically empowering and adaptable to their existing knowledge of Christianity. Further, the clear organizational structure of the AMI, along with its emphasis on religious education and moral development, constituted a stabilizing force in many women's lives—a framework that provided safety and sustained them against the harsh and unforgiving environments of Bronzeville and beyond.

This chapter unearths the lives and experiences of the Four American Moslem Ladies. It particularly focuses on one of the women, Florence Watts—Sister Zeineb following her conversion—and explores how and why she and her peers came to claim Islam through the teachings of Mufti Muhammad Sadiq and the Ahmadiyya Movement in Islam in 1920s Chicago. While Muslim women were undoubtedly present in the United States prior to 1922 when the photo was taken,[4] this image stands as the earliest archival trace of U.S. Muslim's women's *communal* lives and thus, I argue, constitutes a critical, albeit arbitrary, start to a verifiable account of Muslim women's narratives in the United States. In my investigation, I outline the historical conditions that produced ways of being Muslim for the Four American Moslem ladies as at once grounded in the Black experience of the post–Great Migration urban North and facilitated through international networks of diasporic exchange between the United States and South Asia, specifically interracial interactions between Blacks and South Asians in the United States. Through Ahmadiyya Islam, Black women in 1920s Chicago found "safe harbors"—spaces of kinship-shared spiritual desires and of respite from racial and gendered harm—in which they could protect and nurture their bodies, minds, and souls and cultivate religious and intellectual affinities with Muslim women worldwide while using Islam's teachings to navigate and find solace from urban life. Building upon existing histories that have heretofore contextualized the lives of Black Muslims in the early twentieth century through the lens of Black nationalism and Pan-Africanist thought,[5] this chapter considers how the accounting of categories of race, gender, class, and sexuality critically shift Islam's historical meanings in the United States, with particular regard to how Black women were central to the making of Islamic practices and community formation, such as cultivating Islamic religious traditions and institutions and utilizing and engaging "Islam" in ways that specifically addressed their struggles as Black women. Above all, this chapter highlights how the construction of Black American Muslim women's identities during the early twentieth century was deeply informed by the politics of the body, particularly the raced, gendered, and classed bodies of Black migrant women responding to—and oftentimes, *insurgently against*—their circumscription through the discourses and logics of race, gender, sexuality, and class of the time. In their bodies—indeed, because of their bodies—Black women like the Four American Moslem Ladies chose and claimed Islam, not only because they believed in its teachings and tenets, but also because they felt protected and guided by its presence as they enacted forms of affective insurgency that rejected their constant abjection as working-class Black women. For them,

Muslim-ness was fashioned in—and would come to mediate—the contact zone between their bodies and the cultural and political terrains they inhabited in Bronzeville, Chicago, the nation, and the world.

To tell the stories of the Four American Moslem Ladies, this chapter enacts a visual reversal of their image. Instead of *seeing* them as part of an existing narrative (e.g., of Black nationalism, Pan-Africanism, Black men and masculinity, etc.), I instead consider what *they saw* in Islam as Black American women from the South arriving in Chicago in the 1910s and 1920s and how their visions were transformed into insurgent modes of feeling and practice through which they made their Muslim-ness. To put it another way, this chapter offers Sisters Khairat, Zeineb, Ayesha, and Ahmadia as *visionaries*: women who came to look at, inhabit, and experience the world as Black American Muslim women during a time when there was no such thing. To see the world as Muslim women required their continual vigilance and labor, not only in terms of Islamic practices, like praying or fasting, but also in navigating how they as Black women could enact and embody Islamic practices in the racialized and gendered environments in which they lived. To explore their visions, I begin with the story of Florence Watts, a Black working-class migrant woman who moved to Chicago around 1910 and converted to Ahmadiyya Islam in 1922. Through Sister Zeineb's experiences, I investigate the living conditions of working-class Black women migrants in Bronzeville, the neighborhood's shifting religious landscape, the rising status of Chicago as a "global" city and of the United States as empire, and the new forms of emotionality, kinship, sexuality, and mobility that emerged in Black centers of the urban North—all factors that shaped Black women's encounters with and impressions of Islam. I then turn my focus to Dr. Mufti Muhammad Sadiq and his encounters with women in Chicago like Sister Zeineb, exploring how and why his teachings of Islam specifically appealed to Black migrant women. Finally, I close with a historical reconstruction of a typical day in the lives of Sister Zeineb and her peers in Bronzeville following their conversion to Ahmadiyya Islam and imagine how their newfound religious identities shifted their interactions with their neighborhood, the nation, and the world as Black American women.

Before moving on, I find it critical to acknowledge a central factor behind the scholarly inattention to the lives of the Four American Moslem Ladies and, more broadly, to the role of the Ahmadiyya Movement in

Islam in the histories of Islam in the United States.[6] Such elisions stem from the idea that Ahmadiyya Muslims are not "real" Muslims but, even worse, *kafirs* (or infidels) who purposefully distort the teachings of Islam, an idea generally held by Sunni Muslims, who constitute the largest sect of Muslims both in the United States and worldwide.[7] Yet perceptions of Ahmadis as non-Muslims are not only theological but also political, relating directly to the status of the Ahmadiyya in Pakistan, where the group has been the subject of the nation's blasphemy laws, which have led to their ongoing persecution and oppression for the last century.[8] Such differences continue to separate Ahmadi and Sunni Muslim communities in the United States and underscore the highly politicized and sectarian nature of Islam's presence in the historical record and the existing scholarship on U.S. Muslims, as well as the transnational nature of political and theological debates within even the earliest U.S. Muslim communities. In this instance, it is my contention that the marginalization and omission of the AMI has contributed to the making of an implicitly masculinist narrative of Islam in the early twentieth century. This is not only because of its emphasis on male figures such as Marcus Garvey and Noble Drew Ali and, later, Elijah Muhammad and Malcolm X, but also because it ignores how U.S. Muslim women—as well as men, families, and communities—from the 1920s onward lived as Muslims and practiced Islam beyond a starkly political realm. They also lived as Muslims and practiced Islam in the "private" spaces of homes, meeting rooms, and mosques—which were themselves always animated by trajectories of cultural and political power—and in forms that were dynamically influenced by local, national, and international/transnational forces and currents. To initiate a story of U.S. American Islam with the Ahmadiyya Movement in Islam and the Four American Moslem Ladies calls for alternative, markedly different historical narratives, those that relay Black women's embrace and embodiment of Muslim feelings and practices as a form of social movement making—a part of what Robin Kelley has called the "freedom dreams" of the Black radical tradition, which "generate[d] new knowledge, new theories, new questions" and produced "cognitive maps of the future, of the world not yet born."[9] In Ahmadiyya Islam, I argue that the Four American Moslem Ladies found solace and safety, community and kinship, and a map for freedom through which they envisioned their future selves, their *fullest selves* in a future world.

Finding Florence

"Late last night, I sold away and cried," sings Bessie Smith in "Chicago Bound Blues"—"Had the blues for Chicago, I just can't be satisfied." Recorded and released in 1923, the song expressed the thoughts of a Southern woman whose man had migrated to Chicago, leaving "his mama standing there." Without him, she "just can't be satisfied" and ultimately kills herself, a death which will wind up a "big red headline [in] tomorrow *Defender* news," a reference to the *Chicago Defender*, the nation's largest Black newspaper at the time, which had a wide circulation across the U.S. South. As Angela Davis notes, songs like Smith's offered a rare glimpse into "new forms of emotional pain in the post-slavery era" as experienced by Black women[10]—in this case, the pain and longing of a woman pining for a lover who has left her to seek new opportunities in Chicago, a city known as the "Black Mecca" of the North. Owing to her own lack of mobility, she cannot follow him there and thus must deal with the isolation and despair of their separation, a result of the Great Migration. With the "blues on my brain," Smith sings, "my tongue refused to talk / I was following my daddy but my feet refuses to walk." Although she wants to "follow" her man, her body betrays her (a tongue that refuses to talk, feet that refuse to walk). Thus, despite the formal end of slavery, the woman in Smith's song is ironically not "Chicago bound" but instead still bound to the legacies of slavery and anti-Black racism in the South. In these lyrics, we see that, for all its promise, Chicago is also a signifier of the pain and violence of the Great Migration, a "mecca" where the racial and gendered traumas of slavery are not resolved but displaced and diffused in the urban North. Indeed, while Smith's abandoned protagonist commits suicide down South, where her body remains, the news of her death travels far and wide, a "big red headline" for all across the North and South to see.

To Chicago's Mecca, into its endless promise and new forms of pain, a young Black American woman named Florence Watts arrived sometime around 1910. In the photo of the Four American Moslem Ladies, Florence is likely the woman seated on the right, with white stockings and white flowers on her hat, her feet slightly dangling off the floor. This is not entirely clear, however, as the caption reads that the women are named from "right to left." Right to left is the orientation for reading

Urdu or Arabic script, Mufti Muhammad Sadiq's native language(s), and it is perhaps why he indicated the order as such. However, the standard orientation for reading script in the United States (and the West) is, of course, from left to right, and thus one cannot be certain if the caption reflected Sadiq's cultural logics or was simply a typographical error on the part of whomever composed it. As such, it is also possible that Florence is the woman standing on the left, wrapped in a large, plain white sheet, with a dark, unadorned hat.

What can be conclusively known about Florence Watts is that she, along with her peers in the photo, converted to Ahmadiyya Islam in the summer of 1922, around six months prior to the publication of the photo. Her name first appears in the July 1922 issue of the *Moslem Sunrise* among a list of approximately one hundred fifty names listed in the "New Converts" section of the magazine, which also includes the names of other women in the photo, "Mrs. F. Robinson (Ahmadia)," "Mrs. V.C. Clark (Ayesha)," and "Mrs. Parabee Thomas (Khairat)." This particular issue of the *Sunrise* was the first to be published after Sadiq moved the headquarters of his mission to the Bronzeville neighborhood of Chicago in May or June 1922; the previous issue had been published in April, with the organization's address listed in Highland Park, Michigan, the further details of which I will discuss shortly. My focus on Florence here is due to the fact that, of the four women in the photo, she is the only one who has a substantive presence in the historical archive beyond the pages of the *Moslem Sunrise*, one that allows for the reconstruction of the basic details of her life before and after her conversion to Islam. From her appearance in the *Moslem Sunrise*, as well as in the 1880, 1920, and 1930 federal censuses and a 1933 death certificate,[11] Florence Watts emerges as a complex and multilayered individual whose decision to claim Islam was shaped by the overlapping historical forces that impelled working-class Black women to seek work in Chicago and rendered the city an exciting, chaotic, difficult, and dangerous site of encounter from which they sought safety and community in racially and gender-specific ways, including religious conversion.

Unlike many other new migrants, Florence did not come to the city directly from the South but from Washington, DC, where she had been employed as a maid. The nation's capital had been a logical place for Florence to initially seek employment; she had grown up forty miles outside of the District of Columbia, in the small, unincorporated town of Ellicott City in Howard County, Maryland.[12] While Maryland was a slave state, its position at the border of North and South, as well its proximity to the capital city of Washington, DC, made it a critical battleground during the American Civil War. This position produced intense political polarization among the state's citizenry, from those who unabashedly supported secession and slavery to staunch abolitionists, including Frederick Douglass, who was born in nearby Talbot County, Maryland.[13] Florence was born in Ellicott City in 1878, the second to youngest of the six children of John and Elizabeth Sullivan, transplants to Maryland from North Carolina and Virginia, respectively. At the time that John and Elizabeth likely arrived in Ellicott City, around 1870, shortly following the end of the Civil War, the city was "a prosperous farming and manufacturing area," a mill town that served as base for Union troops and in which homes and churches had been used as hospitals for the Union wounded.[14] Perhaps its Union-oriented politics brought John Sullivan and his family to settle there, where John found work in a local store and Elizabeth was a housewife who stayed home with their six children. In the 1920 census, Florence is listed as not having attended school, although it is highly possible that she received lessons at, or attended, the Ellicott City Colored School, built in 1880, the first school for Black children erected through public funds in Howard County, as she is able to read and write.[15]

Prior to her arrival in Chicago, Florence worked as a maid in Washington, DC, where she went by her maiden name, Florence Sullivan, and lived as a boarder in the home of William and Alice Jones, a Black couple. In 1900, Florence is listed in the federal census as being twenty-two-years-old, single, and without children. Because of her time spent in the District of Columbia, we know she was not, upon her arrival in Chicago in the following decades, a newcomer to city life, nor would she have been unaccustomed to the service and domestic type of work available to Black women in Chicago at the time. She also likely had familiarity with the ins and outs of how someone like her might secure housing, ride public transportation, and seek and secure employment. Still, Florence was surely surprised, impressed, or overwhelmed by what she encountered in Chicago's "Black Metropolis," which had emerged during the early decades of the 1900s as a burgeoning cultural, religious, and political center of Black American life. As the terminus of the Illinois Central Railroad, writes Allan Spear in his 1967 text, *Black Chicago: The Making of a Negro Ghetto*, "Chicago was the most accessible northern city for Negroes in Mississippi, Louisiana, and Arkansas," attracting more Black migrants than any other northern city.[16] Indeed, while the city had long boasted a sizeable Black population, including a strong Black elite and bourgeoisie class, following the start of World War I in 1914, Black American Southerners began arriving in the city in record-breaking numbers; between 1916 and 1919, an estimated 50,000–75,000 new Black residents relocated to Chicago. In 1910, the census recorded 44,108 Blacks in the city; by 1920, the number had risen to 109,458. By midcentury, the city's black population had reached almost half a million (comparatively, the total in New York City was 340,000; in Philadelphia, 370,000; and in Detroit, 335,000).[17]

In addition to its accessibility by train from the South, other factors contributed to Chicago's popularity as a destination for migrants, in particular its reputation as a place of limitless Black opportunity, a notion that was advanced in the pages of the *Chicago Defender*. The paper, being widely circulated across the South, frequently trumpeted the city's advantages and actively encouraged Southern Blacks to migrate with the promise of plentiful employment, freedom from racial violence, and general prosperity. The city's promise was also conveyed through the pages of the Sears & Roebuck catalogues (which were also widely distributed in the South), in which the Chicago-based retailer enticed consumers with its images of stylish clothing, elegant home furnishings, and the latest appliances, such as phonographs and nickel-plated stoves. On a more personal note, Blacks across the South heard exciting tales of Chicago nightlife, culture, and money making from the tens of thousands of Black men who had found work as Pullman porters on the Illinois Central Railroad line.

This new Black population from the South fundamentally shifted Chicago's racial dynamics. Unlike Florence Sullivan, many of those who arrived with this massive influx between 1914 and 1920 were unused to, and unfamiliar with, city life and were upset to be met with inadequate wages and substandard housing. Further, the city's racial and economic realities produced new (and exacerbated existing) racial tensions between white and Black Chicagoans. New Black migrants resented the intense anti-Black sentiment they encountered (which they had hoped they had left behind in the South), while white Chicagoans feared and racially antagonized the Black "migrant mob." Such tensions contributed directly to the "Red Summer" race riots of 1919, which left fifteen whites and twenty-three Blacks dead and more than five hundred injured.[18] The riots occurred toward the end of an era that scholars of Black history have called the "nadir of American race relations" in the United States, with riots also occurring in two dozen other towns across the United States that summer. The "nadir" refers to the period following Recon-struction from roughly 1880 to 1920—four decades in which anti-Black violence, lynchings, segregation, and legal racial discrimination reached their height both in the South and beyond, as Jim Crow spread and new and virulent forms of racism emerged in the North.

Through the close of the 1800s, many of Chicago's Black elite had pushed toward integrationist and assimilationist goals. Yet the rise of anti-Black violence in the North, exemplified through the riots, led many to change their course, as the city's Black leaders instead chose to veer toward a "self-help" approach—as opposed to a social justice one—such as building Black owned and operated community institutions, businesses, and political organizations and creating an internal power structure that stood apart from the city's white leadership. In some ways, one might characterize the strategy of Chicago's established Black bour-geoisie as akin to Black nationalism, yet it differed in that the goal of their efforts was not collective Black liberation or freedom but the pro-motion and cultivation of the Black respectability among middle- and upper-class Blacks, that is, the desire to prove that they were "as good as" whites. The logic went: If respectable Black Chicagoans could not look to whites to support their businesses and communities, they would build respectable and well-to-do businesses and communities of their own. These efforts would at once make de facto racial segregation the norm in twentieth-century Chicago through the hardening of racial boundaries within the city, as well as producing the neighborhood of Bronzeville as the nation's most vibrant Black cultural hub outside of Harlem.

"A City within a City"

By the mid-1910s, the South Side of Chicago, once home to significant numbers of white ethnic Germans, Scandinavians, Poles, Irish, and

Italians, was predominately Black. According to Spear, "Chicago's Negro leaders built a complex of community organizations, institutions, and enterprises that made the South Side not simply an area of Negro concentration but *a city within a city*."[19] At the heart of the South Side was Bronzeville, which stretched between 22nd and 63rd Streets between State Street and Cottage Grove Avenue. From the mid-1910s through the 1950s, Bronzeville was the heartbeat of Black life, business, and culture in Chicago, a pulsing urban center that boasted a population of more than 300,000 residents in its seven-mile radius, which was filled with activity both night and day. The neighborhood was home to the leading Black institutions in Chicago, including Provident Hospital (the first Black hospital in country), the George Cleveland Hall Library, and the Wabash Avenue YMCA, as well as celebrities and political figures through the years such as Ida B. Wells, Louis Armstrong, Katherine Dunham, Richard Wright, Lorraine Hansberry, and Gwendolyn Brooks. When the sun went down, Bronzeville was well known for its nightclubs and dance halls, which featured the top stars of the day, including blues singers like Bessie Smith and Ida Cox (who also recorded a version of "Chicago Bound Blues"), as well as Prohibition-era speakeasies, gambling dens, and prostitution houses.

Yet despite this vibrancy, Chicago's South Side was also a harsh, isolating, and difficult place for most Southern transplants. While the lure of well-paying jobs, comfortable accommodations, and leisure and entertainment opportunities characterized the dream of Chicago for migrants prior to their arrival, the reality of what met them there was markedly different, consisting of ramshackle rowhouses, overcrowded living conditions, trash-strewn streets, and so forth. At the Illinois Central train station on Twelfth Street, it was common to see "men in worn, outmoded suits carrying battered luggage, and women clutching ragged, barefooted children, looking hopefully for a familiar face."[20] Whether or not these new arrivals had contacts or relations in the city, most somehow wound up in the South Side Black Belt, where they found "festering slums. . . . Two-story frame houses, devoid of paint . . . in drab, dingy rows, surrounded by litters of garbage and ashes."[21] While many of the Black middle- and upper-class residents, such as Wells, Carter G. Woodson (whose famed Association for the Study of Negro Life and History was established in Bronzeville), and the gospel music pioneer Thomas

A. Dorsey, still kept respectable homes in the area, much of the grandeur that had marked the neighborhood had eroded by 1920, a result of a variety of factors, including race riots, increasing housing restrictions, job scarcity, and the decline of the Black Church as a community and cultural center.

In Bronzeville, Florence Sullivan would find an environment that was not only vibrant and dynamic but also fraught with danger, violence, and racial unease. Bronzeville posed specific hardships and dangers for Black women, whose job opportunities were strictly limited to domestic or service work or low-paying wage work in factories, professions in which they were constantly subjected to the sexual advances of male supervisors and in which they had to spend long hours away from their husbands and children.[22] This was difficult not only because of the desire to be with their families but because they had believed the going North would provide the opportunities to do so. As Jacqueline Jones notes, most black female migrants chose to relocate not only for economic opportunities but also out of deep commitment to family kinship and racial collectivism—that is, to seek out better lives for their families and children and to construct family ties that had been broken by slavery.[23] Although Black women had difficulty finding jobs outside of domestic service, Chicago generally offered a "more diversified female occupational structure" than other Northern cities and thus attracted more single women and wives seeking to work outside the home, which may have been a draw for Florence Sullivan.[24] Yet even if women were able to find work, they were assigned the most difficult and undesirable positions, such as those in the meatpacking and laundry industries, and even those positions were scarce and unstable, with little to no room for advancement. In whatever jobs they could obtain, they occupied the bottom rung of a racialized and gendered labor structure in which they were constantly subjected to physical and sexual violence. Indeed, many migrant women had hoped they would be leaving behind in the South the "unique grievances" of Black women, namely "their sexual vulnerability to black and white men alike," and they had "fled (North) for their own physical safety, and for the safety of their children."[25] Yet while they might no longer have had to deal with the sexual advances and physical violence of white slave masters, Black women now had to confront the aggressive behaviors and sexual advances of their male managers, landlords, bill collectors, neighbors, fellow boarders, and so on. They also constantly worried for the safety of their children. Compared to the small-town South, Bronzeville was full of pool halls, alcohol, night-clubs, and those who frequented them, providing "wide open"—and dangerous—spaces where young people could easily slip away from their elders' supervision, spaces where they might disappear among the teeming "migrant mob."

A series of dramatic events occurred in Florence Sullivan's life from her time in Washington, DC, to her move to Chicago. In the 1920 federal census, Florence is identified as a widow but is married to a man named George Watts and is mother to a daughter, Anerilia Watts, born in Chicago in 1912. Thus a probable scenario is that Florence had married in the District of Columbia to a man who passed away prematurely, which impelled her to move to the Midwest. In Chicago, she met George Watts, a man ten years her senior, and in 1912, they welcomed baby daughter Anerilia. As a family, Florence, George, and their infant daughter did not want the excitement of pool halls and speakeasies but instead the comfort and stability of a well-paying job and a home. By 1920, Florence was working as a live-in cook in the home of Earnest and Carrie Rickitt, a well-to-do couple with four children living in the wealthy white suburb of Evanston located on Chicago's North Shore, a position that kept her away from the harshness of the South Side but also isolated her from other Black people and likely kept her away from her husband and child. It is not clear where George and Anerilia lived while Florence lived with the Rickitts. Perhaps because she grew tired of this separation, the Watts family moved to Bronzeville sometime in 1921–1922, where they were boarders in the home of a Black couple named Pellon and Marie Robinson, whose home was located at 3812 South Prairie Avenue, near the heart of Bronzeville and approximately seven blocks from the subsequent site of the Ahmadiyya mosque. On the South Side, Florence found work as a cook in a fraternity house, and George worked as a laborer. Finally living together as a family, Florence, George, and Anerilia set out to make a life together, to navigate and find community and safety in the bustle of Bronzeville. Yet this posed its own challenges, requiring the couple to find care for Anerilia when they were working and to grow accustomed to living as a family of boarders, likely all three of them in one room, and having to share amenities with the Robinsons. One can imagine that privacy or solace were in short supply, conditions that impelled Florence to seek out spaces of succor beyond her work and home.

A New Sacred Order and the Politics of Respectability

As W. E. B. DuBois wrote in *The Souls of Black Folk*, published in 1903, "The Negro church of today is the social center of Negro life in the United States."[26] In many regards, Chicago was headquarters for the Black Church's social center; indeed, even prior to the Great Migration, the city had long been known as a center of Black American religious life, specifically of Black mainline Christianity. In his study of Black Protestantism in migration-era Chicago, Wallace Best asserts that the city held out a mythic allure to its new arrivals not only as a promised land of higher-paying work, equality, and educational opportunities but also as the destination of their religious pilgrimage from South to North. Best writes that "in escaping the harsh living conditions, severe discrimination, and mob rule [of the South], the migration [to Chicago] was very much a religious sojourn. The biblical imagery of the Exodus, flight from Egypt, and crossing over the Jordan were routinely invoked by Black Southerners to characterize their own migration."[27] These new migrants would bring elements of Southern folk religion into their worship that highlighted themes of exile, sojourn deliverance, and the "moral obligation" of the Church to the community, as well as more animated forms of worship, such as shouting, physical movement, laughter, and weeping to church pews. This ruffled the feathers of many of the congregants of existing mainstream Black churches in Chicago, which generally discouraged expressive worship and viewed community outreach as unnecessary. Yet churches still needed to draw new members. Thus, while Black Church leaders may have disdained migrants as unschooled in the "respectable" bourgeois mannerisms of the North, they would begrudgingly make changes to draw them in, including the implementation of community outreach programs and incorporating entertainment and performance into worship services. Ultimately, the new Chicagoans and their approaches to worship brought about "a new sacred order," one that altered existing class divisions in the Black community and shifted notions of Black "respectability."

Black women intimately shaped the logics and discourses of respectability politics, both in the church and beyond. It is critical to note that, in addition to the social phenomenon that affected Florence Watts's life as discussed here so far—the Great Migration, racial tensions in the North, the evolution of the Black Church—the early decades of the twentieth century also marked growing support across the country for women's suffrage movements *and* the coming of age of the women's movement in the Black Church, which reached its apex between 1900 and 1920. Yet these latter two events worked against each other in some ways; as Evelyn Brooks Higginbotham notes, as "support for women's rights grew in intensity and sympathy, racial prejudice became acceptable, even fashionable in America."[28] Thus Black women, especially in the context of the Church, sought to mobilize the language of women's rights in their efforts to combat structural racism. Yet as new forms of sexuality and mobility emerged for Black women, as expressed in the blues and in other modes of expression, many Black Church women viewed such practices as sinful, reflective of low moral character that would ultimately harm Black communities and the broader Black struggle. In their fight for "equality," female activists in the Black Church "combined both a conservative and radical impulse [that] offered women an oppositional space in which to protest vigorously social injustice . . . situated within the larger structural framework of America and its attendant social norms."[29] These social norms were, of course, dictated by the white gaze; as Higginbotham writes: "There could be no laxity as far as sexual conduct, cleanliness, temperance, hard work, and politeness were concerned. There could be no transgression of [white] society's norms."[30] Such judgmental attitudes and the policing of poor black migrant women's behavior turned away many migrant women from the church. Yet even for women who were not part of a congregation, the Black Church and the politics of respectability functioned as moral and ethical arbiters of social boundaries, barometers of what was proper and improper, "clean" and "unclean."

Still, migrant women like Florence Watts desired community, religious or otherwise, oftentimes in ways that attempted to "re-create the intimacy of village life they left behind."[31] Beyond the church, there were few alternatives. While Chicago had an established network of African American Women's Clubs—from 1890 to 1920, there were over one hundred fifty on record—most were affiliated with churches, and such organizations were generally not welcoming to most working-class migrant women, as they were often unable to accommodate the busy schedules of those who had to both work and manage their households, as well as, oftentimes, caring for extended family and neighbors. Finally, many of the migrant women, like Florence, had encountered difficult situations in their marital and family relationships, whether the death of a spouse, which left one a widow, or divorce or separation, or having children out of wedlock, or extreme poverty or destitution, or drug or alcohol abuse, and so on. While some churches and women's groups were certainly welcome to all, their strong emphasis on respectability discouraged many and sent them toward other spaces of community and kinship, such as those fostered by Mufti Muhammad Sadiq and the Ahmadiyya Movement in Islam. I next turn to Florence's encounter with the AMI and the work of the group's central missionary, Mufti Muhammad Sadiq, to invite Black American migrant women into the AMI's fold.

But before I move on to Sadiq and Florence Watts's meeting, however, it is important to pause briefly and ask, How might Black women in Bronzeville—and Americans more broadly—have thought about Islam and Muslims at the time? What impressions could they have had of Islam prior to their eventual conversions, of the regions and peoples of the "Moslem" world? To respond to these questions, one might consider Chicago's emergence as a global city beginning in the late nineteenth century, a time in which the nation itself transitioned from a modus operandi of nation building to one of empire building. Chicago's international character was exemplified through the World's Columbian Exposition of 1893.[32] At the same time as the exposition, the city also hosted the World's Parliament of Religions, the first interfaith global dialogue that included representatives of both "Western" and "Eastern" faiths, which, while overwhelmed with white European and Christian representatives, also included representatives of Buddhism, Judaism, Hinduism, Shintoism, Confucianism, Taoism, and Islam.[33] The "worldliness" of Chicago arose in conjunction with how the "East" came to figure more broadly in capitalist consumption in the United States, akin to what John Tchen has called "patrician orientalism" in relation to the ways Chinese culture was consumed by wealthy

Americans in the eighteenth century.[34] Islamic and Middle Eastern objects and culture served a similar function; to own or engage with them was a way to express and wealth and status for white Americans.

This consumption of the "East," and specifically of "Moslem" culture, as an exotic commodity coincided with a rise in the notion of Islam as a religious and cultural threat, an idea that came from the efforts of Christian missionaries. By the first decade of the twentieth century, there were numerous efforts by American Protestant organizations to evangelize the Muslim world, fueled by notions that Islam "was a flawed religion that could not save its adherents" and that "the Moslem world was in deep cultural crisis requiring a winsome Christian witness, lest a great moment of opportunity be lost."[35] Further, in the closing decade of the nineteenth century, toward the end of what Mark Twain called the "Gilded Age"—the age when every American "was a potential Andrew Carnegie"—millions of immigrants poured into the country. While most were from Europe, small but significant amounts of Muslims also arrived, mostly from Syria, Lebanon, and the Indian subcontinent. They entered a nation marked not only by its desire for empire, but one of epic inequality, where suddenly rich Americans ostentatiously flaunted their newfound wealth, while countless immigrants and Black Americans lived in squalor. Finally, in the early twentieth century, anti-Asian xenophobia was at an all-time high, as East and South Asian Muslim immigrants who did not phenotypically look "white" experienced intense racism in the forms of violence and hostility, as well as juridical disenfranchisement through immigration and citizenship laws that were constantly changed to prevent their inclusion.[36]

Yet, as already mentioned, Black Americans themselves were perhaps the strongest force in changing the meaning and presence of "Islam" in the United States, as the religion was praised by thinkers like Marcus Garvey and Edward Wilmot Blyden as a suitable theology for Black empowerment.[37] The spirit of Black nationalism animated and amplified the message of Islam for many Black Americans, including those who joined the Moorish Science Temple—the organization founded in 1914 by Timothy Drew, who would later change his name to Noble Drew Ali—and, later, the Nation of Islam.[38] Through Noble Drew Ali, Marcus Garvey, Edward Wilmot Blyden, and Mufti Muhammad Sadiq, "Islam" emerged in the early decades of the twentieth century within the discursive lexicon of Black nationalism and liberation. At the same time, as the nation transitioned to empire at the turn of the century, "Islam" existed concurrently as an exotic oddity, an orientalized marker of a mysterious Middle East inhabited by "Moslems" and an ostensible religious threat to Christianity, reflected in the work of Protestant missionaries. As such, the early twentieth century marked the moment in which "Islam" came represent a number of at times opposed—yet always mutually constituted and imbricated—understandings of its meaning in the United States, of a far away, exotic religion and culture associated with the Middle East; a religious threat; a language and logic of Black freedom; and, later, to white Americans, an insurgent Black threat. For Black working-class women like Florence Watts and others, "Islam" was a term they had heard in political discussions of the day in relation to Black nationalism and Pan Africanism, but it was also one linked to notions of refinement or status, as it signaled a world beyond Bronzeville—a world that offered new imaginative geographies and spiritual horizons in which they could find safe harbor and construct expansive identities beyond the U.S. nation-state, beyond the racist terrains that circumscribed their bodies and minds in the post-Reconstruction United States.

"Pastor, Prophet, Proselytizer"

In 1922, Florence Watts lived just blocks away from the AMI mosque, and before eventually going in, she may have walked by on occasion or wondered about the men and women in "exotic" and "Eastern" dress she saw in her neighborhood from time to time. However, the place where many Black women in Bronzeville likely first "saw" Ahmadiyya Islam and learned of its teachings was on the "Woman's Page" of the *Chicago Defender*. On August 19, 1922, between the monthly column "News of the Music World" and an advice column titled "Advice to the Wise and Otherwise" by a writer calling herself Princess Mysteria, the paper ran a feature story on this page titled "Those Who're Missionaries to Christians," accompanied by the subhead, "Prophet Sadiq Brings Allah's Message into Chicago and Makes Proselytes." The piece detailed the scene of one of Dr. Mufti Muhammad Sadiq's lectures for "a score of worshippers . . . gathered in the newly-domed 'mosque' of the Ahmadia Moslem mission at

4448 Wabash Avenue," a location at the heart of Bronzeville. Elaborating on Sadiq's appearance, reporter Roger Didier offered a description reflective of the orientalist and racial logics of the time:

> Dr. Mufti Muhammad Sadiq, pastor, prophet, and proselytizer, calmly discoursed on the evident inconsistencies of the Christian faith. Dr. Sadiq looks the part, having the appearance of a brown-skinned Jew, cast in a slender mold with sideburns that grow into a flowing beard of gospel likeness. His brow is narrow, but high; the eyes, brown, clear, and alert; the nose, large and domineering, as with Jews of the older type, and a white moustache covers the ample lips, which are a long way from the top of the head and sit securely on what suggests itself is a square and model chin.[39]

Didier then went on to describe Sadiq's wardrobe ("a green baize full-length jacket with scarlet red lining," "a skull cap with symbolic

Figure 1.2. Mufti Muhammad Sadiq. Photograph from the *Moslem Sunrise*, January 1923. Image reproduction courtesy of New York Public Library.

Figure 1.3. Al-Sadiq Mosque in Chicago. Photograph
from the *Moslem Sunrise*, January 1923. Image
reproduction courtesy of New York Public Library.

markings," and "slippers") and offered a careful inventory of the audience
in the room, which included "a huge, brown individual" with "a ferocious scowl," "a dental student from Calcutta," a "fair-skinned Russian
[with] sandy or reddish hair," "the very dark Mr. Augustus who used to
belong to St. Mark's Church in this city," and "half a dozen Garveyites,"
including "one pretty yellow girl and another not so pretty."[40]

Following the careful visual descriptors, the reporter finally turned
to the content of Sadiq's lecture, which the missionary delivered while
"planted rather leisurely against the wall" and "his small fine hands had

just ceased fingering a handsomely bound copy of the Koran." The article is worth quoting at length:

There is but one God, said he. All the others are mere prophets, including Jesus. Mahomet [sic] was the last and the equal of the others. None is to be worshipped, not even Jesus or Mahomet. Only God, the one God, must be served. The Trinity is an illusion—the word is not found in the Christian Bible and its principle cannot be sustained. God created all races, all colors. The Mohammedan faith makes no difference between race or class. One of Mahomet's trusted followers, the chief *muezzin*, was an Abyssinian brought from slavery to the royal household. The sultan had no special seat in the mosque. All worshippers are equal in the sight of God. The Koran is the unadorned word of God, the Bible is much the word of man. Mohammedanism is practical, Christianity is not.[41]

Through Didier's article, one sees the appeal of Sadiq's message to the multiracial, but mostly Black, audience in attendance at the mosque that day. As Moustafa Bayoumi has written of the early Ahmadiyya mission, Sadiq's words conveyed a universalist message that was carefully attuned to U.S. racial logics of the time. Through his exhortations of Islam's egalitarianism—for example, Islam did not make differences between race and class, and the mention of Islam's first muezzin, Bilal, who was Black—Sadiq opened "a critical space for race in the realm of the sacred" that enabled Black Americans to "metaphorically travel beyond the confines of national identities [to] become 'Asiatics' and remain Black . . . to be proud of their African heritage *and* feel a sense of belonging to the participation with Asia."[42] In other words, Sadiq conveyed Islam as a belief system that offered an expansive network of kinship and connection both in the physical and spiritual world, specifically in the direct relationship between the individual and God that would not require Black Americans to forsake the feeling of race pride or anger at white supremacy.

Yet as Bayoumi points out, a strong orientalist logic shaped the appeal of Islam to Black, as well as other, Americans in the 1920s; Sadiq's "slippers" and his "small fine hands" are exotic and attractive signifiers of a faraway "East" that stand in strong contrast to the reporter's descriptions of the "ferocious scowl" and "the very dark" skin of Black audience members. As such, the *Defender* article highlights a critical factor in understanding Islam's appeal to Black Americans, and particularly to Black women: that the allure and promise of Ahmadiyya Islam was largely premised upon the complex relationships forged between Sadiq and other Ahmadi missionaries and the movement's followers. In the case of Florence Watts and the rest of the Four American Moslem Ladies, the relationships were between a South Asian man and Black migrant women. To the latter, it was significant that Sadiq was neither Black nor White—and thus not a bearer or embodiment of white supremacy—and conjured impressions, as Didier's article states, of "a brown-skinned Jew." This description simultaneously allied the missionary to the faraway geography of the Middle East and a non-Christian religion, while positioning Sadiq and his "brown skin" as an intermediary presence within the color-conscious, black-white racial hierarchies of the United States at the time. Combined with his egalitarian message and his exotic aura, Sadiq's racial intermediary status was critical to spurring interest and shaping the appeal of his teachings to women like Florence and her peers.

For two months following the publication of the article, throughout August and September 1922, the AMI's meetings were advertised in the "Churches" section of the *Defender*'s Woman's Page, with this brief listing:

> *Ahmadia Moslem mosque, 4446 Wabash avenue—Sunday evening meeting, 8 p.m. Sermon by M. M. Sadiq of India. All welcome.*

Owing to its placement on the "Woman's Page," Black women—not men—would be the first to learn of the AMI's meetings and thus, convey information about them to their husbands, families, friends, neighbors, and so on. Why the original story on Sadiq, as well as the subsequent listings, were published on the "Woman's Page" of the *Defender* is unclear; it is likely that since much of the paper's reporting on religion and church life ran in the women's section, it was a natural fit to run to piece on the AMI there as well. While there is no way to substantiate that Florence Watts or any of the other Four American Moslem Ladies learned of the AMI through the *Defender*, the timing of the publication of their photograph in January 1923 coincides with their attendance of a meeting in the months following the *Defender* items, connoting that they either saw the ad in the paper and attended a meeting or heard about the meeting from others who saw the advertisements on the "Woman's Page."

The ads most certainly ran at the behest of Sadiq, who carefully cultivated the AMI's publicity efforts and managed every aspect of its outreach and communications. From all accounts, it is apparent that Dr. Mufti Muhammad Sadiq was a quick, and extremely insightful, study—a highly educated, articulate man who recognized and mobilized the political and social landscape around him to advance his work as the first Ahmadiyya missionary in the United States. Sadiq arrived in America on February 15, 1920, landing in the port of Philadelphia on the ship SS *Haverford* from London. Upon arrival, Sadiq was immediately detained by U.S. immigration officials under suspicion of polygamy, owing to the assumptions of the immigration officials that any and all "Moslems" were engaged in polygamous practices. When in prison, the missionary noted the very real affects of racism, in particular, anti-Black racism, in his newfound place of work—an understanding that would indelibly shape his proselytization efforts and the racial composition of those he believed would be most amenable to his message.[43]

Sadiq came to record many of his understandings and observations about race in the United States in the *Moslem Sunrise*, the bimonthly publication Sadiq began after setting up the AMI's headquarters in Highland Park, Michigan (a suburb of Detroit) in 1921. In Highland Park, he connected with a small community of Lebanese and Syrian Muslims, publishing his newsletter in the living room of Muhammad Karoub, a Lebanese businessman who established the first mosque in the Detroit Area.[44] While their denominations differed—Karoub and his community were Sunni Muslims—Sadiq was welcomed into the small immigrant Detroit Muslim community, where they bonded over the shared nature of their Islamic identities. Yet Sadiq felt many of the Muslims he encountered in the United States had lost sight of the true meaning of their faith, which he addressed in the October 1921 issue in the essay "My Advice to the Muhammedans in America." In it, he addressed the "many Muhammadans in this country who come from Syria,

Palestine, Albania, Serbia, Bosnia, Turkey, Kurdistan, and India," which he estimated numbered "in thousands." He observed that for many of these immigrant Muslims, Islam was "not playing practical part in your everyday life [sic]" and lamented that they were forgetting their daily prayers, forgoing the study of Arabic, marrying non-Muslim women, and not passing on their religion to their children. He especially disdained the practice of adopting "American" names: "Retain your Moslem names—Muhammad, Ahmad, Ali, and so forth, and don't become Sams, Georges, James, Mikes, etc."

In addition, despite his mutual respect and cooperation with Karoub and the Highland Park Sunni Muslim community, Sadiq was constantly trying to convince others of the superiority of Ahmadiyya Islam. In the United States, Sadiq realized he could find a far more receptive audience to Ahmadiyya than in his homeland; most in America knew nothing or little about Islam, of orthodoxy and heterodoxy, of the political and cultural debates that fueled varying interpretations of Islam. In particular, Americans were unaware that in Sadiq's native South Asia, the orthodox Sunni Muslim establishment viewed the Ahmadiyya as a heretical movement. While Ahmadiyya religious practices were largely identical to those of orthodox Sunni Islam in basic ceremonial duties, such as prayer, fasting, and almsgiving, Ahmadis diverged from the majority of Sunni Muslims in regard to the notion of Prophecy and their interpretation of Jesus, according the teachings of their movement's founder, Hazrat Mirza Ghulam Ahmad.[45] Thus, perhaps because of doctrinal differences, or simply because his mission outgrew the space of Karoub's living room, in early 1922 Sadiq set his sites on Chicago, purchasing the property on South Wabash with the strong awareness that the movement's message would resonate forcefully with the neighborhood's Black American inhabitants.

Sadiq's Chicago mosque opened to the public in June 1922, and in July the missionary published the first issue of the *Moslem Sunrise* from his new headquarters. Of the move, he wrote in his monthly "Brief Report of the Work in America,"

> Permanent quarters of our Mission have now been established in Chicago where I have bought a large house—a part of which with necessary alterations has been fixed up into A MOSQUE and the rest decorated and furnished as the Mission House and office of Moslem Sunrise.[46]

Sadiq went on to mention that he had been offered the opportunity to set up the AMI's permanent headquarters in Detroit but had declined, stating, "I think Chicago is a better place for our central office in this country than any other city."

In Bronzeville, Mufti Muhammad Sadiq did all he could to "demystify" Islam for American audiences and employed his charisma and intellectual faculties to make a case for why Americans—and particularly Black Americans—should reject Christianity in favor of Islam. Sadiq emphasized Islam's flexibility in the very way he set up the AMI meeting house at 4448 South Wabash, anticipating that the Black Americans inhabitants of the neighborhood would wander into the building from the high-traffic area where the mosque was located, between East 44th and East 45th Streets, just blocks away from the corner of 47th and State Street, one of the busiest intersections in Bronzeville, where "people came to see and be seen, shop, conduct business, dine and dance," and where the "crowds reflected the diverse mix of people living in the black belt; young and old, poor and prosperous, professionals and laborers."[47] As the advertisements in the *Chicago Defender* indicated, the Sunday night meetings were open to all, from the curious to critics, and along with recent converts, Sadiq personally fielded questions and inquiries from all who might pass through. He also lived in the apartment above the mosque, and thus he was always readily available to welcome inquisitive guests who wanted to chat and learn about Ahmadiyya Islam when he was in town.

All this reflected the missionary's acute race consciousness, spurred by his time in detention, as well as his interactions with Garveyites and other Pan-Africanists, through which he learned a great deal on how to speak directly to the hopes and aspirations of Black Americans.[48] In the October 1921 *Moslem Sunrise*, Sadiq penned an essay titled "The Only Solution of Color Prejudice," in which he stated that Islam is the answer to the race problem in America—words that would be famously echoed by Malcolm X in his autobiography in 1965. Sadiq's short piece is notable in the ways it identifies racism as endemic to Christianity and the church. "It is a pity," Sadiq writes, "that no preaching of equality or Christian Charity has so far been able to do away with this evil [racism]." Stating that, "in the East, we never hear of such things occurring between the peoples," Sadiq proclaims that, in Islam, "no Church has ever had seats reserved for anybody and if a Negro enters first and takes the front seat even the Sultan, if he happens to come after him, never thinks of removing him from that seat." He rejects the claim that "Christianity can destroy the color hostilities" and specifically addresses the failure of Christianity in the United States—remarks clearly directed at the Black American community he now saw as his target audience:

> But I ask, has not Christianity failed in this respect right here in America, the very land of freedom, equality, and justice? . . . I believe and it is a well-proven fact that Islam is the only religion that has ever destroyed color and race prejudices from the minds of the people. Go to the East and you will find the fairest people of Syria and Turkestan eating at the same table with the darkest African and treating each other as brothers and friends. . . . If you want to implant the ideals of Universal Brotherhood in the world, come and gather under the . . . Ahmadia Movement in Islam.[49]

"All the Men as Well as the Women"

While the AMI's hopes for racial equality and dignity through Islam have been acknowledged in existing scholarship,[50] issues of gender and women's rights are mostly ignored in discussions of the organization. In addition, whereas certain scholars have rightfully positioned Black women's conversion to Islam in a feminist context,[51] such a lens has not been applied to thinking through U.S. Muslim women's identities in the early twentieth century. Sadiq was an intuitive individual, one who quickly tapped into the ways race and racism shaped the U.S. American landscape and psyche. From advertising on the "Woman's Page" to enlisting women in key administrative roles, Sadiq understood that the AMI could gain the most converts and grow its mission most effectively through the work of both men and women combined, an approach that is reflected in the pages in the *Moslem Sunrise*. Having lived in England prior to his arrival to the United States, Sadiq was familiar with burgeoning discourses of suffrage and women's rights. Although Mufti Muhammad Sadiq likely did not call himself feminist, he certainly presented Islam's teachings in a way that spoke to women's desires for freedom and for the full acknowledgment of their humanity in the early twentieth century, in particular their capacities for intellectual and spiritual development and growth. Indeed, what is striking about the early editions of the *Moslem Sunrise*—indeed, in all of the issues published during his tenure as head missionary in the United States—is their continual focus on women's rights and the gender egalitarianism of Islam.

Sadiq's ideas of gender equity and women's rights were formed in the context of British India during a time when new forms of gender relations were emerging on the South Asian subcontinent as a result of British occupation and colonialism. Beginning in the late nineteenth century, a social reform debate began to take place across India addressing the inferior position of women in society. However, this debate focused almost exclusively on Hindu women, and Muslim women, as well as other non-Hindu women, were mostly sidelined. Yet Indian Muslims themselves expressed strong, and differing, opinions on the status of women, with the two most prominent views being the "modernist" critique of women's inferior position both in India and in Islam, and the perspective of the *ulema*, Muslim theologians who interpreted Quranic verses and the *sharia*. Modernist views "were influenced by Western critiques of Islam—particularly the practice of *purdah* [veiling and seclusion], the lack of women's education, and their discrimination within Muslim law"—and argued for "the abolition of traditional gender roles, reform in Muslim Law, and a greater public role for Muslim women based on the principle of equal rights."[52] The *ulema*'s position, in contrast, "was based on the orthodox Islamic tradition symbolized by the notion of women as *fitna* [potential disorder]," which led to the conclusion that "women's social interaction with men had to be regulated, which in effect translated into a control over female sexuality." The *ulema* supported education for women, but only in regard to the religion. Sadiq's position, and that of the AMI, could be characterized as primarily modernist—advocating for women's education in religion and beyond and for women's increased role in the public sphere. However, the AMI certainly did not support "the abolition of traditional gender roles," and its literature frequently extolled the virtue of marriage and motherhood, which deeply appealed to Black migrant women. What is important to note, however, is that the AMI and Mirza Ghulam Ahmad saw their movement as a corrective to the corruption of the *ulema*, a movement to cleanse Islam of false innovation and cultural and political

perversion. Thus, the movement's, and thus Sadiq's, emphasis on wom-
en's value and import not just in Islam but also in society-at-large, stood
as a challenge to the *ulema*'s conception of women as *fitna*—a rejection
clearly expressed through Sadiq's reliance and investment in women as
important and valued members of the AMI.

Madame Rahatullah

Prior to the AMI's arrival in Chicago, a large number of Sadiq's converts in the United States were white, including a significant number of
white women. In many cases, white women served as a bridge between
Sadiq and his Black female followers, either as actual physical intermediaries or as representative voices of Muslim women through their
writing in the *Moslem Sunrise*. The most prominent of all of the movement's converts, male or female, in the pages of the *Moslem Sunrise*
was a white woman named Madame Rahatullah or, as she was alternately called, "Madam Siddica-tun-Nisa Rahatullah," "Mrs. Mustapha
Thaha" (her married name), "Rahatullah," or "Ella May Garber" (her
birth name, which is on various occasions listed beside her Islamic
monikers). Rahatullah was a formidable presence in the early AMI,
working closely with Sadiq beginning in mid-1921, when she is listed
in the monthly conversion roles as "an American lady in Islam for the
last 10 years [who] has been working for Islam in several places and
now intends to do the Ahmadia Islamic work in New York."[53] As that
description indicates, Rahatullah converted to Islam ten years prior to
Sadiq's arrival in the United States, and she had been searching for an
Islamic teacher when she met Sadiq. She details her journey to Islam
in an extended personal essay in the October 1922 issue of the *Moslem Sunrise*, titled "Islam My Savior," which provides an interesting
glimpse into why a white American woman during the early twentieth
century would convert to Islam, as well as offering insights into the
types of relationships Sadiq cultivated with American women in order
to advance his mission.[54]

 "The good Mufti," Rahatullah begins, referring to Sadiq, "has requested me to write a short synopsis of my life and why I became a Moslem." Born in Indiana "on a beautiful farm where the trees and flowers
welcomed me into the world," Rahatullah encounters difficulties from

Figure 1.4. Mrs. Mustapha Thaha, or Madame
Rahatullah. Photograph from the *Moslem Sunrise*,
October 1922. Image reproduction courtesy of the
New York Public Library.

birth; she has a twin sister who dies at birth, and her mother passes away shortly thereafter, at the young age of twenty-one. Unable to care for her, her father puts young Ella May in the care of her grandparents. When she is ten, her father remarries, and she is sent back to live with him and her new stepmother, with whom she said her "life was a lonely one, always craving for something I knew not what." By age fifteen, she marries and gives birth to a son named Ralph (who would later also convert to Ahmadiyya Islam and adopt the name Basheer). Her marriage soon fails, and she is left to raise her son on her own. It is then that Ella May begins a series of travels "from coast to coast," studying music and eventually enrolling in college in San Francisco, where she "takes up the study of elocution, literature, and oratory." Through her studies, she states her mind catches "on fire" and leads her to the study of Islamic Sufi poetry. In the poems, she "first began to see Islam's light," and her attraction to the religion grows when she meets a Sufi teacher named Sheik Mohammad Majid Gilani in 1915, whom she says "lifted me far above this world." Sadly, Sheikh Gilani dies a year later, in 1916, and Rahatullah says she mourns for the next two years, when she continues to live "only for him." In 1918, however, "a dear soul was sent to lift my soul again." This soul was Dr. Mufti Muhammad Sadiq, whom Rahatullah calls "a friend, a master, and a savior." She devotes her life to Sadiq, the AMI, and to "the submission to one God, the only power which never fails and which never dies." Sadiq also arranges her marriage with a Muslim man named Mustapha Thaha, whom Rahatullah marries in Highland Park, Michigan, on February 6, 1922, just months before Sadiq would relocate to Bronzeville.[55]

While Rahatullah's essay does not explicitly address issues of gender or how Islam appeals to her as a woman, her life experiences of parental abandonment, divorce, and single motherhood indicate she certainly experienced shame and societal ostracism that would have stemmed from her experiences as a young, unwed mother. Rahatullah's attraction to, and eventual acceptance of, Islam was likely linked to her desire for acceptance, belonging, and spiritual and intellectual growth, a sentiment reflected in the deep gratitude she expressed to Sadiq not only for guiding her but also for finding her a "a noble, pure-minded man for a husband," encouraging her writing, and deeming it worthy of publication and praise.[56] While there is no indication of inappropriate conduct or abuse of power on Sadiq's part, Rahatullah's responses reveal the close, even intimate, types of relationships Sadiq had with his female followers owing to how he addressed his female followers as peers and took pains to express the equality of men and women in Islam.

Indeed, the very first quotation from the Qur'an Sadiq includes in the *Sunrise*, Surah 33:35, is one often cited by contemporary feminists as one that demonstrates the radical gender egalitarianism of Islam, which is expressed through the constant repetition of the phrase, in Sadiq's translation, "all the men as well as the women," as the passage explains the means by which a believer may receive God's rewards in heaven, that is,

Surely, (1) *All the men as well as the women* who resign themselves to God and make their will one with the will of the Creator;

(2) *And all the men as well as the women* who believe in God, His Angels, His Messengers and the Day of Judgment;

(3) *And all the men as well as the women* who obey the commandments of God that come direct to them or through his Messengers old and new—all the devout . . .[57]

In addition to constant repetition of "all the men as well as the women" in the passage, Sadiq adds this note to make the point about women's equality in Islam absolutely clear:

Note: Sex makes no distinction in the rules for the uplift of the soul to higher levels of purity, calmness, and union with Allah. Men and women—we are all children of God. To Him we belong and to Him we return. Thus says the Holy Book.[58]

Sister Zeineb

In some ways, Florence Watts's story parallels that of Madame Rahatullah: that of a single woman who arrived in Chicago through a circuitous and difficult journey who would eventually find a community and spiritual home in Ahmadiyya Islam. Florence's life also intersected with that of many Black migrants who were inspired by the pro-Black rhetoric of Marcus Garvey and the United Negro Improvement Association, newcomers to the North lured there by promises of freedom and equality, only to find rampant racism and scant opportunities. Moreover, her life bore similarities to the lives of women of the Black Church, who asserted themselves through the politics of respectability in the 1920s urban North. Florence was surely desirous of full acknowledgment of her humanity, and she sought moral and ethical frameworks to guide her through the chaos and bustle of Bronzeville. Unlike Rahatullah, however, Florence Watts was not an educated, well-traveled white woman, and she likely had not engaged in any previous training or study of Islam, nor had she studied with a Muslim sheikh or been exposed to Sufi poetry. As a working-class Black woman who worked haphazard hours in menial positions, struggling to maintain a marriage and raise a child, it would have been difficult, although not impossible, for her to commit herself to the cause of the United Negro Improvement Association or to any political cause, for that matter. Her schedule and class status would have also made it difficult for her to find stability in the Black Church, where she might have been scrutinized for her class status or been unable to attend services and meetings at set times because of her work schedule. Literate, but minimally so, Florence had few opportunities in her day-to-day life for intellectual, spiritual, or physical development and advancement. And while she may have been far more mobile—"free"—than her parents or grandparents before her, her dreams of seeking a better life for herself and her family were hampered by the reality of supporting oneself and one's kin on a maid's or cook's salary, in environs where she would only ever be a boarder in another's home. Florence Watts would not have the opportunity to travel beyond the United States, to see the world that was becoming increasingly present in the day-to-day lives of early twentieth-century Chicagoans. And in her day-to-day life, in her movements between Maryland and Illinois, Evanston and Bronzeville, she would surely note the incredible disparities of wealth and status of Blacks and whites, and the racial segregation of neighborhoods. She would have confronted the reality of sexual advances and physical violence from male employers and community members and would dream of world where her daughter, Anerilia, might have a better, safer, and more expansive life.

After noticing the AMI meeting house, seeing the ad in the *Defender*, or hearing about the group from friends, Florence Watts might have finally stopped into the meeting house. Sadiq or one of his interlocutors, such as Madame Rahatullah, would welcome her in, show her around the mosque, and gently, little by little, introduce her to the basic teachings of Islam. They might have done so through conversation and by introducing her to other members of the congregation, as well as by offering her copies of the literature the Ahmadiyya Movement freely distributed, which was a hallmark of the organization owing to what Mirza Ghulam Ahmad called the "jihad of words," through which Islam was to spread as the world's dominant religion, not by the sword, but by the pen. Consequently, Sadiq provided reading materials to anyone who might be interested. In addition to the *Sunrise*, this included the AMI's international magazine, the *Review of Religions,* and religious pamphlets that instructed readers on how to perform *salat* (prayer), offered hadith and interpretations (the sayings and actions of the Prophet Muhammad), and the writings and teaching of Mirza Ghulam Ahmad. Moreover, the Ahmadis were the purveyors of the first complete English translation of the Qur'an in the United States, translated by Maulana Muhammad Ali. Florence Watts would have left the Wabash Avenue meetinghouse after her visit not only with new ideas but also with a great deal of reading material, which she could go home and read on their own time and then share with George, the Robinsons, her neighbors, and co-workers.

Then, perhaps on her second or third visit to the meetinghouse, Florence would begin to learn about "Muslim women"—how they dressed, raised their families, interacted with others, and so forth. Sadiq or another teacher would emphasize the equal status of women in Islam, echoing his sentiment as expressed in the *Moslem Sunrise.* After reading over the materials, Florence might note both the focus on race pride and Islam as a solution to the race problem, the egalitarian language, the emphasis on women's humanity. She would also note the similarities between Islam and Christianity, how the stories of Adam and Eve, Mary and Joseph, and the figure of Jesus—although as a prophet, not the son of God—all figured in Islam. She might have been fascinated by images of Muslim women's clothing and dress in South Asia, asked questions about dietary choices and prayer, and met other interested parties, women like Mrs. Thomas, Mrs. Robinson, and Mrs. Clark, the other women in the photo. In the meeting room at the mosque at 4448 South Wabash Street, they would begin to talk about their lives and their histories, and they would set up times to meet again to talk about what they had learned from one of Sadiq's lectures or to discuss the literature they were given. For those who continued to come to meetings, to return to the mosque, eventually they would be asked to profess their faith, which in the AMI was done through the pronouncement of the *shahada*—"La illaha illa Allah, Muhammad rasoolu Allah," which translates to "There is no god but God, and Muhammad is his messenger"—and the signing of the *Bai'at* form, a "Declaration of Initiation" required of all those converting through the AMI, in which they declared faith in Allah, Muhammad as His Servant and Messenger, and Mirza Ghulam Ahmad as "the Promised Messiah." After this, they were Muslims.

One of the first acts they engaged in as Muslims was the adoption of new names. Florence chose "Zeineb"—a name that means a fragrant, flowering tree, or "beauty" in Arabic, as well as being the name of many of the women associated with the Prophet Muhammad, one of his daughters, two of his wives, and a granddaughter. As Sister Zeineb, she began her efforts to live and express herself as a Muslim women in a time when "Islam" was largely illegible to all around them. Walking to the mosque, Florence hurried past speakeasies and churches as she clutched the scarf around her clothing in the manner she had learned from photographs or descriptions of South Asian Muslim women provided to her by Sadiq and his contemporaries. What looks might she have gotten from passersby on the street? What conclusions might they have drawn about her attire? And how did Florence now see the street, the speakeasies, and Bronzeville as a Muslim? With her knowledge that she was part of a global community, that Islam could address the nation's race problem, that women were equal in the eyes of God, that she could reject Christianity and still have a relationship with God, Florence—Sister Zeineb—likely now confronted her environment with a newfound mettle, a moral-ethical framework she believed could protect her and guide her not only from "racism," writ large, but also from the everyday dangers of her life.

As a Muslim, Zeineb expressed her new identity through the comportment of her body, not only in her dress but also in a rejection of pork and alcohol, in how she sought out places to pray, and in whether she was able (or not able) to fast from sunrise to sunset during the month of Ramadan. She necessarily enacted this expression in difficult and unaccommodating circumstances—cleaning homes, working in hot, cramped kitchens, pushing through the bustling streets of Bronzeville, avoiding the dangers of the street and the constant threat of sexual and physical violence. Yet confrontations did not end when she got home, shutting her door to the outside world. As a boarder in a home not her own, she would have to explain her newfound practices to her landlords, as well as to family, friends, and co-workers who knew little to nothing about Islam. They might ply her with questions about why she would make such choice, inquire about the "exotic" Indian man she now called her teacher, or at times, mock and make derisive remarks about a religion that seemed to place its followers outside the fold of

Christian salvation. In explaining, defending, and practicing her new faith in environments that more often than not did not, and could not, recognize or accommodate Islam's existence, Sister Zeineb defined and filled the contours of her identity as U.S. Muslim women *against* the world around her, thus producing the intellectual, physical, and religious insurgency inherent to women's practice of Islam in America. With her newfound "sisters" such as Khairat, Ahmadia, and Ayesha, as well as the global community of women with whom she now shared a faith, Zeineb crafted modes of "Islamic" behavior during a time when there was no such thing.

Whereas Black male converts could mimic the behavior of Mufti Muhammad Sadiq and the other South Asian missionaries who would come after him, Black American Ahmadi Muslim women in the early twentieth century had no such precedents, instead taking the little information they had and fashioning innovative, expansive, and insurgent identities that consistently demonstrated their creativity, resourcefulness, and commitment to Islam. To return to the photo with which this story began, it is clear that, while the Four American Moslem Ladies did not have the fine silks and saris of their Ahmadi Muslim sisters in the Punjab, they instead made do by pulling out and pressing their best linens, putting on their church clothes and hats, and wrapping themselves as regally and as beautifully as they knew how. They innovated and improvised, defying their detractors, and they actively, with purpose, chose Islam. As they looked into the lens of the camera that day, and as they looked out at the world around them every day, they did so with the visions of self-made Muslim women, as working-class Black women working to survive—and striving to flourish—upon the ever-evolving racial, gendered, and religious landscapes of Bronzeville and beyond.

2

Insurgent Domesticity

*Race and Gender in Representations of NOI Women during
the Cold War Era*

The women were carrying on their own conversations, in
low tones; I gathered that they were not expected to take
place in male conversations.
—James Baldwin, writing of the women of the Nation of
Islam in *The Fire Next Time*

To tell a story of American Islam through the lives and perspectives of
Muslim women is an intimate endeavor. This story is necessarily close
to the body, a narrative of how Islam has been embodied, felt, and practiced by women. This intimacy also has much to do with contemporary
American perceptions of the role of religiosity and spirituality in people's lives, with how religion and spirituality are implemented and form
the rhythms of our days, and in how we perform and experience religion
and spirituality in bodies interpellated through race, gender, class, and
sexuality. Because of the First Amendment, many Americans believe we
are a secular nation and understand religion as primarily to be expressed
and practiced in private or domestic space (or only in congregation
with fellow co-religionists). Thus, in a great deal of public and scholarly
discourse, the religious practices of women not only go largely undocumented but also, at times, feel almost taboo, as if to discuss them would
constitute a type of violation or offense. In the case of U.S. American
Muslims, this is further complicated by the fact that, as Islam is a non-
white, non-Christian religion, domestic expressions of religiosity and
spirituality have been, and still are, often *intentionally* kept hidden by its
practitioners, owing to fear of violation or harm.

This was certainly the case with the Nation of Islam (NOI), the
country's most prominent Muslim organization throughout the 1950s

and 1960s, insofar as how their members—particularly NOI women—
expressed their faith and practiced their religion was largely obscured
to those outside of the organization. What did become known of the
NOI's practices in the media and other outlets was carefully mediated
and controlled by the organization's leadership, specifically by the Honorable Elijah Muhammad, who headed the organization from 1934 until
his death in 1975, and by Malcolm X, or El Hajj Malik El-Shabazz, who,
until his break with the group in 1963 (followed by his assassination
in 1965), was the group's most prominent spokesperson. For example,
Muhammad would permit only Black journalists, photographers, and
writers to cover the NOI, owing to his distrust of having white journalists among his community. Muhammad was keenly aware that who
was telling their story mattered, as did Malcolm X, who the cultural
critic Maurice Berger, writing in the *New York Times* in 2012, called a
"visual strategist" and "one of the most media-savvy black leaders of the
period."[1] Their awareness of the media's power consistently guided the
NOI's engagements with the press and other media outlets, including
the ways in which Muslim women appeared in the mainstream press, as
well as in the group's own publications.

As I explore in this chapter, images and representations of Black
Muslim women's domesticity, of the more intimate spaces of their lives,
were issued sparingly yet featured prominently in much of the media
coverage of the NOI from the late-1950s through the 1960s. These
depictions acted as expressions of what I call "insurgent domesticity,"
which performed a specific type of ideological work that rendered the
domestic lives of Muslim women as sites of political struggle amid increasing demands for civil rights and as a response to Cold War gender
politics, in particular against the fear of a "crisis of masculinity" among
white American men. By conforming to certain feminine ideals and
embracing domesticity in these images, Black Muslim women triggered
anxieties for white Americans against the evolving racial and gender
politics of the Cold War era by asserting the moral and spiritual superiority of the Black patriarchal family over white American families
in decay. At the same time, such images were a strong attraction for
new followers to the NOI and Islam, who were drawn to the group's
strict implementation of traditional gender roles and who saw them as
a means to reverse the breakdown of the Black family that had occurred

under slavery. Whether in accounts that portrayed the NOI as a virulent anti-white hate group or those that extolled the merits of Muhammad's teachings on Islam and Black nationalism, depictions of Black Muslim women reflected the deeply politicized nature of NOI Muslim women's domestic lives, as imagined by both the women themselves and the Black Muslim men who mediated their public exposure.[2] Such accounts reveal how the domestic spaces and practices of U.S. Muslim women signified alternative, and insurgent, forms of nation building, as well as notions of transnational encounter and global citizenship.

As with the Four American Moslem Ladies discussed in chapter 1, NOI women certainly made conscious decisions *as Muslim women*, in this case to take on domestic tasks such as cooking, cleaning, and childrearing in order to express their devotion to Islam and to the project of Black nation building. As existing accounts of NOI women show,[3] they did so as well-informed and agential historical actors who saw themselves as enacting deliberate critiques of white supremacy. Yet in doing so, they also necessarily succumbed to a conception of Black female personhood, as the theologian and scholar of African American religion Eboni Marshall Turman writes, that was "dependent on [their] derivative subjugation to Black male power" and produced "a paradox of gender ethics" that "simultaneously and paradoxically" cast Black women as depraved and dangerous *and* as "beautiful Black sisters" who were to be respected, loved, admired, and protected (a sentiment expressed by Sonia Sanchez, as cited in this book's introduction).[4] Whereas the insurgent domesticity of NOI Muslim women was constructed, practiced, and performed against devaluations of blackness and Black womanhood, producing a womanist consciousness among Black Muslim women, it also at times buttressed "a distinct brand of Afro-patriarchy and misogyny" that employed "Islam" as a justification for women's subjugation.[5] Thus, in the depictions of NOI Muslim women I discuss in this chapter, I seek to reveal how such complexities and contradictions around issues of race and gender, the "public" and "private," and between the religious and the political in this particular historical era constructed NOI Muslim women's identities and images in the press and in U.S. culture against the charged racial and gender logics of the Cold War and white anxiety about civil rights.

To explore the insurgent domesticity of NOI Muslim women, I consider a series of representations of the NOI featuring Muslim women that appeared between 1959 and 1963 in the mainstream press, the organization's own publications, and in popular culture and literature. This chapter begins with an examination of the portrayal of Black women in the 1959 *CBS News* documentary *The Hate That Hate Produced*, which introduced the NOI and Malcolm X to America.[6] I then turn to an engagement with the NOI publication *The Messenger* magazine, which also appeared in 1959 and was put together and personally edited by Malcolm X. Following that, I investigate a 1963 photo essay on the NOI in *Life* magazine with both images and an essay by the acclaimed photographer and writer Gordon Parks. I close the chapter by considering the portrayal of NOI women in James Baldwin's classic 1963 text, *The Fire Next Time*, in which the writer describes in detail his dinner with the Honorable Elijah Muhammad at the leader's Chicago home. Throughout my readings and analysis, I continually emphasize Black Muslim women's agency in their engagements with Islam as a lived religion, alongside the arbitration and manipulation of the their images by male leadership in the NOI, the press, and other intermediaries.

Across such various locations in media and culture, such domestic images of NOI women circulated widely in the U.S. public sphere during the Cold War era. While mainstream media outlets generally made the distinction that "Black Muslims" were unlike the Muslims of the "East," oftentimes portraying the movement as "neither legitimately religious nor authentically Islamic,"[7] such differences were neither clear-cut nor adequately explained to the vast number of Americans encountering "Islam" and "Muslims" within the United States for the first time. Nation of Islam members considered themselves and called themselves "Muslims," part of a Pan-Islamic global community who were in solidarity with the Muslims "of the East."[8] I therefore argue that it is critical to examine such representations of Black Muslim women in Nation of Islam and other predominantly African American Muslim organizations *as images of U.S. Muslim women*. In my analysis, I show how the national anxieties and white fears regarding the NOI and Black Muslims during the Cold War shaped Islam's racial-religious form in the United States through the tropes of the Radical Black Muslim Man and the Poor Muslim Woman. As I expand upon later, the ways the "threat" of Black Muslims was described in the media and in state documents (such as the Federal Bureau of Investigation's extensive file on the Nation of Islam) laid the discursive groundwork for descriptions of Islamic Terror that would emerge at the end of the 1970s. In regard to trope of the Poor Muslim Woman, representations of the insurgent domesticity of NOI women revealed how notions of latent danger lurked beneath the stereotype of the Poor Muslim Woman, insofar as her "submission" to Islam connoted the brutal power of the Muslim men who controlled her, as well as her own blind and selfless devotion to Islam.

Before moving on, we should note the critical body of work that already exists on the women of the Nation of Islam. Indeed, of all the subjects of *Being Muslim*, the women of the Nation of Islam are among the best documented in both scholarly and popular discourse.[9] For that reason, I want to emphasize that this chapter is by no means intended to offer a comprehensive account of the lives of NOI women during this time. For example, I do not discuss perhaps one of the most influential Black Muslim women in the NOI, Sister Clara Muhammad—wife of Elijah Muhammad—who ran the organization while her husband was in prison between 1942 and 1946 for draft dodging, nor do I focus extensively on stories of any of the other powerful women in the group, such as Mother Tynetta Muhammad, who wrote a regular column for the NOI newspaper *Muhammad Speaks*. Rather, I focus less on the historical recovery and documentation of NOI's women's experiences—which the existing accounts present beautifully—and instead focus on the ways that representations of NOI women were constructed against and through Cold War era logics of race, gender, religion, and culture and the masculinist framings and norms of the NOI's (male) leadership. As I stated in the introduction, in addition to making central the role of women of color in the production of U.S. Muslim identities and culture, I also seek to explore Islam's significant historical-cultural presence in the twentieth- and twenty-first-century United States as produced and signified by women of color. Here, by examining how the domestic lives of NOI Muslim women were represented as sites of political struggle, I hope to unearth how domestic logics of race and gender have informed the abjection of Muslim women in the United States, in particular how Muslim women signify threat to the nation not only because of their foreign-ness, but also because of how they trigger deep cultural anxieties around race, religion, and gender within the national imaginary.

"The Woman Is Man's Field to Produce His Nation"

In 1923, the same year the image of the Four American Moslem Ladies appeared in the *Moslem Sunrise*, twenty-six-year-old Elijah Robert Poole and his wife Clara moved from Sandersville, Georgia, to Detroit, Michigan. Like Chicago, Detroit was a central destination for 1920s Black Southern migrants, who were lured to the city by the promise of manufacturing jobs, particularly in the burgeoning automobile industry. Between 1910 and 1920, Detroit's Black population grew from 5,741 to 40,838, and by 1930, it had grown to 120,066, making up 7.6 percent of the city's population.[10] As in Chicago, such population growth created a highly contentious racial landscape between the city's existing white residents and the new Black migrants, as well as between the Black bourgeoisie and the laboring classes.[11] These tensions directly affected the Poole family. Once in Detroit, Elijah struggled with the harsh conditions of urban industrial life, in which migrants lived in overcrowded and oftentimes squalid conditions, and experienced constant discrimination in the workforce, health care, education, and so forth. Elijah reportedly had great difficulty dealing with such hardships, bounced from job to job, and on various occasions "succumbed to despair," drinking so heavily that Clara had to often "literally pick him up off the streets of Detroit after repeated spells of drunkenness."[12]

By the close the 1920s, the Pooles had five children, and Clara knew her husband needed to change if their family were to survive. In 1931, she urged Elijah to listen to the teachings of a mysterious and charismatic "Arab street peddler" named Wallace Fard (pronounced "Far-ad") Muhammad, who had been selling exotic silks and goods to Black women in various Detroit neighborhoods.[13] The textiles, however, "were only a means to support his proselytizing mission." Fard was aware that women had much influence in their homes and communities and that they would share his teachings. Indeed, Black women who perused his silks and heard Fard's teachings persuaded their husbands, brothers, and fathers to attend his lectures. Fard told his female customers the silks came from their "home countries," which were not in Detroit, the South, or anywhere in the United States, but in faraway "Asiatic" and African lands where their true history could be found. He taught that Black Americans were descended from the original peoples of the Earth, specifically of the "Asian black nation and of the tribe of Shabazz," which originated "66 trillion years ago." Whites, however, were the product of a mad scientist named Yacub, who grafted them as "a new race of devils." At these lectures, Fard told his audiences that Black people were inherently *superior to whites*, the "white devils," as he called them. Black Americans needed to throw off their identities as "so-called Negroes," in particular the yoke of Christianity, which was the religion of the white man used to brainwash and enslave Blacks. Black Americans needed to adopt their true religion, Islam, as the foundation of a new Black nation.[14]

Fard Muhammad's message would resonate fiercely and profoundly with Elijah Poole, who felt an immediate connection with the speaker. After Fard's lecture, various reports state that when he was introduced to the speaker, Elijah declared, "I know who you are, you're God himself," to which Fard replied, "That's right, but don't tell it now. It is not time for me to be known."[15] Following this meeting, Elijah quickly became Fard's most ardent follower and best pupil, and soon Fard gave him the name Elijah Karriem, which he later changed to Elijah Muhammad. During the next three years, Elijah became Fard's chief minister of Islam, and when Fard mysteriously disappeared in 1934, Elijah oversaw the organization that was now named the Nation of Islam. Quiet and soft-spoken, with a lilting cadence to his voice, Elijah Muhammad would lead the NOI to be the nation's preeminent and best-known Muslim organization until his death in the 1975. For decades, the Messenger of Allah, as he was known, managed the large-scale development of "temples and schools, apartment houses and grocery stores, restaurants and farms."[16] Most important, as C. Eric Lincoln wrote in the first, and still influential, study of the group published in 1961, *The Black Muslims*, Muhammad gave his followers the path to Black self-determination: "a new sense of dignity, a conviction that they are more than the equals of whites," and who has taught them "knowledge of ourselves . . . that makes it possible for us [Black Americans] to obtain freedom, justice, and equality in the world, no matter what the white man thinks, no matter what the white man does."[17]

A main component of NOI doctrine was its teachings on Black women's roles in constructing a Black nation. In Elijah Muhammad's 1965 treatise, *Message to the Blackman in America*, he lays out the organization's beliefs clearly and forcefully in the sections titled "The Black

Woman" and "Protect and Elevate Your Woman." The former section famously begins, "The woman is man's field to produce his nation. If he does not keep the enemy out of his field, he won't produce a good nation. If we love our vegetable crops we will go out and turn up the leaves on that vegetable stalk and look carefully for worms that are eating up and destroying the vegetables. We will kill the worm—right?"[18]

Muhammad then states that Black men must protect Black women and that this is a central imperative of Islam: "Until we learn to love and protect our women, we will never be a fit and recognized people on the earth. The white people here among you will never recognize you until you protect your woman. . . . Our women have been and are still being used by the devil as slaves. . . . Islam will not only elevate your women but will also give you the power to control or protect them. We protect ours against all their enemies."[19]

As the title of the volume indicates, Muhammad writes his book explicitly as a message to the *Blackman*. The Messenger of Allah was plain in his exhortations that, for a Muslim woman to fulfill her religious duties, she has to assume conventional norms of womanhood, such as housekeeping, child rearing, and childhood education, while Black men are obliged to protect, as well as oversee, women so they can fulfill these said religious duties. All NOI Muslim women became members of the Moslem Girls' Training (MGT) and General Civilization Class (GCC), which taught women and girls "how to cook, clean, and ultimately master the domestic sphere. [They were] instructed to embrace not only the rudiments of traditional Islamic cultures and values but a nineteenth-century Victorian image of womanhood."[20]

Thoroughly and unapologetically patriarchal, the NOI's gender politics in the 1930s–1960s did not deter women from joining the organization; instead, they were a strong draw for many Black women. In her memoir about growing up in the Nation of Islam, Sonsyrea Tate writes that her grandparents, who joined the NOI in the 1950s, "liked the fact that in the Nation of Islam gender roles were clearly defined, rules were strictly enforced, and the individual god within in each black person was acknowledged and respected."[21] Black men were to bestow respect and full acknowledgment of Black women's humanity through their reverence of women's roles as wives and mothers. Unfortunately, Black men rarely conferred this respect in the manner women had hoped for and thus advanced misogynist logics of men's superiority over women. Yet Black women nonetheless were attracted to Muhammad's, and later Malcolm X's, proclamations regarding their beauty, purity, superiority, and immense value to the Black nation. In her discussion of Black women's relationships to Malcolm X, Farah Jasmine Griffin attributes their attraction to the charismatic leader and to Black nationalist ideology to what she calls "the promise of protection": the notion that Black men's protection and reverence would constitute a safe harbor for Black womanhood.[22] As Griffin writes, the promise of being seen as "precious," "pure," "innocent," "beautiful," and "revered" had powerful resonances for Black American women because such terms had "been equated with white womanhood and thereby femininity—both privileged spheres in our society; spheres where black women have been historically denied. Poor and working black women, and dark-skinned black women, especially, have been excluded from the discourse of the precious, pure, and protected."[23] This rhetoric of protection, observes Ula Taylor, "helped to camouflage gender inequalities" in the organization.[24]

As Dawn-Marie Gibson and Jamillah Karim note in *Women of the Nation*, women made significant contributions to the organization's development, for example, when Clara Muhammad ran the NOI when her husband was in prison. Gibson and Karim write that general misperceptions and lack of understanding about the lives of NOI women were due to their general absence in the public sphere, which was attributable to "concerns about their safety and dictates about gender spheres [that] resulted in their activism being confined within the walls and boundaries of the NOI's structures and communities."[25] Because of this confinement to the domestic/private sphere, Gibson and Karim continue, "Early Nation women exercised both formal and informal leadership positions in the Nation. . . . Nation women exercised agency *within* their religious setting."[26]

While acknowledging the NOI's patriarchal structure, Gibson and Karim argue that Black Muslim women had more agency and leadership power than in the Black church, in other words, that, even while the NOI was a deeply patriarchal and at times misogynist organization, it also provided empowering and high-ranking positions for its female members. Women were instructed and expected to embrace domesticity as essential to their nature, to submit to men, and to always support and nurture Black male power. Yet as mothers, sisters, and teachers, they held high positions in the MGT, the Nation's schools, and its business enterprises, and they considered themselves to be central to the nation-building project. In these roles, women could exert just as much influence as men, but the exercise of power could only occur through conforming to NOI gender roles, which they understood to be in service of the larger project of Black nationhood.

The Crisis of American Masculinity

The NOI's gender politics were a response and reflection to gender dynamics of white Americans. According to the sociologist Patricia Hill Collins, "Malcolm X's [and the NOI's] view on women reflected dominant views of white manhood and womanhood applied uncritically to the situation of African Americans."[27] For most of the nineteenth century, and into the early decades of the twentieth, white American women's value and worth were premised upon their conformity to Victorian norms of the cult of domesticity, which limited women's sphere of influence to the home and family. "True women" cultivated values of piety, purity, domesticity, and submissiveness, which were enforced through pervasive gender inequality and women's financial dependence upon men. Upon the shifting geographic terrains of post–World War II America, the idea of keeping white women in their "proper place" in the home merged with the language of U.S. American exceptionalism and empire. By the close of the 1950s, as the historian Elaine Tyler May writes, for many powerful white men, "American superiority rested on the ideal of the suburban home, complete with modern appliances and distinct roles for family members . . . a male breadwinner and a full-time female homemaker."[28] Within the "protective walls of the modern home," May explains, "worrisome developments like sexual liberalism, women's emancipation, and affluence would not lead to decadence but to a wholesome family life. Sex would enhance marriage, emancipated women would professionalize homemaking, and affluence would put an end to material deprivation."[29]

The domestic space of the suburban home, with the well-kept wife and the strong and productive working man, functioned as a metaphor for U.S. power in the face of Soviet communism, representative of the "expansive, secure lifestyle that post-war Americans wanted."[30] Just as the sprawling ranch home in the suburbs equipped with the latest appliances could cultivate and foster the vitality and prosperity of the (white and heteronormative) American family, the nation-state, equipped with the world's most powerful military and state-of-the-art weaponry, would foster a strident capitalist ethos of U.S. expansionism that would build wealth at home and spread U.S.-style democracy worldwide. Further, as the sociologist and race studies scholar George Lipsitz has noted, the widespread desire for home ownership and "safe" suburban communities was deeply rooted in possessive investments in whiteness, as the Federal Housing Act of 1934 contained clauses "channel(ing) almost all of the loan money toward whites" as well as "away from older inner-city neighborhoods and toward white home buyers moving into segregated suburbs."[31]

In many ways the focus on whiteness-invested home ownership and the desire for women's domesticity and "wholesome family life" in the 1950s was an anxiety-ridden response to how white women had entered the workforce en masse during World War II. Women filled an unprecedented number of jobs during wartime, a phenomenon that, as the literary scholar Douglas Field writes, would in the postwar years produce "sexual, social, and atomic anxieties that drove men and women together in an orgy of marriage, reproduction, and domesticity, yet created power struggles between the sexes. . . . Conformity inducing suburbs and frustrated men's and women's hidden lives speak of a striking amalgam of 'dis/content' for families in the post-war/Cold War era."[32] In others words, the white, suburban heteronormative family, as films such as *The Hours* (2002) and *Far from Heaven* (2002) demonstrated, was meant to neutralize the threat of the strong, financially independent women who had emerged during the war and to return women back to the home, where they "belonged."

For many, however, it seemed the damage had already been done. In a 1958 *Esquire* magazine article, the historian and social critic Arthur M. Schlesinger described what he called "the crisis of American masculinity" as central to this "striking amalgam of discontent." Schlesinger blamed aggressive women and the mass bureaucratization of society as the central factors driving this crisis, which had made American men weak and ineffectual: "The American woman . . . takes over more and more of the big decisions, controlling them indirectly when she cannot do so directly. Outside the home, one sees a similar blurring of function. While men design dresses and brew up cosmetics, women become doctors, lawyers, bank cashiers, and executives. . . . Women seem an expanding aggressive force, seizing new domains like a conquering army, while men, more and more on the defensive, are hardly able to hold their own and gratefully accept assignments from their new rulers."[33] Schlesinger's words reveal his belief that the crisis of masculinity was attributable to the ways in which women, like Soviet-style communism, threatened to rob American men of their individuality and power. In addition, the large-scale bureaucracies of the corporate workforce were sapping men of their virility—that is, "feminizing" them. Schlesinger proclaimed that men needed to reform themselves from within, arguing that "the key to the recovery of masculinity lies . . . in the problem of identity. When a person begins to find out *who* he is, he is likely to find out rather soon what sex he is. . . . For men to become men again, their first task is to recover a sense of individual spontaneity . . . to visualize himself as an individual apart from the group, whatever it is, which defines his values and commands his loyalty."[34]

The *Esquire* essay reflected what various scholars have identified as the paramount anxieties of white American men during the Cold War:[35] that they were becoming weak in the face of increasingly independent women, while also becoming mindless followers and pen pushers, much like Communists and the masses who followed fascist dictators such as Hitler and Mussolini. In other words, white men could no longer control white women because they had lost the ability, or desire, to control their own destinies; feminism was the by-product of emasculation. When women worked and sought fulfillment outside the space of the home, they were defiling their roles as dutiful citizens of the U.S. nation-state and stripping men of the ability to be their protectors and providers. The crisis of American masculinity during the Cold War arose not only out of the struggle to exert masculinist power against the "feminizing" logics of Communism but also from white men's desire to (re-)assert their power in the home and workplace by once again relegating overaggressive women to the domestic sphere.

Race was tantamount to Cold War gender anxieties, not just in regard to white anxiety but also in regard to how the nation could manage the broader question of race as it related to domestic and international policy. The crisis of "American" masculinity was a crisis of white, middle-class American male masculinity. The types of issues Schlesinger decried were inapplicable to Black men or other men of color in the United States, or, for that matter, to working-class or poor whites. Indeed, in 1955, the lynching of Emmett Till—the event that is often described as the turning point/catalyst in gaining broad-based support for civil rights—represented a "crisis" of masculinity for Black men, and other men of color, more than anything described in Schlesinger's article; their crisis was not about losing their individuality or identity, or the fear of independent women, but the terror losing their very lives. Further, Black men who had fought for the United States in World War II returned home to find that, while their white counterparts were handed the tools to achieve the American dream— mortgage loans, student aid, and other economic resources—they returned to the same racism that their military service was supposed to dissolve. In the Cold War context, such "domestic" problems of race would have global ramifications. As the U.S. legal historian Mary Dudziak states, "From the immediate postwar years until the mid-1960s, race in America was thought to have a critical impact on U.S. prestige abroad. Civil rights crises became foreign affairs crises. Domestic difficulties were managed by U.S. presidents with an eyes toward how their actions would play overseas."[36] By the end of the 1950s, the nation was struggling to reconcile what was increasingly becoming a formal state language of racial equality to the continual and pervasive discrimination against Black Americans, which U.S. leaders realized undercut perceptions of American "freedom" and "democracy." The nation living up to its own democratic ideals, especially in regard to the treatment of Black Americans, was central to the Cold War narrative of American exceptionalism. State needs constrained the very parameters of acceptable civil rights discourse and activism, which Dudziak calls the "Cold War civil rights." In order to project the image of a democratic and ethical nation that held the moral upper hand over the Soviets and could then rightfully exert itself as the world's most powerful leader, the United States had to advance this Cold War civil rights narrative that, while acknowledging the racial sins of its past, demonstrated that it was a country "morally rehabilitated."[37] The high stakes of the narrative led to the cultivation of an "acceptable" civil rights strategy, with the government response to civil rights agitations and activism "driven in part by whether activists supported or detracted from the Cold War/civil rights frame."[38] This frame created an atmosphere in which "those who spoke out of turn, especially to an international audience, were silenced."[39] In the case of the Nation of Islam, which spoke loudly and brashly out of turn, members were both targeted and slandered in attempts to, unsuccessfully, coerce their silence.

The Hate That Hate Produced

The Nation of Islam, along with the Honorable Elijah Muhammad and Malcolm X, initially came to national prominence through the CBS news documentary, *The Hate that Hate Produced*. First airing during the week of July 13, 1959, the report detailed the rise of the Nation of Islam and other forms of Black nationalism against the backdrop of Cold War racial and gender anxieties. Hosted by the journalist and news anchor Mike Wallace, the show was broadcast every weeknight from WNTA-TV, Channel 13, in New York City. Wallace opened the series with these words: "Tonight, a special report assembled by *News Beat* reporters and camera crews in New York and Washington; a fully documented story of the movement for black supremacy among a growing and well-organized minority of American Negroes. The leaders of this movement are crafty, resourceful men who know what they are about. Their followers are Negroes who find in the cause of black supremacy an answer to centuries of persecution.

For that evening and the remainder of the week, Wallace and Louis Lomax, the Black American journalist who collaborated on the report, detailed the rise of what they named "the rise of black racism . . . a call for black supremacy among a growing segment of American Negroes."[40] Of this "growing segment," Wallace announced, "these homegrown Negro American Muslims are the most powerful of the black supremacist groups." Aware that most people in the country knew little to nothing about the difference between the Nation of Islam and "orthodox" Islam, Wallace described the "Black Muslims"—a term advanced by the

CBS report and rejected by NOI members themselves, who preferred to be referred to as simply "Muslims"—with these words:

> They use a good deal of the paraphernalia of the traditional religion of Islam, but are fervently disavowed by orthodox Muslims. . . . They claim a membership of almost a quarter of a million Negroes. Their doctrine is being taught in fifty cities across the nation. Let no one underestimate the Muslims. They have their own parochial schools, like this one in Chicago, where Muslim children are taught to hate the white man. Even the clothes they wear are in sharp contrast to American dress, like these two Negro children going to school. Wherever they go, Muslims withdraw from the life of the community. They have their own stores, supermarkets, barber-shops, and restaurants.

With these words, Wallace conveyed many of the logics and narratives that would come to influence the racialization of "Muslims" in the United States in the ensuing decades, the notions that Islamic ideologies were, for both Black and non-Black Muslims, nefariously and covertly spreading across the country ("taught in fifty cities across the nation"); that Muslims were, above all else, taught to "hate" (in this case, to hate the white man, but more broadly the whole of Western civilization and democratic values); that Muslim women in headscarves (and in this case, even young girls) represented a threat to American values; and that to be Muslim meant to "withdraw from the life of the community," to exist in a "hateful" and cloistered world that signified a rejection of civil society. At the same time, Wallace's words also portrayed Black Muslims as inauthentically Muslim—that they were "fervently disavowed by orthodox Muslims"—and as a radical fringe element in Black America that posed a grave threat to struggles for Black integration and assimilation. In sum, Wallace's anti-Muslim rhetoric was made legible and was enabled through the denigration and demonization of Black nationalism as a viable strategy toward Black freedom, and it delegitimized Black Muslims not only as false Muslims but also as hateful, traitorous, and terroristic Americans.

Perhaps most captivating, and terrifying, to the program's viewers was Malcolm X—handsome, articulate, and unrelentingly critical of the "white devils." In *The Black Muslims in America*, C. Eric Lincoln writes,

"Malcolm X became famous as the [NOI's] chief spokesman through the media. . . . Malcolm's political adroitness . . . tilted with journalists, politicians, black leaders, and any others who cared to subject themselves to his barbed wit and slashing satire."[41] As many have noted, Malcolm was, as the actor Ossie Davis pronounced at his funeral, the "living, black manhood" of Black America, "our own shining black prince." As I further articulate in chapter 3, Malcolm X's presence and actions, in both life and death, definitively shaped Islam's significance in the United States. Less examined is the way he affected the lives of U.S. Muslim women, both within and out of the Nation of Islam and, subsequently, for generations to come, oftentimes in unwittingly negative ways.[42] As Jeffrey B. Leak writes, Malcolm was engaged in constructing a "masculinity in progress," in which he would develop far more complex and progressive views on women's issues and gender by the end of his life.[43] In 1959, Malcolm's understanding of Black masculinity and manhood relied upon "flawed . . . ideological assertions," specifically, in following the teachings of Muhammad, Malcolm conveyed the message that "black male identity would ultimately be determined by the degree to which black men could exercise traditional forms of American manhood,"[44] in other words, that Black men should work to achieve power by emulating the masculinism and patriarchy of white men. However, as discussed in the previous sections, Arthur Schlesinger and others believed that American manhood was on the wane, a trajectory that was making the country weak in the face of the Soviets.

Yet Malcolm X and the NOI appeared anything but weak. As shown in *The Hate That Hate Produced*, Black women appeared ready to join and to accept their subordinate gender positions in the group. Mike Wallace's description of how NOI members wore Islamic clothing, "in stark contrast to American dress," was paired with an image of two girls dressed in the NOI uniform of white headscarves and dresses. The shot of the girls was shown immediately after Wallace stated that children in NOI schools were "taught to hate the white man," linking their blackness, their gender, and their Islamic clothing to the construction of this "hate." As Wallace continued to speak of the of the dangers posed by the NOI, his commentary was punctuated by images of Muslim women and children entering and exiting the Saviour's Day festivities and engaging in other mundane activities, such as shopping for clothing or groceries. Through the inclusion of these images, the news documentary framed the bodies of these Black women and girls with national anxieties around race and gender and, in effect, demonstrated how these "subservient" and "submissive" Black women and girls were actually operatives of Black racial hatred against whites. While white men were unable to control "their" women, *The Hate That Hate Produced* presented a glimpse of a Black American social environment in which the gender troubles of white, middle-class Americans seemed absent. In the NOI, men were empowered and outspoken; women understood and embraced their roles as wives, mothers, and homemakers; and all accepted and willingly embraced domestic gender hierarchies.

The Hate That Hate Produced garnered an intense public reaction, so intense that CBS rebroadcast the program in its entirety the following week. In a 1988 interview about the program, Mike Wallace described the response, saying that the country's top television and cultural critics were "astonished" by the program, which received extensive coverage in *U.S. News and World Report*, the *New York Times*, *Time* magazine, *Newsweek*, and many other local and regional print publications.[45] Ultimately, *The Hate That Hate Produced* introduced the Nation of Islam as an insurgent domestic political presence and produced "Muslims" in the U.S. discursive lexicon as sutured to blackness. It also laid out the ideological groundwork for how Islam and Muslims would exist within the nation's boundaries, as vehicles of harm to white Americans and U.S. liberal democracy. In this logical calculus, images of Muslim women engaged in "traditional" domestic duties in the home and submitting to the power of Black men were rendered insurgent because they were proof that "Islam" was a remedy for the crisis of masculinity plaguing white American men. With their women in check, strong Black Muslim men could shame emasculated white American men in crisis by exerting their own power and virility, thus signifying the imminent possibility of Black political and cultural insurgency.

The Messenger Magazine

Malcolm X understood the power of the media and photography. He was a master of public relations who "provided the mainstream news media with a continuing and histrionic story that would enrapture its readers: a burgeoning black community calling for self-determination, racial separatism, and independence to be achieved 'by any means necessary,' including violent insurrection."[46] Further, Malcolm had an uncanny ability to discern the power of the image; he "knew the cultural currency of photography [and] had an understanding of the long lasting outreach of . . . images as evidence and communication."[47] Just months before the airing of the CBS documentary that introduced Malcolm to the nation, he oversaw the production and publication of *The Messenger* magazine, the first publication of the NOI that only ran for one issue under that name. The following year, *The Messenger* would become the monthly newspaper *Muhammad Speaks*.

Unlike *The Hate That Hate Produced*, *The Messenger* introduced the NOI to the general public on its own terms, and it was meant to operate as a recruitment tool while also educating and fostering pride among its existing members. Two names appear on the publication's masthead: Malcolm X, listed as "Editor," and the renowned Black photographer Lloyd Yearwood (who was not a Muslim), who is credited with "All Photographs and Layouts." Malcolm X worked closely with Yearwood on the layout, which he felt was crucial. In the opening editor's note, X states: "This first edition of *The Messenger* magazine is designed not only to give us a broader view of the Messenger's [Elijah Muhammad's] WORKS and his ACCOMPLISHMENTS, but, the RESULTS of his teaching upon his followers . . . and also his followers' material, moral and spiritual contribution to the communities in which they live, after accepting his leadership."[48] During the production of the magazine, Malcolm felt enormous pressure. In a letter to his wife Betty, dated April 1, 1959, Malcolm writes that editing on the publication "helps to keep me nervous and very hard to get along with" because he hoped that the magazine's success would "eliminate much of the Messenger's [the honorable Elijah Muhammad's] financial needs if properly presented to the public, and on a mass scale."[49] As the NOI grew, so did its financial needs. The purpose of the magazine was to bring in new converts and to increase morale and, thus, increase tithes and donations among existing members.

X was engaged in a "masculinity in process," in which his views on women reflected both his deep political insight and intellectual integrity, *as well as* certain problematic views on women and gender. As some Black feminist writers have asserted, X's views at times expressed the "misogyny at the center of Black Power politics," although his "penchant for truth-seeking may well have enabled him, had he lived, to become a champion for women's empowerment."[50] In 1959, a vision of strong Black families, anchored by images of virtuous Black women engaged in domestic duties, was critical to Malcolm X's "proper presentation" of Black Muslim life. Indeed, images of women constitute more than half of the images in *The Messenger* and epitomize X's belief in Islam as a revitalizing force for Black Americans that could reverse the psychological, cultural, and spiritual devastation of anti-Black racism.

The magazine was organized into thirteen sections, with most detailing site-specific aspects of the group, such as "Department Store," "Dress Shop," "Barber Shop," and "Grocery Store." Two sections focus on the NOI's educational endeavors: One offers a glimpse of the NOI schools, called the University of Islam, and the other outlines Elijah Muhammad's education program. Two other sections provide insight into the NOI's administrative framework, one showing highlights from the annual convention, and the other laying out "Mr. Muhammad's Economic Program (Past-Present-Future)." A section titled "Power of the Press" occupies the literal center of the magazine, on page 20 of the forty-page publication. Beneath a large photo of Malcolm X standing over a spread of major newspapers that takes up almost three-fourths of the page, the start of a story reads, "The time has come for all intelligent 'Negro' leaders to recognize THE POWER OF THE PRESS . . . to realize that THE PEN IS MIGHTIER THAN THE SWORD."

Particularly striking toward the end of the magazine is the section titled "Typical Moslem Family," which features the family of Elijah Muhammad's daughter Ethel Sharrieff and her husband, Raymond Sharrieff, a supreme captain in the NOI and "his most trusted aid." The pictures feature the Sharrieffs in various scenes of middle-class respectability—in a finely furnished living room, at a nicely set dining table, with Ethel Sharrieff and her four children well groomed and beautifully dressed. Their home's attractiveness was attributed to Sister Ethel, who is described as "an expert interior decorator, [who] upholsters her own furniture herself once every year," and who made all the home's "lampshades, curtains, and cornices . . . by her hands." On the page following the family portrait is one of Ethel Sharrieff alone with one of her babies on her lap, meant to emphasize the critical role of mothers in

Figure 2.1. The Sharrieff family, as featured in *The Messenger*, 1959. Image reproduction courtesy of Beinecke Library, Yale University.

the NOI. The caption below the images combines the teachings of Elijah Muhammad with those of the Prophet Muhammad and starts off with the "Eastern Proverb": "TO EDUCATE A MAN IS TO EDUCATE ONLY AN INDIVIDUAL, BUT TO EDUCATE A WOMAN IS TO EDUCATE AN ENTIRE FAMILY." Continuing on, the caption echoes Elijah Muhammad's injunctions regarding women, stating that the proverb "clearly emphasizes how highly the woman is regarded in Islam" and that "young men [must] strive to elevate their women to her rightful place of dignity and respect." It then goes on to cite two sayings from the Prophet Muhammad: "Heaven lies at the feet of the mother" and "One who treats his wife kindly will be with me in heaven." The message of the image and caption is clear: To be a wife and mother are a Muslim woman's tantamount duties and must be embraced in order to gain the dignity and respect of men.

Photographs fill most of the pages of *The Messenger*, while text functions primarily as captions or is interspersed sparingly throughout as a

Figure 2.2. Cover of *The Messenger*, 1959. Image reproduction courtesy of Beinecke Library, Yale University.

means to punctuate or illuminate the images. In fact, each of the publication's forty pages contain photographs. As a primarily visual document, then, it is significant that X chose an image of three young girls in white habits appearing to discuss the contents of a book of Elijah's Muhammad's teachings, *The Supreme Wisdom*, for the publication's cover. In the image, each girl is engaged in a particular type of embodied action in relation to Muhammad's book: The child on the left is intently reading with her eyes lowered, and the girl on the right is closely listening to the girl featured in the center of the photo, who appears to talk enthusiastically about what she is reading. The girls wear similar, but not matching, uniforms, and small individual details stand out on each child. One has a dark vest over her white dress, another wears a blouse with a spray of lace on the front, while the third sports a thin gold necklace that stands out against her clothing. The small caption in the upper left-hand corner states: "In this Issue! Mr. Muhammad's Economical and Educational Program." The photo presents an image of Black girlhood that was rarely, if ever, portrayed in the media or popular culture at the time: girls engaged in the act of education, of self-betterment, and of intellectual exchange. The photo conveys a desire to represent the Nation of Islam and the teachings of Elijah Muhammad as a safe harbor for young Black girls and, thus, for all Black people. In their white habits and dresses, these young women communicated that Islam could bring their embodied presence of purity, hope, modesty, and education to all Black Americans. The magazine's cover announced to its readership that such virtues were at the very heart of the NOI's "material, moral, and spiritual" endeavors. To put it another way, Malcolm X himself decided that Muslim women and girls in the NOI were the best representation of the group's possibility as a vehicle of religious and cultural transformation for Black America.

Produced within months of each other, the images of NOI Muslim life in the *Messenger* stood in stark contrast with the content of *The Hate That Hate Produced*. Wallace and Lomax presented the "Black Muslims" and Islam as a source of latent violence and racial hatred that undermined mainstream civil rights efforts and Black integration. *The Messenger*, in contrast, introduced the group as a family and community-oriented organization that fostered morality and spiritual development. However, both employed images of Black American women and girls as insurgent visions of Islam's potential power to disrupt and transform existing race and gender relations in the United States against Cold War era visions of the nuclear family. Each produced U.S. Muslim women as engaged historical actors who rendered acts of gendered "submission" into forms of religious ritual, political protest, and national threat.

"Inside the Black Muslims": Gordon Parks and *Life* Magazine

By 1963, the "Black Muslims," the Nation of Islam, and Malcolm X had become far more familiar figures in U.S. mainstream media and culture. Along with the NOI, various other expressions of what would soon be called "Black Power" emerged in the first half of the 1960s and constituted the beginnings of a far more radical and revolutionary structure of Black political and cultural feeling in the United States. It was also during this time that internal tensions grew between Elijah Muhammad and Malcolm X, as news of Muhammad's infidelities with young women in the NOI surfaced. By 1962, many in the NOI, including Elijah's wife, Clara, knew of the numerous children fathered out of wedlock by Muhammad with female followers. All of this came to head at the end of 1962, when Muhammad suspended Malcolm from the NOI after the latter's public remarks that President John F. Kennedy's assassination was an example of "chicken's coming home to roost."

Earlier that year, in March 1963, however, the NOI presented an impression of a strong and unified organization in the pages of *Life* magazine. Featuring images by acclaimed the Black American photographer Gordon Parks, the cover of the issue proclaimed "A Negro Photographer Shoots from inside THE BLACK MUSLIMS," a headline that once again, as with *The Hate That Hate Produced*, emphasized the cloistered and putatively racially exclusive space of the NOI, where only a "Negro photographer" might venture to take photos. Parks's photos and his accompanying essay, titled "'What Their Cry Means To Me'—a Negro's Own Evaluation," offered a report on "the internal workings of the movement." In the essay, Parks reveals his skepticism of the NOI and Muhammad's separatist doctrines, listing all of the white men who have aided him throughout his life, and concluding that throughout the course of his career, he has "come to realize the universality of man."[51]

Yet his images effectively conveyed the group's undeniable appeal, which he admitted "struck a responsive chord" to him as a Black man.[52] He expressed a particular fondness for Malcolm X, calling him "the most articulate spokesman in the movement" and at various times mentioning the minister's fierce emotional intensity *and* vulnerability. In the essay, Parks also noted his surprise at the widespread interest of "well-to-do Negro women extolling Black nationalism," such as "one matron" he encountered who was "threaten[ing] to join the New York mosque of the Muslims" amid a group of her peers.[53]

In some ways, the *Life* magazine spread was similar to the one in *The messenger*, allowing Americans to "peek" inside daily life in the Nation of Islam and offering the first widespread view into the lives of NOI Muslim women and families. Unlike *The Messenger,* however, which was meant to circulate only among NOI members and possible converts, *Life* was one of the most popular magazines in the nation, published by the media magnate Henry Luce, the man who also published *Time* and *Fortune* magazines. In the 1940s, *Life* introduced Americans to photojournalism and attempted to provide through pictures what *Time* and other news magazines did through words. With a readership of over two million American homes, *Life* was a mainstay in every barbershop, waiting room, and beauty parlor in the country, as well. Thus, to be featured in the publication was to enter American consciousness and conversation—and to become subjects of discussion and debate, scorn, and/or condemnation. That *Life* devoted fourteen pages of images and texts to the Nation of Islam announced the profound impact of Muhammad's group on the national conversation around race in the early 1960s.

The "story" of the images, the narrative Parks's photos set out to convey, was one of a highly disciplined and well-trained organization whose members were driven by latent anger at whites, as well as anger toward Black leaders and organizations who they believed pandered to whites. Estimating that "there may be as many as 100,000" Muslims in America, the story also depicted this anger as on the rise. Unlike *The Messenger*, the leading image in the *Life* spread was not one of hope, as with the image of the young girls, but a full-page black-and-white grainy close-up of Elijah Muhammad's face adjacent to a page whose headline proclaimed "Black Muslim's Cry Grows Louder: 'The White Devil's Day Is Almost Over.'" In the image and accompanying story, Muhammad emerged as a demagogue who ruled as a false prophet over his followers and led them to harbor a "deep rage at whites." Thus, in one sense, Parks's images revealed the same narrative as *The Hate That Hate Produced*, deeming the NOI a threat to the nation that undercut the peaceful protests of the mainstream civil rights movement and stirred up resentment and anger among Black Americans through Islam. Yet I want to suggest that the pictures also told a story about race, gender, and safety and, in particular, a story about the gendered roles adopted by Black men and women through Islam as a means to seek protection and sanctuary from racial violence and hatred.

Figure 2.3. NOI Women sewing, featured in *Life* magazine, May 31, 1963.

Following the portrait of Muhammad, the next five of the twenty-one photos show NOI men engaged in acts of both spiritual and physical preservation: Members of the Fruit of Islam (FOI), the organization's male-only paramilitary wing, pray with palms upward, pound their chests, "snap fists" in martial arts exercises, and deal with a police dog "like those used against demonstrating Negroes in Birmingham." Immediately establishing the force and discipline of the Fruit of Islam, these images bookend the story, giving readers a sense of what they might encounter when engaging the group. The photos depict Black men ready and willing to attack those might seek harm upon them, especially those who might endanger "their" women. On the fifth page into the article, *Life*'s readers encounter the women of the NOI in a striking two-page spread accompanied by the headline "Wake Up, Clean Up, Stand Up." The women are engaged in the activities of the Muslim Girls Training and General Civilization Class; in the first two, women are shown sewing and teaching in NOI schools. Beside those, in the central image—and perhaps one of the most iconic of Parks's NOI images—we see Ethel Sharrieff standing at the head of a group of MGT and GCC women, who are behind her in a pyramid formation. The women are dressed in starched and immaculately pressed white uniforms, and their eyes all appear trained directly at Parks's camera, their gazes steely, controlled, and unwavering. Unlike the photo of Sister Ethel with a child in *The Messenger*, Parks's picture of Sharrieff here conveys, not the sanctity or high station of wives or mothers, but the sense of anger and insurgency that drives NOI Muslim women's labors as wives and mothers. Protected by the men shown on the previous pages, the women of the Nation of Islam fulfill their domestic and religious duties as Muslims so Black men may build the Black nation that they, as women, so deserve. Ultimately, the Nation of Islam's "promise of protection," to return to Griffin's phrase, is predicated upon the wellness and stability of Black Muslim men to be strong and resilient enough to protect their women from harm.

As the photos proceed, one is shown the constant violence of white supremacy and its harm upon Black male bodies, specifically, by Parks's photos documenting the murder of NOI member Ronald Stokes by the Los Angeles Police Department in April 1962, outside of Los Angeles Mosque No. 27. Seven Muslims were shot, and Stokes, who was unarmed, died. In one image, we see Malcolm X holding a large picture of Stokes lying dead on the ground as he discusses the murder with the press. In the second image, three MGT women, including Stokes's widow, walk stoically past his coffin during his funeral. In the last full-page image, we see a young man in a wheelchair and Malcolm X behind him, selling copies of the NOI newspaper, *Muhammad Speaks*, with the headline "SEVEN UNARMED NEGROES SHOT IN COLD BLOOD BY LOS ANGELES POLICE." Unlike the initial images of the Fruit of Islam, engaged in active and aggressive forms of combat, here we see the vulnerability of Black men in a white supremacist society. The disability of the young man with Malcolm is foregrounded, while Malcolm X's body is small, slightly blurred, and his face in shadow. It is a picture of two Black men in the street proclaiming the relentless racial violence enacted upon their own bodies, in hope that those around them will buy a paper telling their story.

While the Cold War crisis of masculinity gestured toward white men's fears of unruly, independent women and Soviet authoritarianism, such fears were not what drove the NOI. Their crisis was white supremacy and the devastating effects it had wrought on the Black family, Black communities, and Black conceptions of self. As Parks wrote, despite his distaste for the group's separatist agenda, Malcolm X was "right" for being angry and to decry the treatment of Blacks not just in the South but also across the nation: "Because for all the civil rights laws and the absence of Jim Crow signs in the North, the black man is still living the last-hired, first-fired, ghetto existence of a second-class citizen."[54] In the face of this inequality and violence, the NOI sought to insulate and proactively defend themselves from white supremacist harm by conveying the strength of Muslim men and the ardent devotion and committed domesticity of Muslim women. In *Life* magazine, America saw being Muslim in the NOI as a type of racial, gendered, and religious contract, under which Muslim men and women submitted and subscribed to prescribed roles as wives, mothers, protectors, and patriarchs to advance their insurgent devotion to the Black nation, the Honorable Elijah Muhammad, and Allah.

"A Part of Islam": Seeing Muslim Women in James Baldwin's *The Fire Next Time*

Published in 1963, the same year *Life* magazine published its feature on the Nation of Islam, James Baldwin's *The First Next Time* is widely recognized as one of "the most important manifestos of the Civil Rights Movement."[55] In most analyses of the book, scholars and critics commonly foreground the intimate rapport between Baldwin and the Nation of Islam leader, the Honorable Elijah Muhammad, as they dine at Muhammad's Hyde Park home on the South Side of Chicago. Specifically, critics have focused on how Baldwin experienced Muhammad's "appeal as a father figure" and how this mediated his feelings about Black nationalism, to which the writer was drawn but remained "ruefully skeptical."[56] As the essay proceeds, Baldwin—a gay, Black man who was raised by a stern, yet in his eyes, ultimately ineffectual, Baptist minister stepfather—grapples with his fraught relationship to Black nationalism, Black masculinity, and Islam *through* his interactions with Muhammad. Just as he feels the presence of a strong, protective, and effective father in Muhammad, he also experiences the power of "Islam" as a logic and space of racial-gendered belonging for Black men, which leads him to proclaim, "God is black. All black men belong to Islam; they have been chosen. And Islam shall rule the world. The dream, the sentiment is old; only the color is new. . . . The white God has not delivered them; perhaps the Black God will."[57] In these words imagined across the table from Muhammad, in the shadows of the Cold War (which Baldwin describes as "the threat of universal extinction hanging over all the world today"),[58] the writer deeply empathizes with the NOI leader's vision of the plight of the Black man in America. Baldwin's feelings are clear: He wants desperately to believe in Muhammad's message, to find solace under the NOI's wing, although he fundamentally disagrees with the goal of Black separatism. Despite his reservations and intellectual doubts, he feels the NOI's strength in Muhammad's attentive paternalism and senses the father he always longed for but never had. "For where else, after all could I go?" Baldwin asks, concluding: "*I was black, and therefore a part of Islam.*"[59]

While issues of masculinity and religion have been addressed in relation to Baldwin's dinner with Muhammad, less noted has been the writer's depiction of Muslim women in Muhammad's home. Upon arrival, Baldwin almost immediately notes their presence, writing:

> On one side of the room sat half a dozen women, all in white; they were much occupied with a beautiful baby, who seemed to belong to the

youngest of the women. On the other side of the room sat seven or eight men, young, dressed in dark suits, very much at ease, and very imposing. The sunlight came into the room with the peacefulness one remembers from rooms in one's early childhood—a sunlight encountered only in one's dreams. I remember being astounded by the quietness, the ease, the peace, the taste.[60]

This description of Muslim women is ineluctably visual. The scene is assembled like a baroque painting: Sunlight streams through the window, illuminating the purity and contentedness of the women, who are not relegated to a separate sphere per se but who occupy their own space of gendered safety among and in relation to the men in the room, which is, of itself, a racial safe harbor from white supremacy. Baldwin draws the men and women in Muhammad's home through a language of gendered symmetry: The women with the beautiful baby enable the ease and imposing nature of the men in their stead. One may visually assemble an image of the women in white on one side of the frame while the men in dark suits buoy the other.

A bit later on, Baldwin acknowledges the women in the room once more: "The women were carrying on their own conversation, in low tones; I gathered that they were not expected to take place in male conversations. A few women kept coming in and out of the room, apparently making preparations for dinner. We, the men, did not plunge deeply into any subject, for, clearly, we were all waiting for the appearance of Elijah."[61] Through their low tones and subtle meal preparations, the women are always palpably present yet distinct, their movements at once *controlling* and *controlled by* their relationships to the men. Thus, whereas the men must wait for Muhammad to begin their conversations, the women are already "carrying on their own conversation," which is not contingent on the leader's arrival. And it is the women who ultimately produce the feelings of safety ["the quietness, the ease, the taste"] that Baldwin experiences; the women know what they must do to facilitate the events of the evening, and they do not require instruction beyond the "low tones" of their own voices. Ultimately, Baldwin's words offer a portrait of NOI Muslim women as thoroughly and ineluctably a part of the workings and goings-on of the organization, not just as child care or food preparers/servers, but as *active creators* of what it means to feel Muslim and practice Islam in that space and time.

By foregrounding Muslim women in reading *The Fire Next Time*, we are able to see how Black women were central to the production of the perception of Islam as a revolutionary and antiracist religion for Black American men during this time, integral to this space of Black nationalist power and, by extension, to U.S. Muslim spaces more broadly. Baldwin's descriptions of the presence and movements of Muslim women in the text evoke their insurgent presence in both the eyes of Black men as well as the U.S. public during the Cold War and civil rights era. In their "low tones," careful food preparation, the care of children, and the posture and comportment of their bodies in their crisp white dresses and head coverings, Black women affectively respond to the multiple forms of racist, sexist, and economic violence that shape their lives. In the company of other Black Muslim women, with the protection of Black Muslim men, the women of the NOI are seemingly in safe harbor. Yet the presence of the Black Muslim men—their protectors—also forecloses the possibility of women's complete safety, as they must continually fashion their bodies and movements to conform to Black masculinist ideals of Black womanhood, forged out of the terms and limits of Black freedom struggles that they hope to support and advance. Women's ways of being Muslim in the room with James Baldwin and Elijah Muhammad are produced out of insurgent practices of racial and gendered response to multiple scales of violence, embodied rejoinders to the varied racial and gendered environments in which they live, love, and labor. Their ways of being Muslim are simultaneously religious and political practices that require their constant vigilance, discipline, and unwaveringly attention to how racial and gendered power shapes and operates in their everyday lives.

* * *

As I stated at the beginning of this chapter, writing about U.S. women being Muslim requires attention to the intimacy and affect of domestic spaces. In the examples of Nation of Islam women discussed here, I have tried to demonstrate the ways that Muslim-ness was performed for the public eye in the spaces of the home, as well as the ways that

Islam's presence in the domestic United States came to be entangled with the gender politics of Black nationalism during the Cold War. Although there is much about the experience of being Muslim women in the NOI that was specific to that organization at the time in question, considering how their Muslim-ness was constituted and portrayed for the American mainstream offers poignant insights to a broader experience of being U.S. Muslim women. Through their images in *The Hate That Hate Produced, The Messenger, Life* magazine, and *The Fire Next Time*, NOI Muslim women continually engaged Islam as a lived religion in ways that responded directly to how Islam circulated as a racial-religious form in the country at the time. In their case, this form was produced through Cold War logics of race and gender. The Islam of the NOI was a racially charged presence, a signifier of Black rebellion and defiance that challenged state power and troubled the social order. In this calculus, portrayals of NOI Muslim women's ways of being in domestic space expressed those women's longings for protection and reverence from the white supremacist gaze, as well as the desires of Black Muslim men to display the modesty and respectability of "their" women in order to assert power. In terms of how to read NOI Muslim women's agency in the photos, I return to the notion of Muslim womanism advanced by Debra Majeed in the introduction of this volume. As Majeed writes, "Muslim womanism acknowledges womanist concerns for all members of black families" and signifies a "pro-woman, pro-family" stance on gender justice."[62] In their "submission" to the patriarchal norms of the NOI, the images of Black Muslim women discussed in this chapter reflected the unwavering affective insurgency that infused the domestic spaces of NOI Muslim women's lives. Thus they offer a crucial model for how being U.S. Muslim women has been continually constituted as a religious and political act, perceived and practiced in shifting politicized, and always racialized, frames and contexts of history.

3

Garments for One Another

Islam and Marriage in the Lives of Betty Shabazz and Dakota Staton

Your wives are as a garment for you, and you are as a garment for them.
—*The Holy Qur'an*, 2:187

If a woman had a problem in the 1950's and 1960's, she knew that something must be wrong with her marriage, or with herself.
—Betty Friedan, *The Feminine Mystique*, 62

In December 2014, Yasmine Shaikh—a young U.S. Muslim woman of South Asian descent—wrote an article for the *Huffington Post* titled "We Have a Marriage Crisis."[1] The piece discussed how large numbers of well-educated U.S. Muslim women in their twenties, thirties, and forties wanted to get married but were having difficulty finding partners. This issue disproportionately affected Muslim women as opposed to Muslim men, Shaikh wrote, because they were expected to be high-achieving and pursue their educations yet also remain religiously pious and be willing to give up or deprioritize their careers in order to stay home and raise children. In addition, many Muslim men would marry Christian or Jewish women, which is permitted by Islamic law, whereas Muslim women are not allowed to marry outside the faith.[2] Men also often chose to marry women far younger than themselves; for example, a man in his thirties would marry a woman in her twenties, as opposed to someone his own age. Another writer, Hena Zuberi, penned an essay on the same topic in 2013 titled "The Muslim Marriage Crisis." In it, she characterized the number of unmarried American Muslim women over thirty as "an epidemic."[3] Zuberi suggested that race and culture also contributed to the crisis. In South Asian and Arab households, she wrote, many parents required that their daughters marry someone of the same ethnic or cultural background, or they insisted on arranged marriages. They were always focused on the economic status of potential mates and often did not want their daughters to marry Black Muslim men, owing to their perceptions that such unions would negatively affect their class status. Black Muslim families were more open to children marrying outside their race, Zuberi wrote; however, Black men increasingly sought out "the perfect Muslim women . . . in immigrant communities." In both articles, the authors cited the anguish of young, professional U.S. Muslim women, both Black and non-Black, who wanted to retain their Islamic identities, pursue their professional goals, and find suitable Muslim marriage partners to share their lives.[4]

As Islamic and women's and gender studies scholar Juliane Hammer writes, in the postmillennial decade, "American Muslim communities have engaged in vibrant and at times heated debates about marriage, often framed by a discursive claim to 'Muslim marriage in crisis.'"[5] In these debates, Hammer continues, we see how U.S. Muslims "negotiate religion [Islam], vis-à-vis culture[s], and vis-à-vis a homogeneous American societal norms regarding marriage and sexuality."[6] Indeed, as the Shaikh and Zuberi articles show, marrying Muslim in the United States occurs at the intersections of religion, race, gender, culture, class, and nation, when one's understanding of, relationship to, and navigation of, each of these categories plays a vital role in determining the nature and outcome of a union. For example, different logics of race, class, and religion will influence marital relations between two Sunni Muslims from wealthy families of Pakistani origin who subscribe to a belief in the American dream differently than those of union between a Black Muslim and a Latina convert to Islam who might draw from different sectarian traditions and commingle their faith practices with social protest.

Yet at the heart of many of the conflicts and conversations around Muslim marriage in the United States in the late twentieth and early twenty-first century, I suggest, is the tension between Islam's emphasis on marriage as a foundation of faith and U.S.-based secular feminist logics that characterize marriage as an oppressive institution for women. These perspectives are reflected in the epigraphs at the start of this chapter. The first is from the Holy Qur'an, and it offers one of the holy book's numerous citations on male-female marital unions. Of this passage, and more broadly of marriage in Islam, the theologian and Islamic feminist Riffat Hassan writes, "The Qur'an describes the relationship of husband and wife in terms that denote both closeness and quality. It does not regard the husband as superior to the wife. [This passage] illustrates the Qur'anic teaching that the purpose of marriage is to create and live in an atmosphere of love, harmony, and companionship to fulfill the higher purpose of life."[7] In acting as garments for each other, husbands and wives are to be safe harbors for one another, and marriage a space of respite from external harm within which each member nurtures their spouse emotionally, physically, and spiritually. The second epigraph is taken from the U.S. American writer and feminist activist Betty Friedan in her 1963 book, *The Feminine Mystique*, often called the book that launched the second-wave feminist movement. Friedan's quote, in contrast to the quote from the Qur'an, describes marriage as a "gilded cage" for white, suburban women in the 1950s and 1960s, an institution that stifled their dreams and desires and tied women's self-worth to the demands of marriage and domesticity, in large part formed by the Cold War gender logics, which I discussed in the previous chapter.[8] A woman wanting "something more than my husband and my children and my home," wrote Friedan, was understood as having an internal *malaise*, causing women to blame their unhappiness on not being good mothers or wives. Yet, as now numerous Black feminists and other women of color have noted, Friedan's text was also deeply racist and classist in how it centered the experiences of white, middle- and upper-class mothers and wives as universal experiences. As bell hooks said of *The Feminine Mystique*, while it was "a useful discussion of the impact of sexist discrimination on a select group of women," from "a different perspective"—namely that of women of color and working-class women—the book could "also be seen as a case study of narcissism, insensitivity, sentimentality, and self-indulgence."[9] Despite this, Friedan's notions of marriage as stifling and "freedom" as connoted women's ability to enter the labor force to achieve "equality"—as opposed to complimentarity—with men remain central to popular understandings of feminism and women's rights in the contemporary United States.

For young U.S. Muslim women such as the ones discussed in Shaikh's and Zuberi's articles, then, the "crisis" of marriage and divorce in the twenty-first century partially emerges out of the contradictions between notions of marriage in Islam and within second-wave feminist logics such as Friedan's. To return to Hammer's quote above, "U.S. Muslim women have navigated "religion [Islam], vis-à-vis culture[s], and vis-à-vis a homogeneous American societal norms regarding marriage and sexuality." As I have sought to show in this book thus far, women's ways of being U.S. Muslims have continually arisen out of the encounter between their racial epistemologies, Islamic teachings, and the political contexts that shape their daily lives. Societal norms regarding marriage—whether liberal or conservative, in their own racial/ethnic communities or in society writ large—constitute yet another set of circumstances against which U.S. Muslim women must navigate and negotiate, in this case, in regard to how to reconcile whiteness-invested feminist logics within a religious community that is primarily composed of people of color.

Yet Muslim marriage occurred in the United States long before the popularization of Friedan's and other second-wave feminist philosophies, and for many Muslim women, it signified not a site of contradiction but, instead, a space of perceived safety from which they developed ways of being Muslim and practicing Islam in which marriage was central to their religious identities. In this chapter, I consider the lives of two of the best-known U.S. Muslim women of the mid- to late twentieth-century who were engaged in very public marriages to prominent Muslim men: Betty Shabazz, wife and then widow of Malcolm X, and the jazz singer Dakota Staton, who was married to, and later divorced from, the jazz trumpeter Talib Dawud. For Shabazz and Staton, both Black American women who converted to Islam during the late 1950s, the challenges of marrying Muslim emerged not in finding a spouse but in determining how privately and publicly to be Muslim women in the United States when there were no precedents for who and what Muslim women should be. As such, both situated their marriages as essential to their inculcation of Islamic practices and rituals into their oftentimes turbulent lives. As I show here, Shabazz and Staton undoubtedly shouldered the bulk of the labor of their marriages. Shabazz handled all of her and her husband's domestic affairs, including their finances, and she was the primary caregiver of the couple's six children. Staton, as a successful jazz singer, was the primary earner in her marriage as well as the manager of most household duties. In addition, each woman actively worked to showcase their marriages in the public eye, as well as advocating for religious and political causes. For Shabazz, this happened through the advancement of Black nationalism through the Nation of Islam. For Staton, this took place through her and Dawud's efforts to discredit the Nation of Islam as an authentically "Islamic" sect—which I discuss at length in this chapter—to draw attention to Dawud's organization, the Muslim Brotherhood, U.S.A, which was an offshoot of the Ahmadiyya Movement in Islam.

In examining their lives as Muslims, I contend that Shabazz and Staton understood their marriages and religious lives as fundamentally intertwined. In other words, they approached their marriages as religious acts and engaged Islam through their marriages. In making this argument, I do not simply mean that Shabazz and Staton "married into" Islam and thus felt obligated to "be Muslim." While their marriages certainly facilitated and their conversions to Islam, each woman developed religious lives that were at once highly individualized *and* completely connected to their self-conceptions as the wives of Muslim men. In what follows, I demonstrate that, although both women at times felt constricted by their marriages, or by the Islamic organizations to which they belonged, they continually developed their religious lives as married Muslim women and, more specifically, as married Black American Muslim women. Their marriages took place in a time in the 1950s and 1960s when "Islam" had become a signifier of antiracist spiritual consciousness in Black communities, especially among jazz musicians, who viewed conversion to Islam as a means to shield themselves from racist harm and offered an appealing cultural connection to the "East."[10] I examine the struggles Shabazz and Staton encountered in their marriages and how these merged with the development of their own religious and cultural identities as U.S. Muslim women. Neither experienced their marriages exclusively as spaces of safety or of oppression, but rather of both, to which they had to constantly adjust their actions and desires.

Owing to the uneven archives of Shabazz and Staton's lives in the historical record, I employ various methodologies in my approach to each woman's experiences. There is certainly more written about Shabazz than Staton—in particular a comprehensive 2005 biography by the historian Russell Rickford, *Betty Shabazz, Surviving Malcolm X: A Journey of Strength from Wife to Widow to Heroine*[11]—as well as print and media articles covering both her life and her death in 1997. While I draw from these sources, I focus primarily on Shabazz's own writings in this chapter, specifically three letters she wrote to the Honorable Elijah Muhammad between 1963 and 1964—a pivotal moment in which Malcolm transitioned out of the Nation of Islam and became a Sunni Muslim—and I examine a first-person essay she penned for *Ebony* magazine in 1969 about her life following her husband's death. In addition, I cite an interview with the New York–based Muslim community leader and advocate for Muslim women's rights, Sister Aisha Al-Adawiya, who was a close friend and associate of Shabazz in the later years of her life, who is also featured in chapter 5.

In regard to Staton, biographical resources are scarce. As a recording artist, she released over thirty albums and toured extensively around the United States and Europe throughout her career. Yet the singer never achieved the success of her peers in the jazz world, such as the singers Dinah Washington, Sarah Vaughan, and Carmen McRae, which some writers in the popular media attributed to her marriage to Dawud. Thus the primary sources of information about Staton's life come from various articles in the Black and mainstream American press documenting her musical career. In my discussion of Staton, I pay particular attention to her public statements about Islam and the media coverage of a defamation lawsuit she and Dawud filed against the NOI leader Elijah Muhammad. It is particularly important to note Staton's unique position as the only non-NOI-affiliated woman to publicly identify as Muslim during this time period—an aspect of her identity, I argue, that deeply shaped her relationship to being Muslim and that informed her decision to eventually leave Islam. Finally, it is important to point out that Shabazz and Staton were connected through their relationships with Malcolm X, who directly shaped and affected how they formed their identities as Muslims. While Shabazz was, of course, married to Malcolm, Staton squared off against X as a result of the anti-NOI defamation lawsuit, which I address at length here. In the two women's different engagements with Malcolm X, we may observe how male figures like Malcolm X influenced women's constructions of Muslim-ness in both private (e.g., marriage) and public (e.g., the press) relationships, in both positive and, at times, extremely negative ways.

From Black Marriage to Muslim Marriage

In her entry on "Marriage" in *Keywords for American Cultural Studies*, Elizabeth Freeman writes: "As an aspect of modern emotional life in the United States, marriage is . . . the ideological linchpin of intimacy—the most elevated form of chosen interpersonal relationship. At the core of political debate and much critical debate . . . is whether marriage is a matter of love or law, a means of securing social stability or of realizing individual freedom and emotional satisfaction."[12] Freeman goes on to discuss how laws regarding marriage "undergird U.S. citizenship," owing to how they are "implicated in the property relations, racial hierarchy, immigration policy, and colonialist projects that have determined national membership."[13] Indeed, through antimiscegenation laws, antipolygamy laws, prohibitions on same-sex marriage, and so forth, the U.S. nation-state's regulation of who may and may not marry has "provide[d] the very architecture of citizenship," only permitting the *right* of marriage to those it views as acceptable (e.g., white, heterosexual, Christian) citizens. At the same time, however, marriage has also always been a religious institution, and in case of the United States, one that has been explicitly shaped by Christian doctrine and scripture. In spite of the constitutional separation of church and state, marriage as a U.S. institution thus overlaps on uneasy secular-sacred ground, its power granted not only by the state but through Christian ideology that stipulates that marriage makes a man and woman into "one flesh" through God.

Race is critical to understanding marriage in the United States. Black Americans were roundly excluded from the institution of marriage throughout slavery. As the abolitionist William Goodell wrote in his 1853 volume *The American Slave Code in Theory and Practice*, "The slave has no rights. Of course he and she cannot have the rights of a husband, wife. The slave is a chattel, and chattels do not marry."[14] In other words, black fungibility—the notion that Black people were *things* to be traded and sold—was not compatible with marriage, a union that required sentience and personhood in the eyes of the law. The passage of the Thirteenth Amendment and, two years later, the enactment of the Civil Rights Acts of 1866 lifted the prohibition on Black marriage. Along with the right to contract and to own or sell property, "recognition of the slaves' right to marry was an integral part of their transformation into legally recognized personhood."[15] When Black Americans were finally permitted marry, they did so in great numbers; by 1880, 80 percent of Black American families included a husband and a wife.[16] Yet the legacies of slavery "left marriages and families vulnerable to the assault of massive stresses," such as "ongoing economic inequity, high unemployment and underemployment, poor healthcare, and discrimination in housing and education,"[17] conditions that were endemic both in the South and North. In the face of such stresses, concepts of family and marriage became encoded into the discourse of racial uplift and Black progress. For middle- and upper-class Black Americans in the North from Reconstruction through the 1920s, marriage was considered a "signifier for sexual morality in a time when all black people were stereotyped as immoral" and in particular as a way of demonstrating how black women had overcome their "depraved sexuality" in slavery and therefore could not "demonstrate a chastity that was beyond reproach."[18] As discussed in chapter 1, this curtailing of Black women's sexuality was a central aspect of the politics of respectability as cultivated by Black women in African American Women's Clubs in the urban North. Equally important as the control of sexuality was the upkeep of a morally upright domestic sphere structured through "patriarchal gender relations and well-raised offspring."[19] A patriarchal structure was necessary, as was famously argued by E. Franklin Frazier in *The Negro Family in the United States*,[20] because a system of maternal power had developed under slavery and matriarchal women had become a dangerous force, women who were overly oriented "toward consumption" and who were emasculating and demoralizing men.[21] Thus, in order to rehabilitate Black families, Black men must be restored as primary earners and heads of household, which would then lead to the achievement of moral rectitude and racial progress.

The 1920s also saw the widespread emergence of the notion of marriage as an emotional—as opposed to only a practical—relationship. In 1927, the juvenile court judge Ben Lindsey published *The Companionate Marriage*, in which he argued that sexual intimacy and mutual affection should be the cement of marriage, as well as advocating for no-fault divorce and legalized marital birth control.[22] A reflection of women's increasing autonomy in the private and public spheres, as well as the desire for egalitarianism between the sexes, the work of Lindsey and others reflected the belief that marriage itself needed to adapt to the needs of an increasingly individualistic society, as opposed to remaining a traditional institution focused on childbearing, kin, and property relations. For many Black Americans, the idea of marrying for love and sexual desire merged with its meanings as a moral credential and service to the race, imbuing marriage with a multitude of racial and gendered meanings and expectations for both women and men.

Yet whatever Black Americans *expected* of marriage, and the meanings they hoped their union would hold, marriage was, as a lived experience, an intimate relationship between two people. In marriage, men and women grappled with the gendered balance of power inside their homes: who would cook and clean, care for the children, contribute their paycheck to household expenses, and so forth. There were also the issues of feelings and intimacy, how spouses supported and comforted one another, what they talked about, their lovemaking habits, and their arguments. Thus, whereas many women wanted to be supportive of their husbands and to uplift the race, they also frequently struggled against feeling submerged and stifled within their marriages.[23] Such paradigms persisted and were exacerbated by the turn toward domesticity after World War II, as white American men also sought to recapture male dominance during the Cold War through the sequestering of women in domestic space.

It was through such discourses and logics around marriage and gender that Islam entered Black communities and consciousness from the interwar to post–World War II years as a potentially liberatory religious force. As discussed chapter 2, conservative Victorian gender norms undergirded the Nation of Islam's approach to marriage and sexuality; like Frazier, the Honorable Elijah Muhammad believed that Black men needed to be restored to the heads of households in order for the Black family—and thus the Black nation—to thrive. Within the Ahmadiyya Movement in Islam, while such rigid gender roles were not dictated to the same degree, the idea that women should defer to men within their marriages also prevailed. Thus, whereas one could argue that both the Nation of Islam and the Ahmadiyya Movement in Islam advanced heterodox interpretations of Islam, most Black Americans who became Muslim through these organizations learned that marriage was a fundamental tenet of their newfound faith and, in that way, adhered closely to conservative Islamic orthodoxy in its privileging of marriage as a linchpin of religious practice.

As the West Asian historian Judith E. Tucker writes in her book on women and Islamic law, marriage has consistently occupied a "central and pivotal place" within Islam. Marriage is presented in the Qur'an and hadith, Tucker continues, as "one of the most important human relationships" according to Islam's teachings. A common citation from hadith literature states that "marriage is half the faith" of Islam.[24] Yet "Islamic law"—or *sharia*—is not "law" in the Western sense of the term. Instead, to cite the Islamic legal scholar Asifa Quraishi-Landes, who is profiled in chapter 5, *sharia* has a more holistic and all-encompassing meaning and is more accurately defined as "a way of life mandated by God through the Quran and the Prophet Muhammad's example."[25] Muslims are to engage in *itjihad*, or legal interpretation, in order to determine how to implement *sharia* in their lives.[26] Through *itjihad*, Muslim jurists and scholars construct the *fiqh*, or legal rules, of *sharia*, which are constantly evolving and changing through new interpretations and rulings.[27] As such, in regard to issues of women's rights, marriage, gender roles, and so forth, there has always been a wide range of opinions and interpretations of women's rights and the gendered division of labor within Islam. However, while there has always been dissent and disagreement among jurists, the majority of Islamic scholars have interpreted Islamic texts as promoting men as primary caregivers and safeguards of their wives and children, as well the main holders of economic and political power. Such positions aligned well with prevailing beliefs and assumptions around marriage in Black American communities during that time.

Sister Betty Shabazz: Being Muslim through Malcolm

In various accounts of Betty Shabazz's life, family and friends often mention Shabazz's fondness for the story of Hajar,[28] the Egyptian handmaid of the Prophet Abraham's wife, Sarah, who becomes Abraham's second wife and bears him a child, Ishmael (or Ismail). In the Islamic tradition, the story goes that following Ishmael's birth, Sarah becomes jealous and tells her husband to send Hajar and her newborn baby away. Abraham prays for guidance, and God instructs him to heed Sarah's wishes. He leaves Hajar in a bleak stretch of the Arabian desert in what is now the holy city of Mecca in Saudi Arabia, where Hajar and her infant are soon overcome with extreme thirst. Desperate and frightened, her child near death, Hajar begins to search for water and runs frantically between the hills of Al-Safa and Al-Marwah. After her seventh run, an angel appears and tells her that God has heard her cries. A spring appears, from which fresh, cool water flows. This spring is the holy Zamzam, which is located within the Masjid al-Haram, or the Great Mosque of Mecca, and it is visited by millions of pilgrims every year so they may drink a sip of its water.

In *Betty Shabazz, Surviving Malcolm X*, the most extensive biography of Shabazz to date, the historian Russell J. Rickford begins the account by describing Shabazz's affinity for Hajar's tale:

> In the Muslim tradition, brown-skinned Hajar symbolized the virtue of perseverance and faith amid suffering. But for Betty there was something even more personal and poignant; a sisterhood with a woman who had been stranded with a child, bereft but for her trust in God. When Betty made Hajj, or pilgrimage, in the spring of 1965, she reenacted Hajar's quest, running seven times between Safa and Marwah, as do all Muslim pilgrims. Already the mother of four little girls, Betty performed the ritual while pregnant with twins. Only weeks earlier she had become a young and destitute widow, and her life had seemed unsalvageable.[29]

Shabazz's deep connection to Hajar—her "personal and poignant" identification with a woman in Islam who, like her, had also been seemingly abandoned by all but who survived through unyielding faith and perseverance—inspired much of her religious identity and practice as a Muslim woman in the years following Malcolm's X's assassination at the Audubon Ballroom in New York on February 21, 1965. As Rickford states, Shabazz left for *hajj*, the pilgrimage to Mecca that all Muslims are required to make once in their lifetime, in March 1965, shortly after her husband's death. She, along with Malcolm, had moved away from the teachings of the NOI and Elijah Muhammad and had embraced Sunni Islam, and Rickford writes the journey "restored her emotional balance, replenished her sensibility and sense of worth, and deepened her commitment to orthodox [Sunni] Islam."[30] In Mecca, she physically retraced Hajar's steps between Safa and Marwah, infusing and merging her own loss with that of Hajar and placing her body, pregnant with twins, upon a sacred path of Islamic tradition, which would continue after she left Mecca and returned home to the United States.[31] She did so as the wife of a slain Black Muslim man and the mother of six—two still unborn—daughters whom she would raise and teach to practice Islam and be Muslims (even as she herself was still learning how), while also instilling in them a deep knowledge and love of Black people and culture.

Through her *hajj*, Shabazz demonstrated her intention to continue on as a "garment" for Malcolm's spirit, a role she would honor until her death in 1997. Islam, in turn, acted as her garment, and through its practice, she continued on the faith journey she and her husband had embarked upon together, and thusly continued, beyond the NOI. At the same time, her decision to make the pilgrimage, pregnant and in mourning, demonstrated her fierce will, independence, and personal devotion to God. Being Muslim, her actions declared, was integral to her sense of self both as Malcolm's wife and now widow and also as the singular woman who would emerge not in, but *through*, the shadows of his legacy. To fully understand Betty Shabazz's Muslim-ness, I argue, requires an understanding of how deeply her identity as a Muslim woman was interwoven with being Malcolm's wife and how this role led her to make a life for herself, on her own terms, after his death. Islam at once anchored her to Malcolm *and* allowed her to move on from the past. To explore Shabazz's engagement with Islam, I do not retread Shabazz's biography, so excellently documented in Rickford's text. Nor do I delve deeply into the immense body of scholarship and writing on Malcolm X[32] or on Malcolm's writing and speeches themselves.[33] Instead I focus on discerning Betty's personal experiences and strategies in articulating a U.S. Muslim identity at two pivotal moments in her life: during the fallout between Malcolm and the Honorable Elijah Muhammad and in the years following Malcolm's murder, as she sought to construct a life for herself and her daughters. I turn to her personal writings—three letters she wrote to Elijah Muhammad in 1963–1964 and an essay she penned for *Ebony* magazine in July 1969—to trace how she thought of herself as a Muslim, the role of religion and spirituality in her life, and how being Muslim for Shabazz was a continual process of affective insurgency, in which she made her Muslim-ness against the demons of her past, the dangers that confronted her in the present, and the pervasive presence of her husband's memory—of her life with him as a man and of his iconic and enduring status as Malcolm X and as El-Hajj Malik El-Shabazz.

"Your Sister and Servant"

Betty Shabazz's love of Islam and its teachings and traditions, such as the story of Hajar, was always readily apparent, says Sister Aisha Al-Adawiya, who was a close friend.[34] In an interview I conducted in November 2015, Al-Adawiya expressed the need to "reclaim" Betty Shabazz as a Muslim woman. "We"—referring to the U.S. Muslim community—"have to take her back," said Al-Adawiya. "She's not just a woman out there in the world . . . she's a *Muslim* woman."[35] Whereas Betty is often discussed in the same breath as other civil rights era widows such as Coretta Scott King and Myrlie Evers, Al-Adawiya stresses that former's experiences were very different from the latter women because of her Muslim identity. "She was the wife of the most hated man in America at the time: Malcolm X," says Al-Adawiya. "It was not the same for her [than for King and Evers]. There were always elements of danger she had to protect herself and her children from. . . . So she was fierce, in that way. It's not easy being Betty Shabazz." Through the end of her life, Betty actively practiced Islam, even as she earned her PhD in education at the University of Massachusetts, Amherst, and became an associate professor and director of institutional advancement and public affairs at Medgar Evers College in Brooklyn, New York. In the midst of commuting from their family's home in Mount Vernon, New York, to Amherst, Massachusetts, as she was working toward her PhD, Betty would regularly take her daughters to the 72nd Street Mosque on the Upper West Side (officially called the Islamic Cultural Center of New York) every Sunday "like clockwork."

Betty first discovered Islam at age nineteen, when she began to attend Nation of Islam meetings in Harlem in late 1955. She had moved to New York to attend a nursing program at Brooklyn State College in 1953, and prior to that, she had studied at the Tuskegee Institute in Alabama, first pursuing education, then deciding on nursing as her chosen profession.

Her journey from childhood to college was complex and often difficult. Born to a young unmarried couple named Ollie Mae Sanders and Shelman Sandlin in Pinehurst, Georgia, in 1934, Betty—née Betty Dean Sanders—as a small child moved to Detroit with her parents, where she was reportedly abused by her birth mother. After being shuffled around to her grandparents and various relatives, at age 11 she was taken in as a foster child by the prominent Black Detroit businessman Lorenzo Malloy and his wife Helen, who would eventually adopt her and raise her as their own. Helen became the most prominent and influential maternal figure in Betty's life, inculcating her foster daughter with middle-class black bourgeois values that stressed respectability and education as paths toward racial uplift and in which the Black Church—in the Malloys' case, the Bethel African Methodist Episcopal Church—was the bedrock of one's community and cultural life. Betty at once adored and feared her adopted mother and often dreaded her admonitions, which were caustic and critical. Whereas Helen Malloy was the closest person Betty had to a permanent mother figure in her life, their relationship was more cordial and polite than warm and nurturing, and at times it was quite strained. Indeed, Betty's subsequent conversion to Islam and marriage to Malcolm would "shake" her relationship with her foster parents, although this animosity later thawed.[36]

Betty first attended a NOI meeting at the behest of a female co-worker, who lured her there with the promise of nutritious, home-cooked food. Alone in New York, Betty concurred and found herself quickly intrigued by the fiery rhetoric of the minister who was preaching that evening. Yet as Rickford writes, "It was the Nation's masculinity that first enticed Betty." At the temple, she "felt utterly protected among black men, perhaps for the first time."[37] Upon meeting Malcolm X, who was the star minister at Muslim Mosque No. 7, Betty, like most of the other female attendees at the mosque, was smitten. Unlike the other young women, however, her interest in Minister Malcolm was reciprocated, and soon after, the two began to talk, always under the supervision of other Muslims. By 1956, she had converted to Islam and adopted the name Betty X. Less than two years later, on January 14, 1958, with Elijah Muhammad's blessing, the couple married in Lansing, Michigan, Malcolm's birthplace.

The newly married Betty X was a multilayered and highly capable individual, and she brought this complexity into her marriage and role as Minister Malcolm's wife. Keenly intelligent, she quickly learned and mostly accepted her "place" in the Nation of Islam as Malcolm's wife, but she also flexed her independence and expressed scrutiny at some of the organization's practices. While she enjoyed her position as "first lady" at Temple Number Seven and the perks she received as the wife of the NOI's second-in-charge, by the start of the 1960s, she knew that Malcolm received little material compensation for his constant labor and fierce devotion. While Betty and Malcolm rarely disagreed, a central point of contention between them was their finances (a tension portrayed in Spike Lee's 1992 film, *Malcolm X*). Betty also quickly found that being Malcolm's wife rendered her the target of much gossip and jealousy among NOI members, especially the women, many of whom complained about her penchant to not cover her hair or to wear clothing that barely met the group's codes of modesty, such as knee-skimming skirts or short sleeves. Such clucking, however, "never bridled Betty. Invisibility did not suit her, and she continued to sharpen the intransigence that would shape her reputation."[38] Yet Betty was far from being Betty Friedan's notion of a "feminist." While she at times pushed against expectations, she enjoyed being married and relished her role as a wife and mother; even when pushing against the boundaries of women's prescribed roles in the NOI, she understood her marriage and home life as forms of religious duty and practice, as well as being expressions of commitment to Black nationalism and Islam.

By late 1962, Malcolm X's relationship with Elijah Muhammad and the Nation of Islam had soured. He had learned of Muhammad's infidelities with a "coterie" of his secretaries, a discovery that shattered Malcolm and threw him into despair. Betty became worried for her husband's "spiritual and emotional health"; after learning of his idol's indiscretions, "Malcolm had grown increasingly haggard and heartsick" and confided to his wife and others close to him that he was "losing his religion."[39] For Betty, this was a vulnerable time, and a moment in which her devotion to her husband and their family's well-being came first yet in which she also needed to show to those around her, including Elijah Muhammad, that she was *not* losing her religion or her devotion to the NOI. To do so, she felt, would jeopardize Malcolm's standing in the group and thus would put herself and the children in harm's way. It would also forfeit any chance for Malcolm to be recognized—or compensated—for his service to the Messenger. Thus, in the early months of 1963, despite the vitriol directed at her husband, Betty continued to go to NOI events and services at various Muslim temples, including one in the Philadelphia mosque that she was asked to attend by Elijah Muhammad himself.

Afterward, she wrote a letter to the Messenger. During her time in the Nation of Islam, between 1958 and 1964, Betty had often corresponded with Elijah Muhammad, whom she addressed as "Holy Apostle." This was not a simply due to her position as the wife of Muhammad's number one minister, but as a Nation of Islam member. Many of Muhammad's followers, as well as those interested in the group, would write to the Messenger seeking advice and guidance. In this letter, dated February 18, 1963, Betty begins, "Dear Holy Apostle: Hoping when you receive this letter you will be with Allah's will and mercy as he [sic] desires."[40] The letter goes on to note her observations about the Nation's tithing process during services in Philadelphia, specifically her thoughts on how to solicit more donations from members, which she says she arrived at after much deliberation: "I pondered over this many a [day], sometime [sic] one thinks of a lot of things but says few, for fear of being labeled wrong; but truly speaking in general there are a lot of things we could be and are working toward making exact."[41] She strikes a business-like but complimentary tone, telling Muhammad that the passing of the tithing basket should be timed more carefully with the speakers' lauding of his accomplishments, so congregants upon hearing of Muhammad's achievements—his "means and methods, what they have gained" from the NOI—would give more readily. "We need as a Nation a lot of money," Betty says matter-of-factly. "No one needs it more than us."[42] In the context of her husband's difficulties with Muhammad at that time, and Betty's own concerns about her family's financial and physical safety, her words carry multiple meanings, reflecting her caution in addressing Muhammad yet also conveying to him her feelings around the judgment and gossip about Malcolm and their family in the NOI ("one thinks of a lot of things but says few, for fear of being labeled wrong"), as well as their need for financial resources ("We need as a Nation a lot of money"). For Betty, being Muslim is expressed through attention to administrative details that may improve the overall wellness of the group.

After sharing her thoughts about the tithing process, the letter pivots to another topic: Betty's desire to return to school, which she prefaces by expressing to the Messenger how she feels she can be more useful outside of the home:

> I don't do anything now, other than Housework and cooking for my family and guests. They say minister's wives have a full time job keeping the minister happy so he can do his job. I feel this is true, but I also feel I could do more constructive things, although this is a big assignment. If this is what is wanted, this is what I will do; however I would like to go back to school part time. I might be wrong but to me I feel like I am waisting [sic] away. . . . If possible, Dear Holy Apostle, I wish you would give your comment on my going to school part time.[43]

In this passage, Betty carefully conveys reverence to Muhammad and dutifulness as a Muslim woman, alongside her desire to return to her educational goals. Betty had earned her undergraduate degree in psychiatric nursing in 1956 and hoped to advance her studies in the field of education, so she might teach one day. Betty's request to return to school comes at the close of a letter in which the majority is devoted to her display of piety and competence as a "good" Muslim woman; she wants to show Muhammad that she is an asset to the NOI and has the skills to grow the organization. To preface her appeal, Betty is cautious to avoid disparaging "women's work" such as "housework and cooking" but says instead that she can do "more constructive things" if she advances her education. Yet again, she does not overassert herself, telling the Messenger she "might be wrong" about her needs, but she does feel that she is "wasting away." The last line of Betty's appeal is interesting in light of the fact that both she and Muhammad knew of Malcolm's wavering faith in the Messenger at that time. Betty's request for permission from Muhammad to pursue her goals demonstrated her desire to show her family's deference to his authority when he and those around him were questioning Malcolm's loyalties, thus placing Betty and her girls in harm's way. At the same time, knowing of Betty's frustrations with Malcolm's lack of compensation from the NOI, and her worries for his physical and emotional health, the request was also an assertion of strength and independence in the face of a man she believed posed a threat to her husband and family. In other words, she sought to deliver a message to Muhammad that she, Sister Betty, was a strong and capable woman who was undeniably an asset to the Nation and could be just as strong and capable outside of it—or perhaps, even as a force against it. Yet despite this small gesture of defiance, Betty's tone remains restrained overall, as she stresses that she is devout in her faith and believes in Muhammad's leadership. She closes the letter by telling the Messenger she is "praying for [his] continual success," and signs the letter, "Always, with Allah's help, Your sister and servant, Betty."[44]

It is unknown whether Muhammad ever responded to Betty's request, although it is unlikely, because tensions would soon escalate between Malcolm and his mentor. Malcolm had chosen to speak with others in the organization about Muhammad's affairs with his secretaries, an act that led to his censure and widespread disapproval among the NOI rank and file. Following Malcolm's remarks about President John F. Kennedy's assassination on November 22, 1963—that the murder constituted "chickens coming home to roost" of U.S. racism and imperialism—Minister Malcolm was officially suspended from the NOI. This was undoubtedly a period of intense turmoil for Betty, who by then had three children and was expecting a fourth. During this time, from the close of 1963 through spring of 1964, Betty corresponded once again with Muhammad, sending him a short note dated January 5, 1964. In it, Betty strikes a conciliatory tone, once again emphasizing her devotion to Muhammad and affirming her faith. She informs Muhammad that "my husband doesn't know I am writing you this letter" and that she would like request a meeting with the Messenger.[45] She closes by saying, "I love you, the Teachings, and Allah. And I would very much like to talk to you. I have no one that I feel I can talk to but you."[46] The letter is signed "Always, Sincerely Sis Betty."[47] This letter is far less formal than the last, and its tone is slightly desperate. Aware of the rift between Malcolm and his mentor, Betty sought some sort of promise of safety from Muhammad that Malcolm could not at the time. As an NOI Muslim, despite the charges against him, Betty still saw Muhammad, as did Malcolm, as a religious leader, a prophet of God. With Malcolm distracted and oftentimes away from home,[48] Betty composed the note as an act of supplication, a cry for help to the Messenger of Allah.

This intimate, devotional tone shifts dramatically by her next letter to Elijah Muhammad, dated exactly two months later on March 5, 1964. Whereas her other correspondence to the Messenger began with blessings to Muhammad from the Almighty—the February 19, 1963, letter opens with hopes that he "will be with Allah's will and mercy as he desires," and the January 5, 1964 letter opens with wishes that "with the blessings of Allah you are fine"—Betty does not invoke "Allah" or anything regarding the spiritual at the start of her March 5 letter. Instead she writes, "Hope when you receive this letter you will be *as you desire.*"[49] No longer is Muhammad addressed as a deity or in beatific terms. In the paragraphs that follow, we learn that Betty and Malcolm have been chastised by Muhammad and suspended from the Nation. As a result, she and her family have experienced intense backbiting and ostracization from many other Black Muslims, and this is causing her great stress and dismay. She emphasizes that, despite this treatment, she has exercised restraint and decorum—that is, that she has behaved as a good Muslim woman should. The letter, in which she numerically lists the grievances leveled at her, is worth quoting at length:

> I have tried to be pleasant; avoiding un-necessary or embarrassing situations with all Muslims. . . . 1. Some Muslims speak with me, 2. Some over speak, e.g. I was approached three times in one night by a sister talking rather loud [*sic*] about my husband, 3. Some appear to look at me as if I have two heads, etc., but I try to keep myself composed. What can I do? What do they expect of me? I have three children and another expected— their future is always on my mind. I have tried in words or deeds to show no disrespect to any one. I appear to be all alone in the world. . . . When I go to the Mosque, I do what I am told, try to be pleasant, I don't do any- thing to people. I have too many problems myself to be trying to create new ones.[50]

Increasingly frustrated with being a "good" Muslim woman in the face of insults and slights, Betty lays out how she has conformed to Muhammad's teachings and moral code, done what she is told, as a minister's wife should, and yet is looked at as if she has "two heads" and has come to be suspended from the group. In the face of Muhammad's hypocrisy and the threats of those vying for Malcolm's power, Betty is most vexed with what she perceives is a lack of clarity in terms of pre-scribed action for such a moment—*What can I do?*—she asks, clearly frustrated.

In his autobiography, Malcolm X writes that it was during this time, in the early months of 1964, that he began to "arrive at [his] psycho-logical divorce from the Nation of Islam."[51] Although he had been tor-mented by the knowledge of Muhammad's infidelities and felt the sting of his suspension for some months prior, the "divorce" finally occurred because of his knowledge that there were now orders for his death com-ing from within the NOI. For Betty, however, the start of her divorce with the NOI had come earlier, as indicated in the February 19, 1963, letter to Muhammad, when she asked if she could return to school. She knew then that Muhammad and the Nation of Islam would not provide the safety and security—physical, financial, and spiritual—their fam-ily needed. Betty's faith, although strong, vacillated between her faith in Malcolm, who still unwaveringly supported the Messenger at the time, and her own realization that her husband was in danger. In the NOI, with other Black Muslims, Betty had converted to Islam not only because she was drawn to its religious teachings and political messages but also because she became Malcolm's wife. Because of Malcolm, she had demurred to the gossip of others, swallowed her pride, dressed modestly, and written carefully crafted letters to her husband's spiritual father that she hoped would relieve him of stress and advance her own goals. Thus her commitment to being Muslim was always intertwined with her love and devotion to her husband. In the March 5, 1964, let-ter, Betty's tone reflects how, in light of Malcolm's "divorce" from Mu-hammad and the NOI, she could finally express her exasperation and anger that, even though she had done what she was told, even though Malcolm had done all he was told, they had been abandoned. No lon-ger able to believe in the Messenger, "the future [was] always on [her] mind," as she sought to reconcile the moral-ethical framework and the ways of being Muslim she had learned in the NOI to a life without them. Like her husband, who would embark on his *hajj* to Mecca in April 1964 and return to the United States as a Sunni Muslim, Betty Shabazz would also soon undergo her own religious transformation, spurred by the tragic events that led her to take her own *hajj* journey in March 1965.

"All Those Things That Make a Plain Housewife"

As those around her noted, Betty Shabazz leaned toward respectability and middle-class comforts, likely owing to the difficulties of her life prior to living with her adoptive family, the Malloys, and the black bourgeois upbringing she had with them. Following Malcolm's murder at the Audubon Ballroom on February 21, 1965, many in Black nationalist grassroots circles criticized Betty's seeming disappearance to the suburbs of Mount Vernon, New York, where she put her girls in private school and went on to pursue her PhD at the University of Massachusetts. Many in the Black nationalist movement said she was not revolutionary enough and had "became elite and middle-class," moving away from Malcolm's Pan-African revolutionary ideals and toward the "Civil Rights, institutional path."[52] As one companion of Malcolm's remarked

Figure 3.1. Betty Shabazz. Cover of *Ebony* magazine, June 1969.

Figure 3.2. Betty Shabazz with her daughter Gamilah and at her desk answering mail regarding Malcolm, as featured in *Ebony* magazine, June 1969.

stingingly, "She didn't lead a life commensurate with Malcolm's."[53] While such critiques were valid in some ways—Betty was not a revolutionary in the mold of Malcolm, nor did she claim to be—they were also deeply unfair in that they did not recognize or seek to understand that Betty and Malcolm's union was not premised on Betty's "revolutionary" character or credentials. Instead, under the advisement of Elijah Muhammad, Malcolm had been instructed to find a "righteous" wife who would prioritize family life as "the backbone of Islam," which Betty always did. As stated earlier, Betty's sharp wit and intelligence, her outspokenness and independence, and her flouting of the Nation's dress codes and gender norms had already made her the subject of gossip and attacks while in the organization. Thus it was ironic that following Malcolm's death, she was suddenly labeled as too conservative, too meek, and not properly revolutionary.

According to her daughter Ilyasah, in her autobiography *Growing Up X*, much of Betty Shabazz's healing process following Malcolm's death had to do with her embrace of Sunni Islam. The younger Shabazz writes extensively about her mother's faith in her memoir, stating that although "some people might have expected my mother to return to the Christian faith of her youth" following Malcolm's death, "she moved deeper into the faith of her choice."[54] Betty Shabazz was "a devout Muslim" but "extremely private about her faith." Part of this privacy manifested itself in her external appearance; she did not "look" Muslim in that she "did not wear *hijab*—the traditional head covering—in her everyday life, though she dressed modestly as the Qur'an instructs and was always appropriately covered in the mosque."[55] Just as she approached her role in the Nation of Islam, Betty Shabazz also maintained a strong sense of women's autonomy and agency that did not contradict her investment in marriage and family as the cornerstones of her life. Ilyasah Shabazz writes:

> [My mother] did not believe Islam required women to be passive creatures locked away in a house somewhere. She believed she had the support of her religion in doing what she had to do—go out into the world and achieve for herself and for the sake of her family, just as millions of Muslims around the world do. And as she did so, she strove to fulfill the five pillars of Islam; she was conscious of Allah, she prayed, she fasted,

she made hajj, and she gave generously to individuals and to charity. . . .
Islam was a shining, powerful force that sustained my mother through
the darkest periods of her life, and she wanted her daughters to grow up
with that same sustenance. So every Sunday, rain or shine, we went to the
mosque.[56]

In her daughter's words, we see that Shabazz strove to maintain her family's privacy and dignity while also expressing her devotion to Islam and
her husband's commitment to anti-Black racism as a global struggle. The
same care that she took to negotiate her position with Elijah Muhammad
in her letters was applied to her cultivation of her identity as an orthodox Sunni Muslim, yet at the same time a thoroughly Black American
woman, who supported the development of Black cultures and community. Dressing in African style head wraps and stylish contemporary
dresses with appropriately modest necklines and hemlines, Shabazz
sought to live out what she imagined her husband would have wanted
for herself and her daughters, central to which was their identities as
Muslims.

This was likely not an easy task for Betty, who had just begun to
learn about Sunni Islam before Malcolm's untimely death and who
was labeled, along with Coretta Scott King and Myrlie Evers, as one
of "widows" of the civil rights movement—figures forever enshrined
in grief and tragedy. Shabazz cautiously expressed the daily realities
of her life after Malcolm in a cover story featured in *Ebony* magazine's
June 1969 issue.[57] Titled "The Legacy of My Husband, Malcolm X," the
story was one of the only accounts of her life with Malcolm that was
penned by Betty herself. On the publication's cover, as she was often,
and continues to be, depicted in the press, Betty's image is flanked by
the face of her late husband, whose image is replicated on both sides
of her. As a caption with the accompanying stories tells readers, the
depictions of Malcolm are from a portrait that hangs in Shabazz family's living room in Mount Vernon, New York, the bedroom community where Betty moved with her daughters after Malcolm's death. The
cover image of Betty seems to catch her in mid-sentence, responding
to a question or comment. Her arms are clasped, and she wears an orange headwrap, hoop earrings, and a smartly tailored dress cut from an
earth-toned African print fabric. Whereas the images of Malcolm are

clearly painted artistic renderings, Betty's image is vibrant, in motion, and fully enfleshed. On the opening pages of the feature, Betty and her six daughters are featured in a large portrait taken in their home posing under the aforementioned painting of Malcolm X. On both sides of the family portrait are photos of Betty; the one on the left is a close-up of Betty's smiling face, and on the right there are two images, the first of Betty, again smiling and holding her daughter Gamilah at the playground, and the second of Betty sitting before a typewriter surrounded by a "steady stream of letters," as the caption reads, that she received monthly, "mostly from young people who are telling her how much they admired and respected her late husband."[58] Unlike the photos that the public had previously seen of Betty in the press—in mourning and dressed in black, following Malcolm's assassination—the photos in *Ebony* were bathed in warm, natural sunlight, with Betty and her children wearing smiles, or at least contented expressions. Further in contrast with the cover, in which Betty was surrounded by Malcolm's image, the opening pages of the feature showed Malcolm surrounded by images of Betty and his children, indicating that, in this story, her life was framing his, not vice versa.

In the accompanying essay, one of the few pieces of writing Betty published in the mainstream press, the widow began by stating what she believed was the power of her husband's legacy, why Malcolm's ideas "struck a responsive chord among black people, but particularly among black youth."[59] In the second paragraph, she went on to recount inspiring letters from young Black men and women who had written to her saying they identified with Malcolm, and she highlighted one in particular from "a 17-year-old brother in Philadelphia" named Ronald White. She shared that she had met White once on a student panel for a television show appearance, then she quoted the letter in its entirety, which is worth citing at length:

Dear Mrs. Shabazz:
I am writing with an effort to express the joy and honor your presence bestowed upon me. . . . It was a dream come true. When reading Malcolm's autobiography some things lingered on my mind. I had wished someday I could meet someone who was close to Malcolm, never imagining someday it would be his wife. . . .

I figured you to be very plain, shy and *all those things that make a plain housewife*, but I was shocked to when you walked in the door. Your entrance was so dynamic with your graceful smile that said with its expression, "I am black and I am proud and will accept no substitute for freedom." I just can't seem to find in the English vocabulary words to express the happiness your presence brought to me. It motivated and restored my energy to fight on for *the justice for the black man*.[60]

That Betty chose this letter from young Ronald White to frame her essay was certainly deliberate, a way to lead with the attention on Malcolm but then to shift the focus on her ability to continue his legacy. She employs White's letter to reflect the gender expectations of the public toward her as Mrs. Malcolm X, that she would be "all those things that make a plain housewife" but who, as White discovers, is much more. Instead, Betty is "dynamic" and smiling and expresses in her very presence that she is "black and . . . proud and will accept no substitute for freedom." To put it another way, she *is* ready to assume the responsibilities of safeguarding and promulgating her husband's political, cultural, and spiritual work and will do so with dynamism and grace. Yet as the final line of White's letter shows, the political mantle Betty will take up still requires her to maintain her "place" as a Black Muslim woman and wife, as her work will be directed toward achieving "justice for the black *man*," not black people, not black men *and* women. Even with her graceful smile and proud, independent bearing, Sister Betty Shabazz's central role remains to lift up and advance the cause of justice of Black men, which is still implicitly advanced here as critical step in her husband's legacy to achieve Black freedom.

After establishing her own strength and asserting that she can hold her own with those who will be the future of Black struggle, such as Ronald White, Betty's essay moves on to discuss more personal issues, beginning with whether or not she has "gotten over" her husband's assassination. For two years, Betty writes, she and her children could not mention his name or look at pictures of the slain leader. Now, however, she shares, "There is [a picture] in practically every room in the place. . . . I don't think we will ever outgrow [the pain], but I think we have developed the strength to live with it."[61] She begins to discuss the way Malcolm's presence continues to shape how she is raising her children, that his ideas and thoughts on family and child rearing are central in their household:

> My husband had very definite opinions about raising children. He believed that parents should provide proper images for their children and should give them guidelines as to what they can and cannot do. Some of his basic aims were to see that our girls are taught to face reality, to accept themselves, to be able to function under supervision[,] receive some formal training and education and be made to realize it was their spiritual and moral duty to help oppressed people. . . . I still follow his guidelines with the girls. His indoctrination was so thorough even to me, that is has become a pattern for our lives.[62]

In this passage, Betty mentions the role of religion in their lives, saying that the spiritual and moral imperative instilled by Malcolm to help the oppressed is now her responsibility to carry out in his absence. For Betty, the practice of her own spiritual and moral duties have come to be a part of her life through what she calls Malcolm's "indoctrination"—the political and religious ideologies at the foundation of their marriage as Muslims that made central the struggles for Black liberation. For Betty, however, indoctrination was not negative; Malcolm's interpretation of Muslim doctrine was a frame through which she ordered her life, even in his absence.

Yet her words indicate that, while Malcolm fought on the front lines of the struggle, Betty was responsible for implementing the struggle *as practice* into the family's daily routines, to construct Black liberation and Islamic justice as a way to raise children, to run a household, as a basis for marital union, and to imbue moral and ethical values into routine tasks. To put it in terms of Islamic practice, before she even began to study the teachings of Sunni Islam—or, as Betty called it, "the Islamic jurisprudence"[63]—she constructed forms of Islamic *sharia*—those ways of living Islamically—as learned from her time in the Nation of Islam and the teachings of Elijah Muhammad and now in her burgeoning engagement with the global Islam she and Malcolm had accepted at the time of his death. As the essay proceeds, Betty offers further details about how Malcolm's "indoctrination"—and now her interpretation of his interpretation of Islam—structures her family's life, in particular in regard to housekeeping and dietary habits, which Betty, a nurse, stressed as critical to emotional, physical, and spiritual health. She says of her husband's diet: "He had very strict eating habits. . . . As a nurse and because of home economics classes taken at Tuskegee Institute, I had some knowledge of the nutritional value of foods. I prepared a diet for him that included the basic essentials."[64] She goes on to offer a detailed list of the foods she served him ("In the morning, I served him three beverages plus coffee: freshly squeezed orange and grapefruit juice combined with other fresh vegetable juices and a glass of milk with two egg yolks, honey, or brown sugar and a flavoring") and says that her regimen alleviated Malcolm's fatigue and nutritional deficiencies.[65] After detailing his dietary habits, she goes on to convey that Malcolm was voracious reader, a lover of culture and the arts, and firm in his advocacy of Black nationalism as a way of life. Although Betty was accused of pandering to the civil rights assimilationist agenda following Malcolm's death, she does not distance herself from Black nationalism in any way, instead casting it in cultural terms. In addition to "political and economic power," she writes, which are integral to Black liberation, she argues that a love of Black culture is imperative: "This is primary nationalism: a love of the motherland, the family, the language, the folkways and mores of your people. (Call it black awareness, black consciousness or black pride—it's all nationalism.)"[66]

Then Shabazz explicitly outlines her own role in *the fight for justice for the black man*, an interpretation that draws upon the dogma of Elijah Muhammad and the Nation of Islam regarding the role of the Black women yet innovates and builds upon it in ways that address her own reality as a professional woman, a female head of household, and public figure. "The black woman," she begins,

> has the chief responsibility for passing along black cultural traditions to the children. Malcolm had a tremendous respect for motherhood. He used to say that a man should always remember his mother because she bore him in her womb, suffered a lot on his account and reared him while making many sacrifices. The black woman, he believed, is the sustainer of life which she had to be because of circumstances, the emotional supporter of the family, the maintainer and teacher of culture, the vital force in any movement. "If you educate a man," he used to say, "you

educate an individual; if you educate a woman, you educate a family." In the movement he felt that a woman's role should be determined by her qualifications. He did not believe that a woman's role was just in the home and in the bed. . . . Malcolm also felt that black men should be especially concerned about protecting their women collectively; by doing so they were protecting themselves collectively.[67]

Here Betty lays out a framework for her own moral, ethical, and spiritual life as a Black Muslim woman. She firmly accepts and embraces the responsibility and "place" of the Black woman as directed by the masculinist terms of Black nationalist struggle and during the 1960s and 1970s, yet she also asserts the flexibility of gendered space, that is, that women who were "qualified" should not be confined to "home and bed." Yet, hearkening back to chapter 2, we hear her echo the same words Malcolm used to describe the esteemed role of women in Islam in the publication of *The Messenger* magazine, that to educate a woman is to educate a family. For Betty, such maxims of Malcolm's, rooted in both the teachings of the NOI and Sunni Islam, took on a spiritual quality; a critical component of being Muslim meant retaining her allegiance to his values. At the same time, the essay also revealed these beliefs as rooted in Betty's own investments, that she was not blindly following Malcolm's words but had herself come to the understanding that "orthodox Islam [was] the religion which offered the soundest spiritual base for black people."[68]

In the second to last paragraph of the essay, Betty shares that she does not plan to remarry. It was not "feasible," she explained, because she had "six daughters who take up 99 per cent of my time" and because "Malcolm domesticated me into feeling and believing that a woman is supposed to be able to give to a marriage. I don't have anything to give to a marriage at this juncture in my life."[69] By using the word "domesticated" to describe her marriage to Malcolm, Betty indicates how her journey as a U.S. Muslim woman—from the Nation of Islam to Sunni Islam, as well as being a public figure, educator, and social justice advocate—was intimately connected to her embodied experiences of marriage and motherhood, of her identity as a wife and parent. One might argue that Betty Shabazz's articulation of Black women's responsibilities and duties were decidedly "womanist" in nature, expressing her support for Black men while also celebrating the power of Black women. Yet they were also, inexorably, Islamic in nature. Like Hajar, Betty was rendered legible in history through her association with her husband. Yet also like Hajar, one of the most venerated figures in Islam, her marriage fostered her evolution as a consummate representative of Islam, of U.S. Muslim womanhood, as she innovated and fashioned her racial, religious, and gendered identity against shifting political landscapes, all the while translating her belief system into the affective and embodied practices of her and her family's daily life. While Malcolm had begun the journey to Islam at the crossroads of Black freedom struggles, Pan-Africanism, and global Islam, Betty continued on with the journey until her own tragic death in 1997.[70] Thus, not only were Betty Shabazz and Malcolm X "garments for one another," but Betty's understanding of marriage and family itself, and her identity as a wife and then widow, would become a "garment" for her following her husband's death in that it constituted the safe harbor through which she *created herself* as one of the most prominent and well-respected Muslim women in the twentieth-century United States. To put it another way, Shabazz grounded her identity as a Muslim woman in her marriage and prioritized her role as wife in order to protect and fortify herself against, and deftly maneuver, the oftentimes fraught and dangerous political conditions she confronted throughout her life.

Dakota Staton, Aliyah Rabia, and the "True Islam"

On April 19, 1962, *Jet* magazine featured the jazz singer Dakota Staton on their cover. Against a red backdrop, the page featured a black-and-white close-up of Staton's smiling face juxtaposed besides two black ink-line drawings, one of three veiled Muslim women clutching their scarves over their mouths, and the other of minarets. In a small breakout caption to the right of Staton's image, offset in white, the text read, "DAKOTA STATON: Famed singer gives views on religion and polygamy," while along the bottom of the cover, in all capital letters, was the line: "WHY THE SINGER BELIEVES IN FOUR WIVES." Inside the issue, the accompanying story ran under the title, "DAKOTA STATON REVEALS WHY SHE IS POLYGAMY SUPPORTER," alongside a series of images of Staton, who had adopted the Arabic name Aliyah Rabia, with her husband, the jazz trumpeter Talib Dawud, photographed in various scenes of domestic life: Staton cooking, washing dishes, and reading Islamic texts and perusing African art with Dawud in their study. "Despite her success," one of the photo captions read, referencing Staton's singing career, "Dakota firmly believes . . . the role of a housewife comes first in her life."[71] This belief, the article continued, was rooted in her identity as "a devout Muslim who firmly believes in the Islamic God, Allah." This "realization of her role as a woman," Staton said, had "helped her attain success as a concert performer, night club star, and recording artist."[72]

As one of the most popular jazz artists of that moment, Staton had enjoyed consistent coverage in the press since the release of her album

Figure 3.3. Dakota Staton, Cover of *Jet* magazine, April 19, 1962.

The Late, Late Show (Capitol Records) in 1957, which had sold so fast upon its debut that "dealers [couldn't] keep it in stock."[73] The album's lead single, which shared the same name as its title, was a crossover hit, reaching no. 4 on the U.S. *Billboard* magazine charts, very high for a jazz artist, while Staton's covers of jazz standards such as "Misty," "My Funny Valentine," and "A Foggy Day" had earned her comparisons to the reigning jazz queen of the day, Dinah Washington, and drew packed houses and rave reviews every time she performed. (A July 12, 1958, review of a Staton show at the acclaimed New York City jazz club Smalls stated that the venue could not accommodate half the people who wanted to get in to hear and see Dakota Staton, "who has suddenly become a great night club attraction," and stated that she sang and entertained "magnificently.")[74]

Yet this particular *Jet* issue in 1962 was Staton's first *cover* story in which she publicly presented herself as a Muslim woman. As its title indicated, the piece by Larry Still focused not on her musical career or vocal style but on her religious beliefs and practices, as well as her marriage to trumpeter Dawud, whom she said in the interview had introduced her to Islam. In the Black press, of which *Jet* and *Ebony* were the most popular publications—just as in *The Hate That Hate Produced* and in *Life* magazine (as discussed in chapter 2)—"Islam" was sensationalized in specific ways. Staton was not a member of the Nation of Islam, but as a Muslim who "believes in the Islamic God, Allah," what was titillating about Staton's religious beliefs was her subscription to seemingly exotic, and highly orientalist, notions of marriage, specifically polygamy. As with Mufti Muhammad Sadiq, who (as discussed in chapter 1) had been jailed upon arrival in Philadelphia for his supposed support of polygamy, Staton's very identity and presence in the United States as Muslim was bound up with the notion of multiple marriage, which she says she supported in principle but would never practice with her husband "because it is illegal."[75] She went on to tell the reporter, "Man is naturally polygamous, he is supposed to have more than one woman. Allah says he can have four—but some are satisfied with two or three. In this country, everyone knows a married man has more than one woman, but they won't admit it. We're so hypocritical about everything."[76] Staton also emphasized through the interview, as she would in subsequent other interviews, that she believed a woman's primary role should be in the home, "and she should always stay in her place."[77]

Why would one of the country's most popular entertainers, many wondered, espouse views that seemed to directly contradict the value and validity of her work as a jazz vocalist? Why would one disparage the glamor and glitz of the music industry to wash dishes and make soup? As the interview continued, Staton shared with *Jet*'s readers that she had converted to Islam because of "her experiences as a woman" and that it was specifically what she had experienced as "a Negro woman in show business . . . the drinking and the pawing and the familiarity" that had made her a "firm believer in Allah." Being in the music industry, she said, made her "afraid I was going straight to Hell." Being Muslim, thusly, she countered was a far better option, as Muslims did "not let such things [such as pawing and drinking] happen to their women" and because she now had "peace of mind." Since converting to Islam, she continued, she was considering giving up her singing career and "devoting her life to Allah" by "building orphanages and homes for old people in Africa." Staton made it a point, however, to tell the reporter that she and Dawud followed an Islam that was based on "the brotherhood of man . . . not this stuff Elijah Muhammad [of the Nation of Islam] has been telling people."[78]

In 1962, Dakota Staton was the most prominent non–Nation of Islam Muslim woman who had ever presented herself as a Muslim woman in the U.S. public sphere. Like Betty Shabazz, her Muslim-ness was deeply connected to that of her husband, Talib Dawud, who was by all accounts a persuasive and charismatic figure who desired to fashion himself as a U.S. Muslim leader. A performer since her youth, Staton had grown up on the stage, and as her remarks in the *Jet* feature indicated, she had come to realize there was little safety or security for a Black woman oftentimes playing for white audiences and fending off constant sexual advances of men. In addition, headliners such as Staton were constantly expected to conform to feminine beauty standards—which already marked Black women as oversexualized and unattractive—and were frequently ridiculed or mocked for their looks and appearance. Thus Dawud, who was seven years her senior—and thus, Islam—offered her an alternative to the only lifestyle she had known, a seeming safe harbor from the misogyny, racism, exploitation, and judgment of the music industry. Unlike Betty Shabazz, however, Staton was already a public figure when she converted to Islam. Being Muslim actively posed a challenge to her work as a female jazz vocalist working in smoky jazz clubs that served alcohol and in which she was constantly surrounded by male musicians. In addition, whereas Shabazz navigated being Muslim through the rigid structure of the Nation of Islam, which offered clear boundaries on women's roles and taught the religion through the frame of Black nationalism, Staton engaged Islam's teachings—as did the many Black male musicians who also converted at the time—with the explicit aim of constructing herself as a global citizen who could "transcend" anti-Black racism through Islam. As a woman, however, Staton's adoption of a universalist Islam came with restrictive notions of women's mobility and public performance that did not apply to men and rendered her ability to be a "respectable" Black *and* Muslim woman impossible while also pursuing her singing career. Such restrictions ultimately caused her to leave the faith and divorce Dawud, by the late 1960s. Still, for a over a decade, Dakota Staton was also known as Aliyah Rabia, an identity she expressed through her outspoken advocacy for what she believed was a "true Islam," while struggling against attacks on her character, her career, and her music, which came from both within and outside of her marriage. Whereas Betty Shabazz found a lasting safety in her marriage, even after Malcolm X's death, Dakota Staton would eventually shed the garment of her union with Dawud—and Islam—to seek safety elsewhere.

The Late, Late Show

Staton was one of many Black American jazz musicians who converted to Islam throughout the 1950s and 1960s. As Richard Brent Turner writes, most did so through the Ahmadiyya Movement in Islam, whose members included jazz luminaries such as the pianist Ahmad Jamal, saxophonist and multi-instrumentalist Yusef Lateef, drummer Art Blakey, pianist McCoy Tyner, trumpeter Talib Dawud, and many more.[79] Staton, however, was the one of the few female converts from the jazz community, and certainly the best known. In the months following her introduction to the religion through Dawud, after their initial meeting in 1958, Staton converted to Islam through the Ahmadiyya Movement and adopted the name Aliyah Rabia, which in Arabic means "exalted springtime." A few months following her conversion, in February 1959, Staton and Dawud filed for a license to marry in Greenwich, Connecticut. The county clerk refused to authorize the union because Dawud was unable to produce divorce papers from his previous marriage. The couple tried again, and successfully officiated their vows later that year.

Unlike Dawud, it was Staton's first marriage. Born in Pittsburgh, Pennsylvania in 1931, she had displayed musical talent at an early age. Instead of singing in the Black Church, however, as had many other vocalists of the time, she received a formal music education at Pittsburgh's Filion School of Music and "came of age musically in a Broadway-style musical revue" style.[80] By age 18, Staton was the girl singer in a local dance band, and from there, she went on the road and toured with the Pittsburgh-based bandleader Joe Westray. After a few years with Westray, Staton began to do solo shows in Black nightclubs, where in 1953, at a show at Harlem's Baby Grand Club, she was heard by Capitol Records producer Dave Cavanaugh, who signed her to the label. She quickly released several singles, and in 1955, *Downbeat* magazine named her the country's "Most Promising Newcomer"—an accolade that propelled her to widespread fame and led to the production of *The Late, Late Show*. Following its release, wrote one music critic, she quickly became one of jazz's shining stars, joining the ranks of reigning divas such as Ella Fitzgerald, Sarah Vaughan, and Dinah Washington. In other words, at the close of the 1950s, Dakota Staton was at the height of her career, constantly in demand and poised to become jazz royalty.

It was at this time that she met Talib Dawud. The trumpeter was an enigmatic and mercurial character, who at age 18 arrived at New York City from the Caribbean island of Antigua with the name Alfonso Nelson Rainey. According to the anthropologist Robert Dannin in *Black Pilgrimage to Islam*, Dawud entered the prestigious Juilliard School of Music in the early 1940s to study brass instruments and soon found work playing with the Duke Ellington and Louis Armstrong Orchestras.[81] Early in his career, he called himself "Barrymore Rainey" and soon found his most "important musical association [with] the Dizzy Gillespie big bands on the even of the 'be-bop revolution.'"[82] While working with Gillespie, he was introduced to Ahmadiyya Islam in the early 1950s, and he quickly converted, taking on the name Talib Dawud.

Gillespie's band, it seemed, was "fertile ground" for conversion to Islam. In addition to Dawud, other converts included saxophonist Yusef Lateef, saxophonist Lynn Hope, drummer Kenny Clarke, and trumpeter Oliver Mesheux—all members of Dizzy Gillespie's bands. Dawud was said to be particularly effective at proselytization, a sharp and gifted speaker, who possibly had a hand in converting the other musicians who worked with him.

Unlike many of his bandmates, whom Gillespie surmised converted to Islam "for social rather than religious religions,"[83] Dawud was a true believer. Not satisfied to simply be an Ahmadiyya Movement in Islam follower, Dawud established his own Ahmadiyya affiliate organization in 1950, which he called the Muslim Brotherhood of America, Inc., and for which he named himself as president and leader. A few years later, he founded a group he called the Islamic and African Information Center, which based its headquarters in Philadelphia, where he and Staton would move following their marriage. Dawud saw his groups not only as organizations of Islamic learning but also as sites of cultural and religious ambassadorship, for which he was a spokesman and representative of "true Islam" in the United States—an Islam in which, Dawud stated, "there is no racial segregation and discrimination."[84] Beginning in 1959, Dawud wrote regular editorials in the *Chicago Defender* as well as the Chicago-based Black paper *New Crusader*, in which he lambasted Elijah Muhammad and the Nation of Islam for their "false" version of Islam and "his followers' failure to adhere to proper Muslim prayer rituals."[85] As the prime representative of "True Islam," Dawud set out on what he believed was a religious mission to discredit Muhammad, his organization, and followers. The separation of the races, Dawud continually said in the press, had no place in Islam.

Following their marriage in 1959, Staton joined Dawud in taking on Muhammad and the Nation of Islam, with Staton using her access to the media as a platform to decry NOI beliefs as dangerous and false. Following the CBS airing of *The Hate That Hate Produced* (discussed in chapter 2), *Jet* magazine ran an item in their "Entertainment" section stating that, along with pianist Ahmad Jamal, the couple publically denounced "the movement of Elijah Muhammad's Muslims as a vicious misrepresentation as well as slander against the religion of Islam."[86] It went on to cite Staton as clarifying that "there is no connection between

Muhammad's group and the Muslim Brotherhood U.S.A, of which she is a part."[87] As a result of the rising notoriety of the NOI, Elijah Muhammad, and Malcolm X following the news program's showing, Dawud increasingly sought to proclaim himself a U.S. Muslim leader and upped his efforts to act as an ambassador and representative of U.S. American Islam.

Dawud and Staton endeavored to raise their profiles as "true Muslims" later that year. In November 1959, the couple hosted a reception and luncheon in Harlem for the president of Guinea, Sekou Touré and his wife Andrée.[88] Touré's visit was significant to the residents of Harlem and, more broadly, to many Black Americans, as they linked their struggles to anticolonial and Pan-Africanist ideologies and consciousness worldwide. In 1958, Guinea had voted for, and democratically declared, its independence from France, and thus become an independent nation. Touré, a committed anticolonialist and the leader of the Democratic Party, had spearheaded the independence effort and became the nation's president. As the new head of an independent African nation, Touré had emerged on the global political scene alongside the Ghanaian prime minister Kwame Nkrumah, as a leading Pan-Africanist, and actively worked to connect African struggles to those of the African diaspora worldwide, including the Black struggle in the United States. Unlike Nkrumah, however, Touré was Muslim and during his tour of the United States was scheduled to meet with U.S. Muslim leaders, specifically those from the Black community. Staton's star power enabled access to the elite Black circles in Harlem, including the leadership of National Association for the Advancement of Colored People, who were organizing Touré's schedule, and the couple presented themselves as "true" representatives of the U.S. Muslim community.

Yet Staton and Dawud's inexperience in politics and foreign affairs—exacerbated by existing tensions between Black nationalist groups in Harlem and the NOI—marred the event. In their desire to impress, the couple failed to coordinate their stance as orthodox Muslims with the Black nationalist organizations that were also present at the luncheon. According to the Black press in New York, which covered the event extensively, Staton had left it to James Lawson, the president of the Universal African National Movement (a local Black nationalist group), to make some arrangements for the luncheon. But when he did, Lawson dismissed the services of the assigned State Department interpreter for Madame Touré, because the interpreter was a white woman. Lawson then told the press, "We did not want a non-black person interpreting Harlem to Mme. Touré."[89] In addition, Lawson's group (along with Staton and Dawud) declared that "followers of Elijah Muhammad . . . were blocked from participating in any of the affairs" because they were not true Muslim,[90] which led Malcolm X to make a public denouncement of Lawson, Dawud, and Staton. The gaffe would have serious repercussions for Staton, who was seen as inept and a poor representative for her proclaimed brand of "universalist" Islam, and the incident was an indicator of the way her public identity as a Muslim woman would interfere with her singing career, as well as how she would come to square off with Malcolm X, Elijah Muhammad, and the Nation of Islam.

"A Double Life"

Perhaps spurred by the embarrassment of the debacle with the Tourés, or simply because her life had changed, in 1960, Staton set out to present a new image of herself to the press as a Muslim woman. Although she had released four albums since *The Late, Late Show*, none had replicated its success. That year, she would record four more and would be constantly performing and touring. It is interesting to note that these albums took on a far more somber and introspective tone than Staton's previous albums, which had been decidedly upbeat, driven mostly by uptempo swing rhythms. Her first release of the year was titled *Dakota Sings Ballads and the Blues*, a collection of standards that opened with the poignant George Gershwin ballad "Someone to Watch over Me." Around this time, from the close of 1959 to early 1962, Staton appeared in a host of news stories and features that foregrounded her newfound happiness as a married woman and emphasized her love for the domestic arts, as well as highlighting her disapproval of Elijah Muhammad and the Nation of Islam. A December 10, 1960, piece in her hometown newspaper, the *Pittsburgh Courier*, surmised that Staton led "a double life": "On stage, the singer is every inch the trouper. She prefers peace and quiet, as far from the glitter as possible. Whenever her schedule permits her to be at home, she delights in preparing her husband's meals . . . despite a busy schedule, [she] pursue[s] her hobby of preparing authentic

African dishes . . . collects antiques and paintings . . . [and] reads historical novels."[91] Another article, published the following month in the
New York Amsterdam News on January 7, 1961, offered almost the exact
same narrative, also stating that Staton led a "double life" of "belting out
songs" on stage while being an "anti–instant package food user" who
"shops for her own fresh groceries and makes careful selections . . . she
will return food to the store in a second if she feels it is not of good quality and worth the high price she paid." An accompanying photo called
Staton "a beautiful picture of domesticity" and shared that she had just
penned a cookbook of African dishes.[92]

Like the women of the NOI, Staton's practices of domesticity mirrored
the norms of middle-class white women during the Cold War, complete
with a white apron tied around her waist, hair perfectly coiffed, stirring
a steaming pot over the stove. Yet unlike the middle-class white women
depicted in Betty Friedan's *The Feminine Mystique*, who sought work
as escape from suburban drudgery, Staton had been working her whole
life. By the time of her marriage to Dawud, Staton had endured the sexism, misogyny, and scrutiny of being a female jazz performer for years,
as well as the grueling performance and touring schedule of all working
musicians. To cook and clean—for example, "whipping up tasty African
dishes for her husband, far from the glare of the footlights"—was undoubtedly a relief for Staton, a space of respite from labor.[93] Yet Staton
did not explicitly state to the press that her desire to serve her husband
dinner and her penchant for domestic duties had anything to do with
Islam until the publication of the *Jet* cover story in April 1962. Besides
a few minor news items in which Staton had clarified that she was not
part of the Nation of Islam and that she disapproved of Elijah Muhammad's version of Islam, the *Jet* article explicitly identified her as a Muslim
woman to the American public. To make this pronouncement, Staton

Figure 3.4. Dakota Staton, featured in *Jet* magazine, April 19, 1962.

did not wear a headscarf or discuss her worship practices as a Muslim; instead, she signified being Muslim through her devotion to marriage and her affinity for housework, as well as her agreement with "exotic" practices such as polygamy.

Interestingly enough, however, Staton made clear that she thought assuming such gender norms were not only integral to "the realization of her role as a woman" but also to her goals as "a concert performer, night club star, and recording artist," as her work would enable her to channel her talents toward charity or philanthropic work someday. Although some surmised that Staton was simply parroting the views of Dawud, these words reflect how Staton herself, as Aliyah Rabia, saw Islam a means of merging her "double life" as a jazz artist *and* private individual who craved the safety and sanctity of domestic space. Staton's embrace of Islam and her marriage to Dawud were not acts of giving up her career to be subjugated in the home but in fact constituted what she saw as a path toward "having it all"—a means to affectively live as a religious and spiritual being that allowed her safety and security while also continuing to express her talents and abilities as a musical artist. Further, her marriage to Dawud enabled her access to a political voice and community that she, as a Black female jazz vocalist, would not have likely accessed otherwise.

"Injunctive Relief"

Following the *Jet* feature, Staton's profile as a U.S. Muslim woman would rise even further as she and Dawud decided to singlehandedly take on what they saw as the "falsehood" of the Nation of Islam's brand of Islam. They claimed their decision was due to religious, as well as deeply personal, reasons: After the broadcast of *The Hate That Hate Produced*, Staton said her career had suffered because the public had come to associate her with the Black Nationalist and racially separatist politics of the NOI, which led to less bookings for her to perform. Thus, on June 4, 1962, Staton and Dawud filed an action in the U.S. District Court in Philadelphia, "seeking to enjoin Elijah Muhammad from claiming to be a Muslim and to prevent him from further use of the terms Islam and Muslim in connection with the sect which he heads."[94] In an interview with the *New Pittsburgh Courier* concerning the suit, Staton told the newspaper:

We . . . seek injunctive relief against future declarations by Elijah [Muhammad] that what his organization teaches is actually based on the religion of Islam as taught in the Holy Qur'an, or is, in fact, in any way related to the Islamic religion as contained in the Holy Qur'an. . . . Our first concern is that the words Islam and Muslim to the American public have come to be synonymous with the Black Muslims. Because we openly profess to be believers in Islam, we have on many occasions been erroneously linked [with the NOI]. . . . My career as a singer has suffered irreparable harm as a result. . . . The unwitting actions of the press in linking us with this man who declares that all whites are "devils" has caused a drop in my bookings, and further has made some disc jockeys refrain from playing my records.[95]

Staton's words and charges reflect the strategies through which she sought to make her Muslim-ness legible in public space. Unlike the women of the NOI and Betty Shabazz, Staton saw her practice of Islam

Figure 3.5. Dakota Staton with Talib Dawud and Arthur Gottschalk, Republican state senator from Illinois, at the May 31, 1962, press conference. Press photo in author's possession.

not as a component of Black nationalist struggle but as a religious orientation she could implement and integrate into her career as a successful jazz singer. When "Islam" became a politically charged racial presence owing to Elijah Muhammad and the NOI, Staton sought safety *from* Black nationalism, not within it, and sought relief through the courts, in effect asking the state to litigate a definition of "true" Islam.

A week prior to the filing, on May 31, 1962, Staton and Dawud held a press conference to announce their intentions, where they were represented by a Republican state senator from Illinois named Arthur Gottschalk. As their affiliation with Gottschalk demonstrated, in order to seek legal counsel and monetary support for the case, the couple had joined forces with prominent white detractors of the Nation of Islam, such as Gottschalk and the conservative syndicated columnist George E. Sokolsky, who wrote a series of columns following the case in July 1962. Arguing in support of the couple, Sokolsky used their case to denounce the NOI, writing, "Should this case, asking for a permanent injunction, be pursued to a conclusion, it could be that this curious and dangerous native American sect might be completely exposed. It is about time. . . . The Black Muslim movement is a political cult designed to separate Negroes from Whites and to create major troubles in areas in the United States where Negro masses congregate."[96] Sokolsky's words indicated that he cared little about Staton's claims that her career had been negatively affected or about the doctrinal differences she and Dawud put forth. Instead, he saw their case as merely a way to delegitimize the NOI.

After they filed the suit, Malcolm X charged back at the couple, but primarily at Staton, whom he attacked through a discourse of morality, or her alleged lack thereof. Comparing her to the "respectable" women of the Nation of Islam, X said, "Even the non-Muslim public knows that no Muslim sister who follows Mr. Muhammad would think of singing sexy songs, half-naked in a night-club where people are getting drunk and expect people to still respect her as an example of religious piety. . . . She is over-rating herself and underestimating the intelligence of the public."[97] Further ridiculing Staton, X called the suit "ridiculous" and a "publicity stunt," saying that its only purpose was to regain the spotlight for Staton, who had "grown very unpopular" and was just seeking to raise her profile.[98] In addition to X's sentiments, Staton and Dawud said they had also experienced physical retaliation from the Black

Muslims because of their opinions; they had been the victim of an acid attack, and that there had been a bomb threat made to their mosque in Philadelphia.[99]

The case took an undeniable toll on Staton. In a press photo taken at the May 31 press conference, Staton sits with her arms clasped, next to Dawud and Gottschalk, who appears to be making a statement. She wears a rather plain, demurely patterned dress, her hair is loosely coiffed, and her face is without makeup. Whereas Dawud and Gottschalk look out into the audience, Staton's eyes are downcast, seemingly fixed on a spot on the floor, the sides of her mouth turned down in a frown. Her expression is strikingly somber; she looks exhausted, dejected, and perhaps most of all, simply, sad. The image is a far cry from the smiling, apron-wearing, domesticated Muslim woman and musical superstar she had sought to present herself as over the course of the past year. The Philadelphia court eventually dismissed the case, and in its aftermath, Staton's career suffered irreparable damage. Her record label, Capitol Records, dropped her as an artist after 1962, and although she signed another contract with United Artists the following year, she would record only two albums in the next three years, neither of which performed well in sales. In 1965, Staton and Dawud moved to London, where she recorded one album on London Records. Their primary reason for moving, they said, was to flee the attacks of the NOI. The couple would divorce by the end of the decade, and Staton stopped practicing Islam during that time.

Upon her death in 2007, many music critics proclaimed that Staton had simply married the wrong man and that this had robbed her of her rightful recognition as "one of America's great vocal stylists."[100] While Dawud certainly influenced Staton, her words and images in the public eye also revealed her intense desire for Islam and its gendered structure, as she interpreted it, to operate as a safe harbor from the music industry, through which both Dakota Staton and Aliyah Rabia could exist in harmony. Ultimately, it was not only Dawud who hurt her career but also the antagonisms against which she had to articulate herself as a Muslim woman in the United States *beyond* the question of race—beyond Black nationalism. As a non-NOI Muslim woman, Staton was not only illegible to the U.S. American public as a Muslim woman but also rendered persona non grata by Black Muslims who attacked her career, talent, and character. While she sought to find sanctuary in her domestic life with Dawud, in which she performed forms of domesticity she believed reflected her practice of Islam, Staton would finally find a garment not in her husband or in Islam but in her own music making, which she resumed when she returned to the United States in the 1970s.

* * *

For Betty Shabazz and Dakota Staton, "Islam" was a guiding force in their marriages and in their identities as Muslim women insomuch as they understood their marital bonds as acts of worship, as well as their acceptance of women's "domestic" positions in their relationships. At the same time, both women adhered closely to notions of Black women's "responsibility" to uplift the race through marriage through their seeming embrace of domesticity and submission to their husbands. In addition, Islamic doctrine—whether as taught by the Honorable Elijah Muhammad, by Ahmadiyya missionaries, or by other Muslim leaders or guides—offered guidelines that each woman implemented to the best of her abilities in her daily lives. For Betty Shabazz, this meant carefully navigating—and at times, subverting—the power structure of the Nation of Islam while presenting the appearance of a "proper" Muslim wife in order to secure safety and stability for herself, Malcolm X, and their children. For Staton, being Muslim was expressed in negotiations between her career as a successful jazz artist and performer and her self-presentation as a deferential and devoted Muslim wife, as well as in her decision with husband Dawud to pursue a lawsuit against Muhammad and the NOI in 1958. Neither were simply oppressed or "imprisoned" by marriage, as the women described in Betty Friedan's *The Feminine Mystique* were. They employed their marriages as platforms for the construction of their public images as U.S. Muslim women and as conduits for religious practice. For each woman, being Muslim and practicing Islam was essential to how they engaged Islam in both private and public spheres and, ultimately, to how they incorporated—or rejected—Islamic practices and "Muslim-ness" into their daily lives.

4

Chadors, Feminists, Terror

Constructing a U.S. American Discourse of the Veil

At the end of 2002, the year following the 2001 U.S. invasion of Afghanistan and four months prior to the initial strikes of the second Iraq War, hip hop magazine *OneWorld* featured a cover photo of rapper Lil' Kim. In the photo, Kim wore thin, intercrossed scarlet strips of fabric that clung to her erogenous zones, and on her head, a billowing, blood-red burqa covered her face, except for her eyes, which looked directly at readers through bright blue contact lenses. The words "Race Matters" snaked down the cover's right side, referencing the accompanying interview with Kim penned by the writer Rebecca Walker (the daughter of Alice Walker), titled "The Bluest Eye," an allusion to Toni Morrison's novel of a young Black girl's desire for whiteness. In the introductory pages of the magazine, the editor's note offered readers a glimpse of Kim before the photo shoot. When asked whether she thought her attire might be considered offensive or too politically charged in light of the U.S invasion of Afghanistan, Lil' Kim replied, "Fuck Afghanistan. Let's shoot this."

The image went viral immediately. Internet message boards lit up with both praise and insults for Kim; some called her a fearless crusader for women's rights, and others labeled her a warmonger and an Islamophobe. For Kim's supporters, the rapper's overt sexuality was a right of U.S. citizenship. One commentator wrote that Kim was "a beautiful young woman making money. . . . This is America she can wipe her ass with a burka if she feels like it." Additional support for Kim arose from an unlikely locale, the conservative Internet message board *Free Republic* (www.freerepublic.com), self-described as "America's exclusive site for God, Family, Country, Life, and Liberty constitutional conservative activists." In a lengthy thread, *Free Republic*'s netizens praised the rapper by writing "My respect for Lil' Kim just went up 100%," and "Generally I am *far* from a fan of rap/hiphop. But if this girl is outraging

Figure 4.1. Lil' Kim. Cover of *One World* magazine, December 2002/January 2003.

Muslims, she's doing good work." While the site's target demographic of white conservatives did not traditionally support "hip hop"—or more broadly, Black—culture, most did agree that when having to choose between "hip hop" and "Islam," the former was preferable. One message board member asked, "What is worse for African Americans? Islam or hip-hop? I'd go with Islam." This sentiment was quickly followed by a flurry of posts in affirmation and agreement.

Commentators who were critical characterized *OneWorld*'s decision to run the photo in wartime as part of, as one person put it, "the 'hate-the-Muslims' ideology" that "made it OK for Bush to bomb innocent ppl [*sic*] in Iraq." Some critics deemed Kim a crass sexual provocateur who represented all that was wrong with hip hop. They noted Islam's central role in hip hop culture and antiracist struggles and expressed their points of view by employing derogatory and sexist language: "Lil' Kim is a tramp and a slut, and that is what tramps do: push people's buttons." "Lil' Kim—Most of your fellow rappers are Muslim! . . . You really want to start with Muslims?" Another commentator, calling herself "SISTAH MUSLIMAH" and who self-identified as a Black American Muslim woman, addressed those who perceived Kim to be an advocate for women and/or an American hero by saying, "I have viewed the cover of *OneWorld* magazine and as a Muslim woman, I am offended. . . . I am sad that all women will not be offended. . . . It's blatant disrespect. It's an outright mockery of the Islamic ideal of modesty. In a magazine that titles itself *OneWorld*? *Whose* world???"

Beyond the online message boards, news outlets reported that "Muslims worldwide" were furious and called for boycotts of *OneWorld* and other business ventures of Russell Simmons, the magazine's publisher and owner and overall hip hop mogul.[1] The one group that actually boycotted Simmons and his magazine was Islamic H.O.P.E ("Helping Oppressed People Everywhere"), a Los Angeles–based community organization named and led by the activist and Black American Muslim Najee Ali, the son-in-law of the late U.S. Muslim leader, Warith Deen Muhammad. Ali had harsh words for Simmons, asserting that the photo betrayed Muslims worldwide as well as Black Americans. Ali demanded an apology from Simmons and told the press, "Mr. Simmons should be ashamed of his exploitation of Lil' Kim (and she of herself). . . . Russell Simmons has stood with Louis Farrakhan and had him host hip hop meetings for peace. Does he want to build bridges with the men of Islam, but disrespect the women?"[2]

I argue that Lil' Kim's *OneWorld* cover signified an important moment in the evolution of the "discourse of the veil" in the United States. A term first coined by Leila Ahmed in *Woman and Gender in Islam* (which I discussed in the introduction), the "discourse of the veil" refers to the fetishization of the headscarf as a primary—if not the preeminent—signifier of Islam as culture in the West.[3] In her examination of debates around the veil in late nineteenth-century Egypt, Ahmed demonstrates how "the issues of women and culture first appeared as inextricably fused" both in Arabic discourse written by men as well as in the discourse of British colonizers in Egypt, in other words, how the veil came to encapsulate women as a symbol of Islamic culture for Brown and white men. Specifically within European colonial discourse, the fetishization of the veil became a central component of "colonial feminism"—a term discussed in the introduction of this book—a description of "feminism used against other cultures in the service of colonialism."[4] Through colonial feminism, the colonizer employed the discourse of women's rights to show how "other men, men in colonized societies or societies beyond the borders of the civilized West, oppressed women," thus rendering those in the colonized society culturally and morally inferior.[5] In the late nineteenth century, Ahmed writes, a new colonial discourse of Islam emerged in the West, in which, "Islam was innately and immutable oppressive to women, that the veil and segregation epitomized that oppression, and that these customs were the fundamental reasons for the general and comprehensive backwardness of Islamic societies. . . . Veiling—to Western eyes, the most visible marker of the differentness and inferiority of Islamic societies—became the symbol of both the oppression of women and the backwardness of Islam, and it became the open target of colonial attack and the spearhead of the assault on Muslim societies.[6]

In *Being Muslim* thus far, I have spoken little of the Islamic headscarf, or, as it is alternately called, the *hijab* or *khimar*.[7] This is mainly because the scarf was not a central issue or concern for the women discussed here. Some wore it, some did not, some wore it sometimes, or some wore it only in prayer or formal occasions. For the women of Ahmadiyya Movement in Islam during the early twentieth century, head coverings were made of blankets, bedsheets, and whatever else was available to them. The women of the Nation of Islam wore uniforms with white head coverings, which many said resembled nun's habits, although they also donned less formal scarves and clothing that reflected the styles of the day, as was reflected in the clothing of Betty Shabazz and Dakota Staton. For Muslim women immigrants to the United States who began arriving in larger numbers following the passage of the Hart-Cellar Act, otherwise known as the 1965 Immigration and Nationality Act, many women did not cover or ceased to cover their heads when they came to the United States. If they did, they generally did so in the styles of the lands from which they came. Thus, owing to the still relatively small numbers of Muslims in the United States, both Black and non-Black; the absence of contentious geopolitical conflicts between the United States and Middle East nations through the close of the 1960s; the predominantly Black American presence of Islam in the United States until the mid-1960s; and national gendered logics in which "feminism" had not yet entered the mainstream consciousness, there was little discussion of the veil and Islam's treatment of women in U.S. popular culture or in mainstream media throughout the close of the 1960s and even through most of the 1970s. Consequently, while U.S. Muslim women wore, or did not wear, the headscarf during those decades, they largely did not have to confront widespread perceptions of the veil as a symbol of women's oppression by "Islam" in their day-to-day lives.

This would change by the close of the 1970s, when the specter of "fundamentalist" Islam would enter the national imaginary through the figure of the Ayatollah Khomeini in Iran and specifically in relation to the rise of the Iranian women's movement in March 1979. It was in this moment—as I examine in this chapter—that a distinctly U.S.-based discourse of the veil emerged that would come to shape national conversations around Islam, race, and gender in the years to come. Critical in the construction of the U.S. discourse of the veil, as I will show, was the presence of women of color, particularly Black and Third World feminists, who challenged white second-wave feminist activists who sought to take up the cause of "oppressed" Muslim women in Iran while ignoring the voices of women of color in the United States.

With that in mind, I want to return to the photograph of Lil' Kim on the cover of *OneWorld* to further elaborate upon its significance in the U.S. discourse of the veil. Unlike the other chapters in this volume, this chapter does not consider the specific experiences or representations of U.S. Muslim women but instead looks at the relationship between white women, women of color, competing notions of feminism, and racialized and gendered notions of Islam within the national cultural imaginary. As I demonstrate in what follows, Black Muslim women—and, for that matter, the history of Black American Islam—were vanished in the media's and mainstream feminists' conversations around Muslim women in Iran in 1979, as the headscarf emerged in the United States as the central signifier of the "oppression of women and the backwardness of Islam." The orientalized conception of Islam that emerged out of Iran at the close of the 1970s overshadowed associations of Islam with Black nationalism or racial separatism, and it forcefully jettisoned Islam into the Orient. Indeed, following the assassination of Malcolm X in 1965, the Nixon administration's crackdown on Black dissidents and activists throughout the 1970s, and the death of the Honorable Elijah Muhammad in 1975, Black American Islam largely retreated from the headlines, and Islam as a religion of fundamentalist religious clerics, conniving oil sheiks, and veiled women clad in black from head to toe took its place.

This post-1970s racial-religious form of Islam was very much in place at the time of the September 11, 2001, attacks on the World Trade Center and Pentagon. It was the logic that drove the increase in hate crimes against Muslim women following the 9/11 attacks, specifically those who wore the headscarf, and led a number of U.S. Muslim community leaders to declare the permissibility of women removing their headscarves if they feared for their safety. What was significant about Lil' Kim's *One-World* cover image and the discussion surrounding it, then, was how it at once mobilized both the historical legacies of Black Islam—in which women's modesty operated as a type of political insurgency (as discussed in the previous chapters)—as well as affirming and advancing the colonial orientalist logics of the discourse of the veil. In other words, the image simultaneously highlighted Islam's presence in the United States as a Black protest religion while also advancing the imperialist logics of the discourse of the veil. As the online commentary at the *Free Republic* message board demonstrated, the veil (or in Kim's case, the burqa) signaled Islam's inferiority and barbarism, a characterization that was employed to justify the War on Terror. Kim's nudity was meant to highlight the oppressive nature of the veil, insofar that she, as an American woman, was assuming a defiant stance against the sexism and misogyny of Islam.

What rendered the image more than another iteration of the discourse of the veil, however, was Lil Kim's racial identity as a Black woman. Prior to 9/11, the Islamic veil had received little scrutiny in relation to Black women's bodies. In addition, the image's placement on the cover of a hip hop magazine highlighted Islam's significance in hip hop culture; the journalist Harry Allen and Public Enemy affiliate once called Islam "the unofficial religion of hip hop." Yet owing to the presence of a Black woman in an Islamic veil, the image did not stress the masculinist empowerment ethos of groups like Public Enemy or rappers like Nas; instead, it referenced the ways Islam had operated in Black women's lives as Black liberation discourse and religious presence, while also obfuscating these significances through a reinvigorated logic of U.S.-based colonial feminism. In the photo's contradictory logic, the spectacle of Lil' Kim in a bikini and burqa represented a "clash of civilizations" between Islam and the West.[8] Departing from former iterations of the orientalist opposition between East and West, the West this time was represented by a Black female rapper. Her race-d body triggered a discourse of the veil that sanctioned the procedural movements of state terror while also indexing the ways Black Islam would *not go away*. The presence of Lil' Kim in a bikini and burqa on the cover of a hip hop magazine titled *OneWorld* demonized Islam through the discourse of the veil while also provoking an articulation of Black Islam's historically *insurgent* racial-religious presence in the United States. While Lil' Kim said "Fuck Afghanistan," the image solicited responses from women such as Sistah Muslimah, who reminded us of the lives and labors of Black Muslim women, and from figures such as Najee Ali, who referenced the insurgent legacies of Black Islam. Thus, even as the rhetoric of terrorism marginalized Black Islam, Kim's photo showed the persistence of a critical counternarrative of Islam in America, which conveyed Islam's insurgent racial politics and the critical role of women of color within them.

The Iranian Women's Revolution, March 1979

I turn to the story of the Iranian Women's Revolution of March 1979 as reported by the mainstream U.S. media and the feminist publication *Ms.* magazine in order to unearth the origins of the contemporary U.S. discourse of the veil. In my analysis, I describe how "chadors, feminists, and terror" became entangled in national conversations around Islam and Muslims and how this was predicated upon white second-wave feminist desires to ignore the voices of Black and other women of color feminists within the United States. The American discourse of the veil emerged directly out of this moment. Taking place shortly after the overthrow of Shah Mohammad Reza Pahlavi and after Ayatollah Ruhollah Khomeini's rise as the Supreme Leader of Iran, the Iranian women's protests marked a moment in which the U.S. nation-state—which had been an ardent supporter of Pahlavi's regime (while, Pahlavi, in turn, had been an indispensable ally of the United States)—seized onto a specific explanation why Khomeini was a tyrant, why Iran was in turmoil, and why Islam was the enemy. From that moment on, "women's rights" became a rallying call employed by the United States to explain the ills of the Middle East and the "terror" of Islam. Eight months prior to the saga of the Iranian hostage crisis in December 1979, media coverage of the women's movement in Iran produced the racial and gendered contours of the U.S. discourse of the veil that would shape conversations around Islam and Muslim women throughout the 1980s and 1990s. It recast long-standing orientalist narratives of a barbarous Islam and oppressed Muslim women upon American discourses of nationalism, civil rights, and second-wave feminism, and it positioned Muslims and feminism at opposite ends of a seemingly irreconcilable divide between Islam and America.

"Out of the Mists of the 13th Century"

On Thursday, March 8, 1979, less than a month following the Ayatollah Ruhollah Khomeini's rise to power, Iranian women took to the streets of Tehran for International Women's Day. While the marches, rallies, and speeches of the day had been planned well in advance, a spate of recent actions and comments made by Khomeini on the status of women in the newly minted Islamic republic—including a reported remark in which the Ayatollah stated that all working women should be required to wear the chador, the black head-to-toe covering which left only a woman's face exposed—fueled a maelstrom of anger among many of the women in Iran's capital city, who showed up masse in the day's heavy snows to protest the clergyman's views. Up to thirty thousand women joined the day's protests, many of whom belonged to Iranian progressive and leftist organizations. Some had been central organizers and participants in the revolutionary struggles that had overthrown the monarchy of Shah Reza Pahlavi, who many on the left saw as corrupt, authoritarian, and a puppet of the U.S. government. During the revolution, many leftist middle-class Iranian women—most of whom had traveled extensively or been educated in Europe or the United States—had taken up the chador as a sign of solidarity with their brothers and sisters in struggle.[9] Wearing the chador had been a means of displaying the unity of the opposition during the revolution. Most women, however, had not expected to continue wearing it after the shah's downfall, nor had they thought veiling would become an official policy of the newly installed Islamic state. Many of the women therefore felt not only anger but betrayal over the Ayatollah's remarks, frustrated that a revolution that had promised women so much had gone back on its word.

The U.S. media had closely followed the events of the Iranian revolution, from the early rumblings among the anti-shah forces led by Khomeini (who had been living in exile on the outskirts of Paris, in early 1978), through the shah's forced departure from Iran in mid-January and Khomeini's triumphant return on February 1, 1979. Throughout these reports, the press expressed a deep skepticism that the revolution would succeed, constantly stressing the ragtag nature of Khomeini's supporters and the power and might of the shah's military. On April 2, 1978, the *New York Times* reported that "the Shah looks secure in his nearly absolute power," and as late as December 13, 1978, the paper stated that President Jimmy Carter was "asserting that the Shah of Iran would be able to overcome his present difficulties and maintain power."[10] In piece after piece, the media described the shah as a dedicated reformer who modernized Iran, brought immense wealth to the nation, and liberated women while describing his challengers as "the strangest revolutionaries ever to challenge a ruler."[11] Of the reporters who did challenge and criticize the Shah's rule, their words "hardly had the sound of ringing condemnation," generally only stating that the shah had not been as effective as he should have been.[12] A question posed by the *New York Times* aptly described general U.S. bewilderment toward the events in question: "How could Iran, with its oil and strategic situation between the Soviet Union and the Persian Gulf, between Europe and the Middle East, fall under the sway of a holy man out of the mists of the 13th century? How could the Shah, a monarch who commanded more tanks than the British Army, more helicopters than the United States First Calvary in Vietnam, be pressured so neatly out of power? To many Americans and Europeans, the whole thing must seem mad."[13]

Such sentiments framed the coverage of the women's movement from the very start—a notion that Iran had "fallen under the sway" of a religious madman after being in the hands of the enlightened, modernizing Shah and that the protesting women were the first in the nation to "come to their senses" about what was going on. These narratives detailing the Ayatollah's "madness" and demonstrating how enlightened Iranian women were "coming to their senses" became quickly apparent when the story of the Iranian women's protests broke on U.S. television on the evening of March 8 and in most of the major papers the following morning of March 9, 1979. On television screens across the nation, the three major news networks—CBS, ABC, and NBC—displayed images of hordes of chador-clad women and a graven-faced Khomeini in order to demonstrate, as ABC's Tehran correspondent Jack Smith put it, the "hysteria of the revolution,"[14] while the procession of protesting women marching in the day's heavy snows for "women's rights" and "freedom," mostly with hair uncovered and wearing Western-style clothing, were the manifestation of, in the words of CBS reporter Mike Lee, "Iran's simmering post-revolutionary tensions."[15] In major newspapers across the country, the story broke more gradually, as a handful of papers such as the *San Francisco Chronicle*, the *Washington Post*, and the *Los Angeles Times* ran lead stories on the protests on March 9, while the *New York Times* and *Chicago Tribune* reserved the bulk of their coverage for their March 11 Sunday editions. Throughout the week, the coverage ebbed and flowed, as bursts of reporting following the major demonstrations staged by women in Tehran between March 8 and March 13, which on some days constituted the lead story of the day while on others was delegated to a quick news item or short article to run down the day's details.

Both the TV and print coverage were quick to focus on the chador as their central image early in the week. In addition to the barrage of footage of women of chadors in every report, American journalists also explicitly utilized the rhetorical trope of the veil to frame their reporting on the events. Introductory remarks by NBC news anchor David Brinkley for the network's March 8 report typified the type of standard orientalist assumptions that characterized the coverage early on, as he began, "The chador is the traditional veil and cloak worn by women in conservative

Moslem countries, a symbol of modesty and a station inferior to men. In Iran, the Ayatollah Khomeini has ordered, at least the women who work for the government, to get back into it. Those accustomed to Western clothes don't want to. Today, several thousand of them went to the prime minister's office to protest."[16] This equation of the veil and "a station inferior to men" was apparent in the print media's headlines as well. *Los Angeles Times* reporter Charles T. Powers echoed such an emphasis on the chador as he characterized the situation in Iran as one in which "the Ayatollah Ruhollah Khomeini, as the moral and political power in Iran, has embarked on the battle of the veil,"[17] while headline after headline employed the veil as its central trope. "Veiled Warning: Modern Iran Women Cool to Holy Edicts" read the headline on the cover of Power's *Los Angeles Times* piece, while the *New York Time's Sunday Magazine* ran a feature titled "Iran's 'New Women' Rebel at Returning to the Veil"[18] and an Associated Press piece in the *San Francisco Sunday Examiner and Chronicle* on March 11 named the protests "an unveiled threat" toward Khomeini.[19] Every article provided a definition of the chador: "a black wraparound garment," a "full-length cloak," "the head-to-toe veil Orthodox Islamic custom dictates," "a shapeless, full-length Moslem veil," and "the traditional head-to-toe covering of Moslem women."[20] They also offered stark orientalist oppositions between "the medieval principles of old Islam" and the modern female protestors dressed in "tight jeans or Western dresses," "skirts and jeans," and "blue jeans and jackets."[21] Reporters continually employed the veil to paint a firm dividing line between Khomeini's "Islam" and "modernity," especially on the op-ed pages of papers across the county. Following the very first day of the protests, the *San Francisco Chronicle* ran an editorial characterizing Khomeini as gripped by "righteousness" and "religious fervor," asserting that the revolution had occurred owing to the shah's efforts to "bring his country too rapidly into the twentieth century" and arguing that the Ayatollah "had better yield women the equality they are winning almost everywhere else in the modern world."[22] The *Chicago Tribune* spoke of "a conceptual gap" between Khomeini's followers and the female protestors, a gap that "seems unbridgeable" because, concluded reporter James Yuenger, "It spans centuries."[23] Charles Powers in the *Los Angeles Times* named the events a "battle of the veil" in which "the basic question is whether an Islamic revolution means a step backwards in time."[24]

The American media's fascination with the chador was not surprising. Playing upon the same colonial feminist tropes I mentioned at the start of this chapter, reporters employed the binarizing colonial logics of East and West that Edward Said had meticulously described in *Orientalism*, published the previous year in 1978.[25] Yet unlike the various colonial milieus Said discussed in his work, there was no active colonizing mission on the part of the United States in Iran in 1979 (although one could make the case that oil politics, an ever-strengthening U.S.-Israel alliance, and a general desire to expand U.S. markets constituted a contemporary form of U.S. imperialist occupation of the Middle East). Thus, while this new discourse of the veil mimicked British and other European colonial feminist tropes in a number of ways, the contexts through which news of the Iranian Women's Movement emerged in the United States— historically, ideologically, and culturally—were vastly different, reflecting very different conceptions of race, gender, and nationhood from in its previous iterations.

The Defiant Women of Tehran

The central figures in the media's narrative of Khomeini versus the women of Iran, were, in fact, the "modern," Western-educated, and un-veiled women of Iran. These were women the media consistently portrayed as wearing jeans and skirts, holding hands with their boyfriends, and, most significantly, as acting unambiguously "defiant" in the face of Khomeini's edicts and Islam's religious strictures. In fact, beyond the continuous spotlight on the chador, the most frequently featured item in all the week's coverage was the "defiance" of the female protestors. On television, reports showed women engaged in passionate debates with men on the streets of Tehran, pumping their fists in the air, demanding "liberation." In piece after piece in the print media, reporters spoke of how "thousands of women in Iran marched in Tehran in *defiance* of the veil," how "thousands of Iranian women [were] *defiantly* marching on Prime Minister Mehdi Barzagan's office," how the "*defiant*, fist-waving women threatened further demonstrations," how every march that was staged "took place in *defiance* of [Khomeini's] government," "and how the women were all "dressed *defiantly* in anything they wanted to wear."[26] Television and print reports described in detail ferocious standoffs between women and male Khomeini supporters,[27] while television images emphasized that the women were under constant threat. This threat was signified through pictures of "fanatic" mobs of snarling Iranian men who seemed to surround the protesting women at every turn. For example, ABC illustrated this dynamic on the opening night of its coverage by showing the image of a lone, bareheaded woman arguing passionately while surrounded by a group of angry, gesticulating Iranian men.[28]

Media images of the protests generally depicted the women of Iran with their hair uncovered and wearing stylish Western attire, such as Jackie-O style sunglasses, flared jeans, and fur-collared coats. Television coverage offered sound bites of young Iranian women telling the camera in flawless English that they were marching for "freedom"[29] and "liberation," and saying that since the end of the revolution, Khomeini had turned "against women," and was now "a dictator" and "a fanatic."[30] The women were also often shown with their fists raised in the air—reminiscent of the salute which had become the symbol of the Black Power Movement in the U.S. during the late 1960s-early 1970s.

However, the female protestors featured in the U.S. media's images were definitely not Black. Nor did they even look particularly Arab or Middle Eastern, as had women featured in American depictions of postrevolutionary women of Algeria in 1962 (who had also employed the veil as a symbol of opposition to French colonialism and struggled with a return to "traditional" Islamic values and gender roles following their revolution) or in the images of women in Iraq and Afghanistan in our contemporary era. In fact, many of the fair-skinned, straight-haired Iranian women featured on U.S. television news reports and print media appeared phenotypically white. For example, on *NBC News*'s March 12 broadcast, the segment on Iran featured a long, lingering shot of a heavily made-up blond female protestor, whose eye shadow, glossed lips, and feathered hair almost rendered her an Iranian version of a Charlie's Angel, one of U.S. television's most popular shows at the time. A cover story for the *New York Times Magazine* on the issue of women and Islam in Iran featured as its central image a photograph of a woman named Susan Kamalieh, a sandy-haired "liberal" Iranian female painter, who, according to the reporter Gregory Jaynes, loved skiing, lived with her boyfriend, drank beer with her friends, and painted "in a pair of sandals, jeans, and a denim shirt," often "slip[ping] one bare foot out of a sandal and scratch[ing] the back of one calf with her toes."[31] Liberal Western morals and "feminist" values like Kamalieh's figured prominently in most U.S. media accounts. In another *New York Times* article, the reporter Youssef Ibrahim quoted an unnamed Iranian female technician at the protests expressing her frustration at the constant comparisons the "religious fanatics" were making between the female protestors and women in the United States: "They are calling us American dolls because we don't want to wear the chador. They say our moral character is flawed because we wear Western clothes. . . . Doesn't [the Ayatollah] know that his Islamic women can also fool around under the chador?"[32]

Thus, in the eyes of the U.S. media, the protesting women of Iran looked, thought, and acted a great deal like U.S. American women circa 1979, in particular, the white, educated, middle-class and unmistakably "defiant" second-wave feminists currently involved in their own "battle of the sexes"—for example, Gloria Steinem, Betty Friedan, and Kate Millett, who had spearheaded the feminist movement and sexual revolution in the United States throughout the late 1960s and into the 1970s. In fact, the media's representations of Iranian women filling the streets of Tehran could almost be mistaken for their coverage of white American women who had marched in equality drives and "Women Power" protests throughout the earlier part of the decade, save for the occasional woman in chador or the bearded mullah at the edges of each image's frame. Demands for "equal rights" were listed in almost every news report as the central goal of the women of Iran—Iranian women were repeatedly reported as wanting the same things as women in the West: "equal civil rights with men; no discrimination in political, social and economic rights, and a guarantee of full security for women's legal rights and liberties," reported the *New York Times*,[33] as well as rights of "education, abortion, child-care, divorce, and employment," reported the *Washington Post*.[34] While these demands certainly did reflect the desires of many of the Iranian female protestors, few news reports discussed the needs of the vast majority of Iranian women living outside the urban centers, who were mostly poor and working-class peasant women, and whose lives were still plagued by the same issues they had struggled with before the revolution, such as poverty, hunger, and lack of opportunity.[35]

Hence the U.S. media's reporting on the Iranian women's movement explicitly rehashed the terms, antagonisms, and goals that had characterized the women's liberation movement in the United States just a few years prior. In these accounts, the protesting women of Iran were the international doppelgangers of "liberated" women in the United States, desirous of the same equal rights feminism as white American feminists. However, in this case, the "enemy" of women's empowerment was not American patriarchy and misogyny but the patriarchy and misogyny of Islam. Subsequently, the postrevolutionary struggles of the women of Tehran were cast not only through the binaries of East versus West, or even Islam versus. modernity, but through a new binary of "Islam" versus "feminism." Through its reporting on chadors and Islam in March 1979 Tehran, the media cast the two concepts as diametrically opposed entities—women were marching "to protest the increasingly antifeminist overtones of Iran's fundamentalist Moslem revolution"[36] and mounting "a growing feminist revolt [as] a direct challenge to . . . Khomeini,"[37] while all who opposed the protests or supported Khomeini's views were, whether they knew it or not, inherently "antifeminist," "anti-woman," or "male chauvinist pigs." In this way, supporting the "feminism" of the women of Iran, as the press uniformly did at the time, became not only a means of supporting "feminist" ideals in general but also a way of asserting nationalist pride in the face of fundamentalist Islam—an equivalence that would become increasingly deployed in the years to come.

Kate Millett versus the Ayatollah Khomeini

Equivalences between feminism and the nation were enabled by the historical moment at hand. In 1979, feminism in the United States was enjoying a moment of widespread public acceptance in which issues of gender equality at work and at home, sexual autonomy and freedom, and abortion rights had moved out of the realm of the "radical" and into the space of national "common sense"—if not in actual practice, than at least through mainstream cultural rhetoric and the formal language of the state. For example, in 1977, twenty thousand delegates gathered in Houston, Texas, for the first federally financed conference on women's rights, while women's studies departments were being established at universities and colleges across the country. In 1978, President Carter issued Executive Order no. 12050, which ordered the establishment of a National Advisory Committee for Women, while Congress passed the Pregnancy Discrimination Act, which as its name suggests, banned employment discrimination against pregnant women. In addition, two major cities—San Francisco and Chicago—had female mayors (Dianne Feinstein and Jane Byrne, respectively), a historical first. In the cultural arena, films like *Kramer vs. Kramer* (1979), *Norma Rae* (1979), *Coal Miner's Daughter* (1980), and *9 to 5* (1980) reflected how shifting gender roles and female empowerment, as well as the anxieties surrounding them, were at the forefront of popular national consciousness. Their success revealed the public's hunger for portrayals on how "feminism" was reshaping American life.

This widespread appeal of popular feminism spurred a great deal of public interest in the radical feminist activist and author Kate Millett's journey to Iran. Millett's story constituted a significant portion of the week's news coverage of the women's protests, in particular in the print media. Millett—the author of *Sexual Politics*, the 1970 text often regarded as the first and most prominent manifesto of the U.S. women's liberation movement[38]—had long been involved with the Committee for Artistic and Intellectual Freedom in Iran, a U.S.-based anti-shah organization, and in early 1979, she was invited by a group of Iranian feminists to speak in Tehran for the events of International Women's Day. While Millett's initial arrival in Iran in early March did not make the news, she quickly became a focal point for the U.S. media after reportedly commenting that the Ayatollah Khomeini was a "male chauvinist pig" on March 11, 1979—a statement that was roundly repeated in the U.S. press on March 12. Millett made headlines again a few days later when news outlets learned of the Iranian government's plans to expel the feminist from Iran, after which the press closely followed the events of Millett's arrest, detention, and subsequent expulsion from Tehran.[39]

Prior to her Iran coverage, Millett's profile in the press had been decidedly unflattering. Following the publication of *Sexual Politics*, a piece in the *New York Times* dubbed her the "Karl Marx of New Feminism,"[40] while her general portrayal in the mainstream media was that of an aggressive renegade who had positioned herself as "a high priestess of the current feminist wave"[41] by advocating for the complete abolition of sexual difference, decrying the traditional nuclear family as "patriarchy's chief institution,"[42] and labeling Freudian psychology as a counterrevolutionary force infused with "male supremacist bias."[43] In addition, Millett was described as a typically "unfeminine" feminist, a woman who swore "like a gunnery sergeant" and worked as a sculptor in a Bowery loft in New York.[44] In its August 31, 1970, edition, *Time* magazine featured Millett on its cover, with the cover story calling her the "Mao-Tse Tung of Women's Liberation," who had come along to take on the role of "ideologue to provide chapter and verse for [second-wave feminism's] assault on patriarchy" and whose 1970 text had supplied a "coherent theory to buttress [feminism's] intuitive passions."[45] It included a quote from George Stade, a professor at Columbia University, who stated that reading Millett's work was "like sitting with your testicles in a nutcracker."[46] Portrayals like these reflected early national attitudes and opinions of the women's liberation movement as a radical fringe group of man-hating women who had traded their "femininity" for, as one article described Millett, a "casual dashiki-workpants-sandals lifestyle."[47]

Yet such views had evolved a great deal since the start of the 1970s, a shift that was apparent in the press's later assessment of Millett. From the beginning of the coverage of Millett's journey to Iran, she was often described as a courageous patriot—a far cry from the portrayal of almost a decade prior when she had been compared to Marx and Mao. Calling her "one of the few Americans daring to speak up publicly in what has become an extremely anti-American revolution,"[48] journalists delighted in Millett's characterization of the Ayatollah Khomeini as a "male chauvinist pig." They cited Millett's words in their headlines (e.g., Reuters, "U.S. Feminist Calls Khomeini 'Chauvinist'") and on the air (both David Brinkley of NBC and Walter Cronkite of CBS reported on Millett's comment in their broadcasts on March 12 and March 15, respectively), although in reality, Millett's full comment had actually discouraged usage of the term. Asked by a reporter at a press conference she organized to introduce her Iranian feminist colleagues whether she thought the phrase could be applied to Khomeini, Millett had replied that it could be, although "it would be germane. . . . It would be a simple idiot way of describing him."[49] However, she continued, "when we are dealing with something as serious as this, when people's lives are at stake, we should avoid banal phrases."[50]

The lack of context in reporting Millett's comment demonstrated the press's desire to depict the events of the women's protests in distinctly American terms, downplaying the fact that the left-leaning women of Iran were actually wary of Millett's presence in the region. As one Iranian woman commented: "I think [Millett] has no right to talk for Persian women. . . . We have our own tongues, our own demands. We can talk for us. . . . She and no one else who is not Iranian can say anything that we should listen to about Iranian women. She does not know us. I do not know what she is doing here."[51]

Yet the reporting of such sentiments was rare, save for a few accounts that did so in order to demonstrate Iranian and/or Muslim women's inability to comprehend the benefits of Western feminism. For example, the *Washington Post* reported on March 12 that at the press conference in which Millett made the comment about Khomeini's chauvinism, she had magnanimously invited those women who had been heckling her to join her on the podium. The women had declined, however, because, the *Post* explained, "talking out problems—and the techniques of consciousness-raising—have not caught on Iran."[52] Such hostility toward Millett's opinions were contextualized within the mood of anti-American, "xenophobic post-revolutionary times," not the fact that Millett seemed to continually speak of the goals of Iranian women as nothing more than an offshoot of the U.S. women's movement. At one point, Millett said at a Tehran press conference that "*our* rights of education, abortion, childcare, divorce, employment in the professions—all the things *we* have fought for since the commencement of the women's rights movement in 1847—are in great jeopardy *in this society*."[53] Of course, Millett's citation of 1847 as the beginning of the women's rights movement was a reference to the actions that led up to the Seneca Falls, New York, convention of 1848, the first women's rights convention in the United States. The "we" she referred to in her statement did not include the women of Tehran, yet somehow what was going in "in this society" of Iran posed a grave threat not only to American feminists but to the entire history of U.S. feminism.

On March 15, 1979, Millett was refused entry to the Intercontinental Hotel in Tehran, where she had been scheduled to hold a press conference that day. After being formally asked to leave by the hotel's manager, Millett decided to hold the conference instead on the sidewalk in front of the hotel, where she discussed the recent report that the Iranian deputy premier Abbas Amir had said she would be expelled from the country for "provocations against the revolution." The *Los Angeles Times* reported that Millett appeared flustered and tense throughout her interviews, her "hands . . . shaking in nervous reaction to the confrontation in the lobby" she had just had with the Intercontinental's manager.[54] The paper then went on to report that a single Iranian women "heckled" Millett as she spoke, telling her that she did "not have the right to decide what is happening in Iran."[55] Two days later, on March 18, when Millett was detained by the Iranian government and ordered out of Iran, the Tribune Wire Service reported that Millett told *ABC News* that she was "absolutely terrified" and could "not understand why I have been treated like this. . . . I came in friendship to help my sisters."[56] "Iran Expulsion Terrifying, Says Kate Millett," read the headline on the second page of the *Los Angeles Times* on March 19. Another story that day quoted Millett as telling the Associated Press that she "had never been so terrified in my life" and that the experiences of the last twenty-four hours, during which she had been deported from Tehran to Paris, "had made her understand the true meaning of human rights."[57] Three weeks following her expulsion from Iran, Millett told *Los Angeles Times* reporter Nancy Rivera that she was still bewildered as to why she had been ejected from the country, saying, "I never did anything illegal or even impolite. I had gone there in peace and in the best will in the world, being thrilled by the insurrection and the hopes of a democracy in Iran. I'm still in a kind of state of astonishment."[58]

Thus, in a space of week, the U.S. press transformed Kate Millett from a brash, outspoken feminist who had come to Iran to defend the nation's women from Khomeini into a terrified and defeated victim of fundamentalist Islam. As these stories show, by the end of her trip, Millett had been stripped of her feminist agency, confused and trembling over how her good intentions toward the people of the region could have been so misconstrued. This was the power and barbarity of Khomeini's brand of Islam, the U.S. media coverage told us: It was an ideology that could make even an iconoclast like Kate Millett shudder in its wake. While Millett had begun her journey to Iran and with the best of intentions, she was thwarted by malicious foes gripped by fundamentalist ideology and religious fervor who were thus were unable to stomach her "modern" ideas about women's rights and international feminist solidarity. Instead, these enemies of American-style freedom terrorized, captured, and ultimately rejected Millett and her feminist ideals. Indeed, Millett's story was a harbinger of the captivity narrative of the hostage crisis that would grip the nation at the close of the year—that of an American caught, held, and terrorized by Islamic militants. Except in this case, the hostage was not only Millett but white American "feminist" subjecthood as well, a subjectivity that was part and parcel of "our" national identity and was posited as such in direct opposition to fundamentalist Islam. As the U.S. public looked on at the events of that week, what had happened to Kate Millett appeared to be a clear indication of the type of treatment "American" values such as "democracy," "equality," and "feminism" would receive in the Islamic Middle East, and it provided ample justification that "Islam" should, from here on out, like the Soviet Union, be viewed as a dangerous and formidable enemy of the United States.[59]

"The Hegemony of (White) Feminism"

Race was rarely mentioned throughout the week's coverage, both in the stories of the Iranian women's protests or in the saga of Kate Millett. None of the news reports made connections made between "Muslims" in Iran and "Muslims" in the United States, a group the media had previously placed under such intense scrutiny in their coverage of Black Muslims and the Nation of Islam (as shown in chapter 2). Indeed, the press was oblivious to its rhetorical inconsistency around "Muslims," to employing "Muslim" in an entirely different racial register than it had just a few years prior. Yet many of the same logics employed to render the threat of the Radical Black Muslim Man were repackaged to describe the Ayatollah Khomeini and the angry "hordes" of Iranian Muslim men hounding women in Tehran's streets. And whereas American feminists had paid little attention to Black Muslim women in the United States, not expressing any concern for their choices or well-being, the freedom of Iranian Muslim women suddenly became a central priority of mainstream feminist groups.

This aligned with the general inability and/or studied refusal of many feminist organizations to deal with domestic issues of race or to take up issues of racial inequality as part of a feminist agenda. By 1979,

Nixon-era law-and-order politics, through aggressive politicking and imprisonment tactics and surveillance programs like COINTELPRO,[60] had greatly diminished the effectiveness of Black Power and Third World revolutionary movements in the country. Also, by the close of the 1970s, the conservative factions of American politics who would usher in the Reagan years had already begun to roll back the Great Society civil right reforms of the Lyndon B. Johnson presidency—for example, the Bakke anti-affirmative action case of 1978.[61] Perhaps most significant was the discursive "racial project" of color blindness, in which conservatives attempted to control the racial narrative by stating that they no longer saw race. Indeed, the only discussion of race that appeared in the coverage of the protests was through the persistent language of "equal rights" that pervaded the news of the women's struggles, such as in a *Chicago Tribune* editorial published following the close of the protests, which stated that "Iranian women have no choice but to make it abundantly clear they will not surrender their hard-won rights and freedoms in the name of religion or revolution and dewesternization. They deserve the sympathy and support of all who value human rights—and who would be protesting in their behalf if they were blacks being forbidden to participate in major areas of national life."[62] Thus, in the eyes of the *Tribune*'s editorial staff, the struggle for African American civil rights was a battle that *had already been won*—Black Americans were no longer "being forbidden to participate" in all aspects of U.S. civic life and therefore "we" could move on to the project of sympathizing with and supporting the women of Tehran.

This discursive transfer of Islam's significance from the realm of Black domestic politics onto the global stage was enabled by the fact that the "feminism" deployed by the national media during its coverage of the women's protests in Iran was also conspicuously "un-raced." In it, "feminism" referred to a white, middle-class movement and ideology untouched by the ferocious internecine debates about issues of race, class, and sexuality that had been spurred on by the writings, theory, activism, and direct challenges of women of color, specifically Black and Third World feminists, to the racism, classism, and homophobia of mainstream second-wave white feminism at the time. Yet such a construction was advanced not only by the mainstream news media but by prominent feminist organizations and publications, such as *Ms.* magazine.

Before I turn to *Ms.* magazine's coverage of the Iranian women's protests, paying close attention to how race informed constructions of feminist activism and the women of Iran, it is critical to note the nature of the coverage of Black and women of color feminists within the mainstream feminist press. By the close of the 1970s, Black and Third World feminists had become increasingly vocal in their criticisms of the mainstream, and overwhelmingly middle-class and white, feminist leadership and their political agenda. Since the early 1970s, Black women and other women of color had defined and developed their own definitions of feminist principles through intersectional analyses that simultaneously addressed "multiple" and "interlocking" systems of oppression that circumscribed their lives and experiences. In 1977, the Combahee River Collective released their landmark "Black Feminist Statement," which articulated how their experiences as women of color constituted forms of knowledge production and named identity politics as a site of political struggle.[63] Black feminists joined with other women of color feminists to, as Maxine Baca Zinn and Bonnie Thornton Dill have written, contest and challenge "the hegemony of feminisms constructed primarily around the lives of white middle-class women." In their work, they took to task unitary theories of gender that did not acknowledge women's existences "not merely as gendered subjects but as women whose lives are affected by our location in multiple hierarchies."[64]

The effects of such internal debates played out on the pages of *Ms.* magazine in 1979, as the publication opened the year with the front page of its January issue featuring a full-page photo of Michele Wallace, the young Black American woman writer who had just published *Black Macho and the Myth of the Superwoman.*[65] Perhaps one of the most controversial texts among feminists at the time, *Black Macho* addressed black male sexism within Black Power movements and cultural constructions of Black women. Calling it "the book that will shape the 1980s," *Ms.* magazine ran an eight-page excerpt of Wallace's text in its January 1979 issue. In addition, the magazine's editors stated on its table of contents page that this issue was to "inaugurate a series of special reports by and about black feminists that will feature personal voices and contemporary perspectives on the sexual politics of black womanhood."[66] Along with Wallace's excerpt was another blurb stressing that the magazine would continue to focus on Black women for the many issues to come.

"Next month," the editors stated, "the special report by and about black feminists continues. The February *Ms.*—and other issues to come—will include additional personal voices and contemporary perspectives on the sexual politics of black womanhood."[67] The extended excerpt, the list of Black women's organizations, and the editors' repeated declarations of commitment to the perspectives of Black women revealed *Ms.* magazine's pointed desire, at the start of 1979, to present itself as a publication that was sensitive to issues of race and ready to engage with Black and women of color critiques and perspectives.

Yet *Ms.* magazine's discussion of *Black Macho* did not acknowledge any of the harsh criticisms of the book from other Black feminists. Among these was a scathing review of the book from poet June Jordan, who wrote in the *New York Times Book Review* that Wallace's work played directly into the hands of the white feminist establishment. In her review, Jordan wrote, "You do have to concede champion qualities to Miss Wallace's capacity for unsubstantiated, self-demeaning, historical pronouncement" and summed up the text as "nothing more nor less than a divisive, fractious tract devoid of hope or dream."[68] Palpable throughout the review, perhaps even more so than her frustration with the text, however, was Jordan's anger with the way *Black Macho* had been held up by the white U.S. feminist establishment at a time when "American mass media rolled the camera away from black life and the quantity of print on the subject became too small to read."[69] Citing a string of recent events, such as the Bakke decision and the passage of California's Proposition 13,[70] Jordan asserted that in 1979, more than ever, "collective affirmation [and] political resistance" was needed from the Black American community in order to counter the "swift and radical reversion to national policies of systematic exclusion and disablement of black life" that had taken place in the United States throughout the 1970s.[71] At review's close, Jordan stopped just short of implying that the text's popularity was due mainly to the desires of white feminists—and in turn, all white Americans—to sweep the issue of anti-black racism under the nation's rug: "Why did Michele Wallace write this book? And, I wonder, how does it happen that this book has been published—this book and not another that would summarily describe black people to ourselves, and to the other ones who watch us so uneasily. . . . It is something to think about, indeed."[72]

While Jordan's opinion was only one among many, the magazine's singular focus on Wallace's text certainly hinted towards *Ms.*'s desire to declare itself in solidarity with Black women without engaging in any sort of sustained critique of white women's racism. This desire to assert sisterhood without simultaneous self-reflection became even more clear in the magazine's February issue, when the magazine ran four short pieces by the writers Alice Walker and Audre Lorde and the activists Sandra Flowers and Christine Bond, entitled "Other Voices, Other Moods," in what it called its "Continuing Series on the Sexual Politics of Black Womanhood." While all four of these featured authors were known as outspoken critics of white racism—and in particular cases, the racism of white second-wave feminists—the published pieces only took to task sexism in the Black community (Walker and Flowers), ignorance in the Black community (Bond), and homophobia in the Black community (Lorde) as the premier agents of Black women's oppression. The issue featured no Black feminist critiques that addressed the continuing legacies of anti-Black racism or white supremacy in the United States, nor did it acknowledge the existence of racism within the mainstream women's movement itself or attempt to link the feminist cause with any type of antiracist goals.

Furthermore, following the February issue, this series was suddenly and unceremoniously dropped. Without apology or explanation, no pieces having with anything to do with race ran in the March 1979 issue, and for the remainder of the year, *Ms.* magazine offered no more articles on "the sexual politics of black womanhood," unless one counted an essay on raising an only child penned by Alice Walker for the August 1979 issue[73] or an excerpt from Toni Morrison's 1979 commencement speech at Barnard College, published in the September issue.[74] Instead, the magazine chose to turn its eye toward less contentious issues, such as women in the workplace, balancing a career and motherhood, women's financial independence, fashion, and female health. With titles like "How to Buy a Home on Your Own" (March 1979), "How To Get Dressed and Still Be Yourself" (April 1979), and "Is Success Dangerous to Your Health? The Myths—and Facts—about Women and Stress" (May 1979), the majority of the stories published for the rest of the year addressed the grievances of white, middle-class women and explored how such women could live their lives guided by feminist ideals. In addition, most of the subsequent stories in *Ms.* magazine functioned in a decidedly "domestic" framework, focusing on feminism in U.S. contexts and rarely linking the predicament of women in the United States with other women around the globe. Profiles and features were of white women (e.g., Jacqueline Onassis, Barbara Walters, Patty Hearst, Jane Fonda), and analysis of the feminist movement was grounded in discussion of various U.S.-based organizations and institutions (the labor movement, women's colleges, women's art collectives, etc.). Thus feminism seemed a resolutely white, middle-class American affair.

"The Beginning of a New Unity"

The one "international" story, however, that did find its way into the publication that year concerned the women's movement in Tehran. On the cover of *Ms.* magazine's June 1979 issue, beneath story titles such as "How to Find a Feminist Therapist" and "Dolly Parton Has the Last Laugh"—ran the headline "Iran: The Women's Revolution Goes On." The accompanying piece, written by the longtime feminist and political writer Mim Kelber, opened with the question "Was the revolution a beginning of Women of the World United?"[75] It then posed another question to its intended audience of American feminists: "Do we know . . . that Iranian feminists need our support—and vice versa?" The article went on to provide a summary of the events leading up to the protests of International Women's Day on March 8, 1979—the participation of Iranian women in the revolution, the deposal of the Shah, Khomeini's rise to power, and his subsequent conservatism and calls for women to return to the veil.

To her credit, Kelber generally offered a rich and complex portrait of the Iranian women's movement, noting from the start of the piece that "feminism" in Iran was not a Western import, that "Persian queens ruled long before the Koran, and feminist activists existed as early as the 19th century in Iran."[76] Kelber also attempted to avoid the simplistic characterizations that much of the mainstream press had engaged in that rendered the shah as modern and pro-woman and Ayatollah Khomeini as backward and sexist, informing *Ms.* magazine readers of the despotism of the shah, the torture and persecution of political prisoners under his rule, the Central Intelligence Agency's involvement in the coup that overthrew Prime Minister Mohammed Mossadegh and installed the shah in 1953, and the numerous rapes Iranian women suffered at the hands of SAVAK, the shah's secret police. She stressed that women had voluntarily taken on the chador during the revolution and did not over-emphasize or fetishize the significance of the veil throughout.

Two central points that emerged from Kelber's piece, however, that demonstrated how women's actions were directly linked to the fates of U.S. feminists were that (1) Western/American feminist involvement with this issue was central to the success of Iranian women's goals, and (2) the struggles of the women of Iran would ultimately be a boon for the feminist cause worldwide. Pinpointing Kate Millett's participation in the March 8 protests as a pivotal moment, Kelber wrote, "Not until Kate Millett, the guest speaker invited for March 8 by the Iranian feminists, had arrived did press attention begin—and only then did police pro-tection follow. The lesson was not lost: international attention could be helpful to the women's struggle to keep the anti-Shah revolution demo-cratic."[77] At the article's close, Kelber offered a resounding "yes" to the question she had posed at the start of the article, as to whether the Ira-nian women's protests signaled the start of a new phase of the feminist movement. "For the women in Iran," she concluded, "for women all over the Islam [sic] world threatened by a growing religious fundamentalism, and for international feminism, the five days in March can and must be the beginning of a new unity."[78]

Statements such as these echoed sentiments expressed by Millett at the time of her visit to Tehran—when asked by a New York Times reporter why she had come to Iran, Millett replied, "I'm here because it's inevi-table. This is the eye of the storm right now. Women all over the world are looking here. It's a whole corner, the Islamic world, the spot we thought it would be hardest to reach, and wow, look at it go!"[79] In addition, at a New York demonstration staged in front of Rockefeller Center on March 15, 1979—"the first large-scale show of solidarity with those agitating for women's rights [in] Iran"—featuring prominent feminist activists such as Gloria Steinem, Betty Friedan, Bella Abzug, the actress Marlo Thomas, and the author Susan Brownmiller, organizers called the day's events part of an "international feminist action," which coincided with demonstra-tions across America and in Paris, London, and Rome.[80] Perspectives like these demonstrated the importance white U.S. feminists placed upon their own participation in an "international" feminist struggle such as the one taking place in Iran, as well as their belief that these "five days in March" would bear strong significance upon the very future of Western feminism.

Thus the "growing fundamentalism" within the "Islamic" world provided the necessary catalyst to spur on "the beginning" of this new international feminist unity. Such a notion once again emphasized the fundamental opposition between "feminism" and "Islam" and implied that if the tenets of second-wave equal rights feminism could flourish in this "Islam world"—in particular, in the Middle East where feminists like Millett had thought it "would be hardest to reach"—then that was certainly a sign that Western-style feminism was ready to go global. Furthermore, Millett's unfettered enthusiasm in her characterization of Western feminist participation in Iranian women's struggles as "inevitable" and the events in Tehran as "the eye of the storm," alongside Kelber's confident assessment that the struggles "can and must" signal the start of global feminist unity, revealed the sense of destiny many second-wave activists felt in regard to what was going on in Iran. For while certain of feminism's tenets were enjoying a moment of widespread acceptance in mainstream America in 1979, the organized feminist movement itself was, in many ways, in decline, as "feminism" became more of a lifestyle and a way of thinking as opposed to an activist agenda—a development that would ultimately result in what Susan Faludi later famously named the "backlash" against feminism that took place in the ensuing Reagan years.[81]

This desire to "spread" feminist ideology internationally was readily apparent in an essay by *Ms.* magazine founder and original publisher Gloria Steinem in the magazine's end-of-year December 1979 issue. Titled "The Way We Were—and Will Be," Steinem's piece detailed the ideological and cultural shifts caused by the feminist movement throughout the 1970s, from the initial blossoming of consciousness to the proliferation of feminist consciousness, from "the supposedly "easy" matters like equal pay, women in political office, and equal access to education to the supposedly "controversial" ones like the Equal Rights Amendment, a woman's right to choose abortion, and the question "Would-you-work-for-a-woman?"[82] Steinem told a tale of women coming into their own sexuality, into their own power. The essay detailed how feminism had transformed every aspect of American life—from relationships to families, work and finance, to politics, language, and the very conception of sexuality. By the article's close, Steinem offered this synopsis of the decade in question: "The 1970s were a decade in which women reached out to each other: first in consciousness-raising groups that allowed us to create *a psychic turf* (for women have not even a neighborhood of our own); then in movement meetings and a wom-an's culture that created *more psychic territory*; and finally *across national and cultural boundaries*. The 1980s can build on these beginnings."[83] In other words, Steinem characterized the American second-wave feminist movement as an ever-expanding enterprise. It began with the establish-ment of "psychic turf" within the minds among the circles of privileged white women, then increased through the conquering of more "psychic territory" throughout the West, and was set to grow even more "across national and cultural boundaries," for example, into Iran and the Mus-lim world. While perhaps unintentional, Steinem's description of the feminist movement's desire for expansion and territory was jarringly imperial, a portrayal that demonstrated how the movement wished to expand its borders beyond the domestic realm and to claim and settle upon more territory beyond national boundaries.

Yet the energy and enthusiasm emanating from white middle-class U.S.-based feminists in support of the women of Iran and against the enemy of fundamentalist Islam took place against a pointed lack of en-ergy and enthusiasm on the part of these same activists in regard to addressing issues of racism and elitism. As Combahee Collective head Barbara Smith pointed out, in 1979, white feminists appeared "tired of hearing about racism" and, like so many post–civil rights era white Americans, had deemed themselves "not racist" because of how, to quote Smith once more, they felt they were "capable of being civil to black women . . . because I do not snarl and snap at black people."[84] Furthermore, few feminist critiques of the Ayatollah's edicts and funda-mentalist Islam were combined with indictments of U.S. involvement and oil politics in the Middle East—the central catalysts to the devel-opment of movements of religious fundamentalism. As a result, from the "feminist" perspective, a flattering portrait of the nation emerged, one in line with the vision of a free and just nation imagined by the mainstream press in its coverage of the Iranian women's protests and a nation that needed to rightfully protect "our" women against Islam and

Muslims. By constructing themselves against the enemy of fundamentalist Islam, white American feminists turned away from what Margaret A. Simons has called "a schism in the sisterhood," and they shut the door on acknowledging U.S. Muslim women as agential subjects who had long engaged Islam to seek racial and gendered freedom.[85] Instead, these mainstream feminists insisted upon a teleological discourse of progress in the movement in which they moved uncritically towards a "global feminist unity" premised on unitary and universalizing notions of second-wave ideology. In doing so, white feminists at the close of the 1970s unwittingly allowed their cause to be subsequently aligned with the Islamophobic rhetoric that would come to dominate the ensuing Reagan years and continue into the post-9/11 era.

* * *

The U.S. discourse of the veil mobilized existing orientalist and colonial feminist logics around Islam, gender, and veiling. These were reinvigorated upon the racial, class, and gendered terrains of the late 1970s and directly shaped how Muslim women would be seen and discussed in U.S cultural discourse in the decades to come. Even as white middle- and upper-class feminists critiqued patriarchy and gender inequality in the United States, they did so by turning a blind eye to the perspectives and concerns of Black and other women of color feminists. White feminists also refused to acknowledge their own racial and class privilege, unwilling to critique their own possessive investments in whiteness—that is, the material investments gained through their privileging of their whiteness over their ability to empathize and build solidarity with women of color. The media coverage of the 1979 Iranian women's revolution demonstrated how such racial tensions animated national "feminist" desires to empathize with the women of Tehran and, more broadly, with the "plight" of Muslim women. The desire for global solidarity with Iranian Muslim women on the part of the U.S. feminist establishment both jettisoned the problem of gender inequality to distant lands and papered over racism in the United States as an ongoing social problem.

This rhetorical approach coincided with rise of conservative strategies to nullify the civil rights gains of the 1960s and 1970s, in particular the discourse of "color blindness," which in our contemporary era has morphed into the logics of "postracialism." As Michael Omi and Howard

Winant wrote in *Racial Formation in the United States: From the 1960s to the 1990s*, the period between the 1960s and 1980s "represented anything but a slow, steady evolution to a 'color-blind' society" but was instead a period of "racial upsurge, failed consolidation, and reaction," during which "the forces of racial reaction seized on the notion of racial equality advanced by racial minority movement and *rearticulated* its meaning."[86] When Ronald Reagan assumed the presidency in 1980, these forces of racial reaction doggedly propelled the color-blind racial project forward, and "feminism" did not resist the ride. As such, the discourse of the veil gained further purchase in the following decades. The best-known example of this was Betty Mahmoody's autobiographical account of her marriage to an Iranian Muslim man, *Not without My Daughter* (1987), which detailed her husband's transition from a seemingly sweet and loving man to a rabid Islamic fundamentalist who kidnaped their daughter during a trip to Iran.[87] Other examples of this literature "of the veil" includes a number of travelogues written by white American women who went to the Middle East to explore "the hidden lives" of Muslim women, such as Geraldine Brooks's *Nine Parts of Desire: The Hidden World of Islamic Women* (1995), Jan Goodwin's *Price of Honor: Muslim Women Lift the Veil of Silence on the Islamic World* (1994), and the anonymously penned *Latifa, My Forbidden Face: Growing up under the Taliban—a Young Woman's Story* (2003).[88] In addition, the books in Jean Sasson's *Princess Trilogy* (1992–1999), which offered the "true story of life behind the veil in Saudi Arabia," were all bestsellers during the 1990s, as were her other books beyond the series, with titles such as *Mayada, Daughter of Iraq: One Woman's Survival under Saddam Hussein, Love in a Torn Land*, and *Growing Up Bin Laden*.[89] This popular literature of the veil blossomed into a full-fledged genre following the 9/11 attacks, as Americans sought out literature that explained "Islam" and its strange customs, and it consistently reinforced sexism and misogyny as aspects of Islam while championing the United States as a beacon of democracy, quality, and women's rights."[90]

Thus this avowedly "feminist" and racially evasive discourse of the veil produced the Poor Muslim Woman as a recurrent racial-religious form in American popular culture throughout the 1980s and 1990s. Since its initial emergence in 1979, the trope of the Poor Muslim Woman, alongside the notion that "Islam" and "feminism" are mutually opposed and competing ideologies, has become a preeminent logic against which U.S. Muslim women must construct their identities and practice Islam in the United States. Following the 9/11 attacks—and repeated during the 2016 U.S. presidential campaign and after the election of Donald Trump as president—Muslim women in headscarves were, and continue to be, singled out as objects of scorn and derision, people who have not been recognized as U.S. citizens. Yet it is important to note once more that notions of Muslim women as oppressed, and of Islam as inherently misogynist, repeatedly function through the disavowal of Islam's racial legacies in the United States. Islam can only be positioned as inherently oppressive through an elision of the choices and agency of Black women and other women of color who engage Islam as acts of racial and gendered insurgency. As the conversation around the image of Lil' Kim at the start of this chapter demonstrates, blackness undoubtedly complicates this opposition between Islam and feminism and troubles assertions that Muslim women are oppressed. Indeed, in moving toward a more accurate and holistic understanding of U.S. Muslim women's lives and experiences, I argue it is critical to challenge the false oppositions of the discourse of the veil through the acknowledgment of the stories of women of color in their engagements with Islam.

5

A Third Language

Muslim Feminism in America

All women speak two languages
The language of men
And the language of silent suffering.
Some women speak a third,
The language of queens.
They are marvelous
And they are my friends.
—Mohja Kahf, "The Marvelous Women"[1]

In the early 1990s, the American journalist, filmmaker, and scholar Elizabeth Warnock Fernea set out "in search of Islamic feminism."[2] Her journey took her around the world, from Austin, Texas, where Fernea was a professor of comparative literature and Middle Eastern Studies at the University of Texas, "to the Middle East, North Africa, Central Asia, and back again."[3] She documented her search in a 1998 volume titled *In Search of Islamic Feminism: One Woman's Global Journey*, which she wrote from the perspective "of an American feminist with long-standing interest in the Muslim world."[4] Unlike other travel literature by women (and specifically white women) written in the 1990s about women in Islamic societies (as I discussed at the close of the previous chapter), Fernea did not confine her journey to what she called "the Muslim world." After eight chapters detailing her experiences in Uzbekistan, Morocco, Kuwait, Turkey, Egypt, Iraq, Saudi Arabia, and Israel/Palestine, her ninth and final chapter was titled "The United States: Coming Home." Fernea framed the chapter by asking, "How do Muslim peoples, and particularly Muslim women, manage to practice their religion in countries which are not part of Dar al-Islam [home of Islam]. . . ? How do they accommodate themselves to states in which they are in the minority? . . . So what about America?"[5]

In her study of American Muslims and notions of Islamic authority, *Islam Is a Foreign Country*, the anthropologist and American studies scholar Zareena Grewal points out the fallacy of the notion of "the Muslim world." The term is generally used interchangeably with "the Middle East" (a term also steeped in colonial orientalist logics), despite the fact that 80 percent of the world's 1.6 billion Muslims live outside of that region. In addition, as Fernea's usage demonstrates, the "Muslim World" is also applied loosely, imprecisely, and at the discretion of whomever employs the term. In her case, in addition to countries in the Middle East/North Africa region that are generally lumped together under its usage, Fernea includes Uzbekistan and Turkey, which are certainly Muslim-majority nations, but not Pakistan or Bangladesh, which are as well, or Indonesia, which, with 205 million Muslims, constitutes 13 percent of Muslims globally and is thus the largest Muslim country in the world. "Ultimately, the term 'Muslim World,'" Grewal writes, "implies both that Muslims live in a world of their own and that Islam is an eastern religion and there is a foreign place—a distant, contiguous part of the world—where Islam properly belongs."[6] This places, or displaces, U.S. Muslims—and, indeed, all Muslims who do not live in such "foreign" places—outside of "Islam." Thus Grewal proposes an alternative, transnational notion of the Muslim world, which she defines as "a global community of Muslim locals, both majorities and minorities who *belong* to the places where they live and who, in their totality, exemplify the universality of Islam."[7]

Grewal's definition supplements and builds upon the influential work of the religious and Islamic studies scholar Aminah Beverly McCloud. In her 1995 book *African American Islam*, McCloud theorizes expressions of African American Islam as lived and negotiated between the concepts of *'asabiya* and *ummah*, two terms she borrows from the writings of Ibn Khaldun, a thirteenth-century North African Arab philosopher who is often called one of the founders of the social sciences and history as scholarly disciplines. *'Asabiya*, explains McCloud, "refers to kinship relations, which exert themselves in a feeling of tribal solidarity, common ethical understandings, and ultimately, in community identity. . . . African American Islam can be viewed as the history of a people attempting to create *'asabiya* in a hostile environment."[8] *Ummah*, like *'asabiya*, "is a concept that refers to group affiliations, and in general

Arabic usage . . . has been employed to designate a community, a nation or a generation."[9] Yet *ummah* also holds distinctly religious connotations, she continues, "referring to a 'community of believers' who struggle in unison to submit their will to the Will of Allah. . . . *Ummah* is thus a more general concept than *'asabiya*, unifying Muslims across specific national, ethnic, and cultural boundaries."[10] In much of contemporary Islamic discourse, McCloud observes, being part of the *ummah* is positioned as opposed to affiliations of *'asabiya*, that is, the notion that one must forgo "tribal" affiliations (of race, nation, culture, etc.) in order to be a "Muslim." Yet she argues, in the case of her study, that it is precisely the "interplay and tension" between *'asabiya* and *ummah* affiliations for African American Muslims that "[shape] the growth and development of individual Muslims as well as Muslim communities."[11] To blend McCloud's words with Grewal's, *'asabiya* produces the terrains upon which, and through which, Muslims *belong* to the places they live, while *ummah* bridges Islam's multifaceted manifestations and adaptations as expressions of its universality. In the case of Muslim women of color in the United States, I propose that *'asabiya* is made up not only of the racial and ethnic communities through which they identify (and are identified by) and to which they belong, but also by the ways logics of race and gender—and notions of gender justice—are constituted within these communities. Place-based race and gender logics influence and produce their engagements with the *ummah*, as U.S. Muslim women strive to articulate Muslim identities across multiple scales of the body, community, nation, and world and construct domestic and transnational moral geographies of Islamic practice that shape their quotidian lives as well as the arc and reach of their spiritual desires.

As I have noted throughout, women's desires for safety and freedom, whether signified through the term "feminism" or "womanism," have been integral to the history of Islam's presence in the United States. Womanism—as I discuss through the work of Debra Majeed in the introduction[12]—is a term that was coined by Alice Walker to identify the intersectional position of women of color who supported racial and gender justice yet sought to distinguish themselves from the elitism, classism, homophobia, and racism of white, second-wave feminism.[13] Majeed theorizes *Muslim womanism* as way of living Islam that is attentive to the lived experiences and perceptions of justice by Black Muslim women. "Feminism" has broader, and also far more highly contested, multiple, contradictory, and fraught meanings, due to its linkage to formal movements for women's political enfranchisement as well as scholarly discourses of feminist theory. Yet "feminism"—whether one understands it as an emancipatory ideology, a tool of colonial rule, or a type of secular innovation—constitutes, and has always constituted, an integral part of the both the *'asabiya* and *ummah* affiliations of U.S. Muslim women's lives. To be a U.S. Muslim woman, I argue, is to engage in a relationship with feminism/womanism, which is shaped by one's racial epistemology and is refracted through one's understanding and practice of Islam.

Whereas Fernea traveled to a foreign "Muslim World" as an "American feminist" in search of Islamic feminism, I locate the feminist/womanist expressions of Muslim women as part of the history and fabric of American Islam. Yet, as I also discuss in the introduction, citing the work of Margot Badran and miriam cooke,[14] "Islamic feminism" has emerged as a term that connotes a specific body of activism and scholarly thought that was first identified in the 1990s and has mainly focused on women-centered interpretations of Islam's holy texts as a means to enact gender justice-oriented social reforms. Thus I do not name (although one certainly could make a case to) or signify the experiences and narratives of the women discussed in this book as "Islamic feminism." Instead, I prefer to call them expressions of *U.S. Muslim feminism*, which I define as a critical strand of gender justice discourses of U.S. women of color, alongside Black feminism, women of color feminism, and womanism in the United States, which encompasses the ways U.S. Muslim women have engaged Islam in various forms in order to secure gendered agency and freedom. While U.S. Muslim women such as the ones discussed in this book have certainly engaged in Islamic feminist praxis (e.g., how Betty Shabazz incorporated the story of Hajar in her life), many have also adopted Islam *because of* their desires for gender rights and racial justice and did not seek to reinterpret but instead to follow its (at times, patriarchal) teachings in order to achieve such goals. Being Muslim further refined their understandings of justice and offered them religious, ethical, and embodied structures through which they could translate these desires into lived praxis. Muslim feminism compliments Majeed's concept of Muslim womanism to encompass both how U.S. Muslim women have articulated feminist discourses and practices through Islamic paradigms and the ways "Islam" has signified the potential for gender freedom for women of color in the context of the twentieth- and twenty-first-century United States. Muslim feminism is the impulse of gender justice in American Islam, of how Black women and other women of color inhabit Muslim-ness as a religious identity infused with social, political, and cultural resonances. ~~U.S. Muslim feminism is therefore an expression of the affective insurgencies of American Islam, of the lived ways women make their identities and practice their faith against tropes of Islam's shifting racial-religious form in the nation's cultural and political imaginaries.~~

In this final chapter of *Being Muslim*, I present the voices of four U.S. Muslim women whose stories are culled from interviews I conducted between late 2013 and early 2016. Each of these women inexorably *belong to the places where they live*, not just in regard to their location in the U.S. nation-state but also within racial and ethnic space, diasporic communities, generational bonds, cultural affiliations, and their relationships to gender and women's rights and, specifically, "feminism." Unlike many of the women previously discussed in this book, the women I bring together here explicitly understand social justice activism as a central component of their lives as Muslims, and each describe clear understandings of gender justice that they have developed through scholarly and professional endeavors, religious training, and lived experience. Yet their narratives, I argue, are closely intertwined and emerge out the stories that have preceded them in *Being Muslim*, and they are made possible through legacies of women who strove to be Muslim as a set of moral and embodied practices that functioned as affective insurgency and social critique. As I hope the words of Sister Aisha Al-Adawiya, Dr. Asifa Quraishi-Landes, Dr. Laila Al-Marayati, and Sister Hazel Gomez demonstrate, Islam acts as an insurgent ethos in their lives, one intertwined with their desires for racial, gendered, and religious freedom, formed in response to the social and political contexts of the time, and understood as an expansive moral and cultural geography employed to negotiate the tension between *'asabiya* and *ummah*, between the places they live and the universality of Islam.

I begin with the voice of Sister Aisha Al-Adawiya, a close friend of Dr. Betty Shabazz, whose words are featured in chapter 3 and who currently directs the organization Women in Islam in New York City. Al-Adawiya is a well-known activist and community figure in New York City, and her group hosts the Dr. Betty Shabazz Awards every year. Her voice bridges the stories of the women discussed previously in this book to the ones that follow. Her journey of being Muslim began with her understanding of Islam as form of Black consciousness and has involved into a universalist ethos that still centers the lives and well-being of Black—and, indeed, all marginalized—people as central to her religious practice. I then turn to the stories of Dr. Asifa Quraishi-Landes and Dr. Laila Al-Marayati, both of whom were part of the U.S. Muslim women's delegation to the Fourth World Conference on Women in Beijing, China, in 1995. In China, they presented platforms in which they attempted to articulate the collective needs and issues confronting U.S. Muslim women though discourses of "feminism" when there was a great deal of resistance to such framing. Quraishi-Landes, a South Asian American Muslim woman originally from the Bay Area, is currently professor of law at the University of Wisconsin and has written extensively on Islamic criminal law and Muslim family law in the United States, with a focus on women's issues. Al-Marayati is a Palestinian American physician specializing in obstetrics and gynecology in Southern California and spokesperson for the Muslim Women's League, a Los Angeles–based group that advocates for Muslim women worldwide. She also leads humanitarian efforts to support Palestinian children in the West Bank and Gaza. Hazel Gomez, the next voice featured, is a Latina Muslim, Islamic scholar in training, and activist based in Detroit, Michigan. As Latinos are converting to Islam more than any other racial/ethnic group in the United States, Gomez discusses some of the specific issues confronting U.S. Latina Muslims and explains how she engages broader forms of antiracist and feminist consciousness. In closing, I share some thoughts on how their experiences refract the lives and legacies of the women discussed throughout this volume.

Before moving on, I want to note that, in Fernea's book, in her search to find Islamic feminism in the United States, she interviewed Amina Wadud. In their conversation, Wadud highlighted the centrality of Islam as the "motivating factor for all I want to do in life," as well as pointing out the "ethnocentricity" in U.S. Muslim communities and, in particular, anti-Black racism among South Asian and Arab American Muslim communities.[15] Wadud is perhaps the best-known "Islamic feminist" in the world, although she prefers to be called "pro-faith, pro-feminist" because "my emphasis on faith and the sacred prioritize my motivations in feminist methodologies" and because she believes that "feminism" is not a term that was meant to include her as an African American woman.[16] She is the author of the landmark text *Qur'an and Woman: Rereading the Sacred Text from a Woman's Perspective*, which was first published in 1992 in Malaysia, in the United States in 1999, and has since been translated into several languages worldwide.[17] When I began the research for this book, Wadud's was one of the first texts I read, as I wanted to understand, as someone working in the fields of race and gender studies, how a scholar of Islam would engage notions of patriarchy and male dominance in the *Qur'an*, especially in regard to passages that many scholars interpret as condoning the physical chastisement of women by their husbands or unequal inheritances for sons and daughters.[18] Wadud does so in a hermeneutical reading of the Qur'an, in which she "examines verses on women in light of the entire Qur'an . . . and in light of [the Qur'an's] continuing movement towards greater social justice." Ultimately, she argues that it is the patriarchal interpretations of the Qur'an—and not the Qur'an itself—which must be challenged and that "the Qur'an must be continually reinterpreted because its general principles are eternal and newly applicable in changing context, and thus its interpretation can never be final."[19]

In the more than twenty years since it was first written, *Qur'an and Woman* has become a classic text of Islamic feminism. Its *tasfir* (exegesis) of a holistic hermeneutics of the Qur'an focusing on women and social justice has opened up countless other spaces in the United States, and the world over, for conversations about race, gender, and Islam, including this book. Yet, as also stated in the introduction, Wadud has been a controversial figure at times, primarily because of her leading of a mixed-gender *jummah* prayer in New York City in March 2005,[20] as well as her outspoken support of LGBTQI Muslims and her advocacy for HIV and AIDS education in Muslim communities. As a Black Muslim woman, born to a Methodist minister in the South and who converted to Islam in the 1970s, and as a mother who "refused to really fit the role into the role of the preacher's wife," Wadud occupies a singular space in which her intellectual work and activism bridges the space between discourses of global Islamic feminism worldwide and U.S. American Islam.[21] In August 2016, I had the opportunity to meet with Wadud at her home in Northern California's East Bay, where we spoke about her work with Sisters in Islam, a Malaysia-based women's rights organization that she co-founded in the early 1990s, and Musawah, a global organization dedicated to, according to its website, "equality and justice in the Muslim family."[22] While the interview was conducted too late to incorporate in its entirety in this chapter, as we spoke, it became abundantly clear that Wadud's intellectual and activist labors have undoubtedly changed the landscape for how Muslims in the United States and beyond talk about gender justice in Islam. As such, her presence runs through this entire volume, in particular in her continual quest to articulate what she described in our conversation as a *"living Islam—a voice that continually changes by the people who live it."* Part of living Islam, as Wadud writes in the final chapter of *Inside the Gender Jihad*, is a belief shared by the women throughout this book, the notion that "God created women fully human. Anything, anyone, or any system that treats them privately or in public as anything less than that is destroying the potential harmony of the entire universe."[23] This notion of women as fully human within Islam's teachings is critical to each of the women whose stories follow and is deeply integrated in their ways of being U.S. Muslim women.

Sister Aisha Al-Adawiya: "I Chose to Live"

Sister Aisha Al-Adawiya is from the South. "I was born and raised in Alabama in a Christian family," she tells me, as we sit in her office at the Schomburg Center for Research in Black Culture in Harlem, where she is the program administrator for the Scholars-in-Residence Program.[24] Images of Malcolm X and Betty Shabazz hang on the walls, aside Islamic art and calligraphy. Al-Adawiya says she "grew up in the church and sang in the choir." While she is describing the segregated South in the 1940–1950s, a place she says was "very segregated, and very unequal," she also recalls a sense of safety in her childhood. "I was a very sheltered, spoiled baby child," she laughs, and tells me that owing to segregation, all her role models were Black. "People who looked like you provided your everyday life services. So those were our role models: the teacher,

Figure 5.1. Sister Aisha Al-Adawiya

the doctor, the lawyer. These were all Black folks, and many of them were neighbors." In a way, segregation buffered Al-Adawiya from the world, a type of protection from white supremacy that was further reinforced by her family, who sought to shield her from racism's ills. But they knew they could not protect her forever. "Families tend to protect their children. So you don't really realize what oppression is until you start to venture out into the world and you experience things personally. So I just didn't know that we were oppressed or poor then. . . . But that was my world, and that's who I was."

In the early 1960s, Al-Adawiya left the South and set out for New York City, where she hoped to pursue a singing career. Her parents, who reluctantly allowed her to go, sent her to live with an aunt in Brooklyn. "When I landed in New York," she says, chuckling, "I tried to do everything in one day." Her aunt was a very devout Christian who engaged Al-Adawiya in long conversations about religion and God; she recalls that they "had very beautiful talks about God and all the beautiful things that you would expect people of faith to talk about." Yet even amid the hustle of the city, she found herself searching spiritually, wanting something more. It was then that she first encountered Malcolm X and the Nation of Islam, as well as Pan-Africanist and Black nationalist messages "of pride about Africa, being African." These messages made a strong impression, Al-Adawiya said, because "you never heard anything about Africans besides them being backward, being monkeys. . . . So to hear that, that talk about the history of African peoples, before slavery—that message that groups like the Nation of Islam were putting out there, that was very, very powerful."

She learned about the Nation of Islam because she needed a haircut. As a young woman, she wore her hair short, and her aunt recommended she go to a barbershop on the corner close to the apartment to get it shaved. The shop turned out to be owned by NOI members, and Al-Adawiya heard about the teachings of Elijah Muhammad, Black self-determination, and Black power: "So just imagine, here's a young girl, walking into a barbershop that's owned by the Nation. It was classroom time. I was completely open to everything, and they wanted to expose and teach me to what they were doing. They were trying to uplift the community." She began attending various meetings, lectures, and concerts with the brothers from the barbershop, and soon she "began to have some self-awareness as a young African woman." Soon after, she moved to Greenwich Village, where, in the context of the social movement, culture, and political shifts of the mid- to late 1960s, "everything was changing." In the midst of the tumult, many young people engaged in destructive behavior, through drugs or alcohol, but many "were looking for another way, another path. A big part of this was searching for a new spiritual identity, something to hold onto in the midst of all the madness going on around us. You had to choose to live a healthy life or possibly self-destruct. In the late 1960s, that feeling was very real and palpable. So I chose to live."

It was then that she began to learn about Islam. She recalls wandering around bookstores and looking for books on world religions. Many of her friends were becoming Hindus or Buddhists, and one day she came across a book on Sufism (the mystical branch of Islam) by Idries Shah, which she found interesting.[25] Soon after, she came across a copy of the Qur'an. At the same time, her political consciousness was further developing, especially in regard to embracing one's blackness. Over time, says Al-Adawiya, "I saw myself changing. Taking certain steps. We were becoming conscious on many levels because we'd been brainwashed. Talk about the 'mis-education of the Negro'! It was profound. Over time, my dresses started to get longer. I started to wrap my hair. And though I never joined the Nation, I knew Malcolm was the thing. He was the person I was focused on—his message and teachings about cleaning up one's self: 'Wake up, clean up, and get on God's side.' After that, I decided to get serious about Islam."

To learn more about Islam, she headed up to 72nd Street and Riverside Drive, which was the former site of what is now the Islamic Cultural Center of New York, on 3rd and 96th Street. She was immediately impressed and moved by the diversity of the mosque's congregants ("It was like the United Nations in there!") and soon after began attending classes, where she studied Arabic, hadith, and Islamic sciences. One day, in between classes, she wandered to the third floor, where members could sit and have lunch or socialize. Still relatively new, she struck up a conversation with a woman who told her that all new people attending the center had to answer a question: What brought you to Islam? So the woman asked Al-Adawiya the question, to which she blurted out, she says without thinking, "*I'm just following Malcolm.*" To which the woman replied, "Well, meet Mrs. Malcolm X!" Betty Shabazz was sitting right next to her. The two women quickly became friends.

By then, Al-Adawiya was clear about pursuing the path of Islam. She appreciated its structure, yet also its flexibility, the way in which it addressed both the minutiae and largesse of life. She was also deeply moved and compelled by its teaching on women and gender:

> In Islam, I found a religion that talked about all aspects of our existence, even the mundane stuff. I believe that Allah calls us to this religion. Allah chooses us. I don't think I could ever read enough books, or listen to enough lectures, and then make the choice myself. I'm thankful that Allah chose me, honored me with this religion. And in reading about Islam, I came away with understandings about women, about being a woman, that were so powerful. That's what I was looking for. I could still speak, I had an agency, but now I had something informing my actions. Islam helped me set my bottom line, which freed me up to just fly. What I

mean by that is that it helped me make decisions about what I was going to do and what I was not going to do. Having a bottom line was very powerful for me. Now I could really fly based on that [an Islamic] paradigm.

She notes that because of her conversion to Islam, she stopped singing. Primarily, she says, this was because she no longer wanted to inhabit the spaces she had to go as a singer (similar to Dakota Staton's situation, described in chapter 2). "I didn't want to go to bars and taverns to sing. . . . The music business—it was a very toxic industry for women. So I had to make a decision, and I just didn't find a path for it in my life." Yet she said she was able to find other paths for her creativity in Islam, for example, she shares, in her name. As a Muslim, she adopted the name Aisha Al-Adawiya, which she says she chose "very consciously." She selected the name Aisha after one of the wives of the Prophet Muhammad, often called "Mother of the Believers" and known for "her prowess and greatness." She chose Al-Adawiya to honor the female Muslim saint and Sufi mystic Rabi'a al-'Adawiya, who was born in A.D. 713 in Basra, Iraq, and who is reported to have been the first human being to articulate the concept of Divine love in Islam, the notion of "loving God unconditionally, regardless of desire for reward or fear of punishment."[26] Additionally Al-Adawiya chose two middle names, Habiba and Latifa, which mean "beloved" and "gentle," respectively. "Creating and choosing my name," she says, "was one of the most powerful things, most empowering things I've ever done."

As the founder of Women in Islam, Inc., an organization of Muslim women focusing on human rights and social justice, Al-Adawiya leads the annual Dr. Betty Shabazz Award, which honors women "who exemplify dedication and leadership to chart a new course for Muslim women and Muslim communities."[27] She also organizes the yearly commemoration of Malcolm X at the Schomburg Center while traveling widely to advocate for Muslim women and human rights worldwide. She says that being a U.S. Muslim woman is a continual story of gender justice, which requires improvisation and creativity at every stage, and a long-standing commitment to engage and evolve:

So many Muslim women in the United States, and elsewhere else, I'm sure, come into Islam looking for empowerment, just like men are. And when they found it, they joined a journey. And most—not all—stayed with Islam. I'm one of those. I chose it. And I've found a way to create this story that is about women having their own agency. *This story does not always look like what Western feminism thinks it should look like. But that doesn't mean it is not, and has not been, equally concerned, working for, and telling the story of women's liberation.*[28]

Asifa Quraishi-Landes: "We Need to Get This Right"

Asifa Quraishi-Landes speaks quickly. In the little over an hour that we speak on the phone—she in her office at the University of Wisconsin, where she is a professor of law, and I am in my office at Rutgers—we cover many topics, including how we have "known" each other for years but have never actually met in person.[29] Quraishi-Landes was a founding member or AMILA, or American Muslims Intent on Learning and Activism, a Bay Area–based Muslim advocacy and education group that I was a part of in the early 2000s. By then, Quraishi-Landes had moved away from the Bay Area, where she grew up and eventually attended the University of California, Berkeley, where she started AMILA with a group of friends. For years, I had encountered her thoughts and writings on email Listservs and, more recently, on Facebook, where we became "friends." During our conversation, she spoke of growing up as a U.S. Muslim girl during the 1970s and 1980s, as well as her evolving relationship with issues of gender and feminism, in particular as a result of her trip to the 1995 World Conference on Women in Beijing.

Quraishi-Landes tells me about her parents, explaining that her father was an immigrant from South Asia who was raised in India but moved to Pakistan after the partition of India by Britain in 1947. Unlike a vast majority of immigrants from South Asia who arrived in the United States in the late twentieth century, he did not come after the passage of the 1965 Hart-Cellar Immigration Act, which lifted quotas on immigration from most parts of South and West Asia. Instead, he moved to California in the mid-1950s to attend college. There, he met her mother, a white American woman from a working-class farming family, who was first in her family to attend university and who converted to Islam. They married in 1960, and Quraishi-Landes was born seven years later, in 1967.

Quraishi-Landes's father entered the business school at Stanford University in Palo Alto, California, and there he was instrumental in starting

Figure 5.2. Asifa Quraishi-Landes

the Stanford Islamic Society. Even in the liberal environments of the Bay Area in the 1960s, he encountered racism. "My dad," Quraishi-Landes says, "he was dark enough to be considered black by anybody who was white American. So white people definitely thought of him as black, and he encountered a lot of job discrimination." Both of her parents were very interested in how to adapt Islamic practices to an American context. For example, her father was interested in getting his business degree "because he wanted to help build an Islamically based economy in the U.S.; part of what he was doing was working on sharia-compliant banking, way before anybody else was talking about Muslim finance."

Quraishi-Landes grew up in the Stanford Muslim community in the 1970s, which she says was made up of "a bunch of graduate students, all friends of my dad's, very international." From all over the world, these students even started an Islamic school (the Stanford Islamic School) for their children to attend on weekends, where they taught religious texts in Arabic. As a result, Quraishi-Landes laughs, she learned the language in a number of accents: "I didn't realize until I finally took Arabic in college that I was saying one story with a Turkish accent and another with a Pakistani accent and another one with an Egyptian accent. It was because I was following whatever grad student they could find to teach us our classes!" During this time, her family also hosted Friday prayer services and Islamic holidays at their home because "there were no *masjids* in that part of the Bay Area when I was a child." She recalls her mother trying to find henna to celebrate Eid al-Fitr (the festival of breaking the fast the end of Ramadan), as was the custom in South and West Asia. When she was unable to find it, "she tried little creative things like [using] mercurochrome, you know that red dye you put on a cut?"

Watching her parents improvise and construct Islamic practices and ways of living deeply shaped Quraishi-Landes's understandings of Islam and what it meant to be Muslim:

> It was clear from the beginning—and this may be part of why I'm a lawyer now—is that with every issue that came up in our lives, there were these questions. How are we going to do this Islamically? How are we going to live as Muslims in America? And the answers often involved talking about what is *culturally* Islam versus what is *actually* Islamically required. We had that conversation a lot, and I remember directly asking my father when he would say, "I want you to wear these clothes." I remember specifically saying, "Well, is this because it's the Qur'an that says that, or is this what they do in Pakistan?" He wanted me to wear [foreign clothing] every day, and I'm like, "I'll do it if God says so, but if it's just the clothing that's your style, well maybe I'd rather wear jeans." So that from a very early age, I was constantly analyzing the things that were being asked of me that were different than the norm outside the house. I was enough of a believer to say, "Look, if this is Islam, no problem. But if it's culture, that's a lot to put on a ten-year-old." *But being Muslim was always the most important thing, figuring out how to do Islam in America was the most important thing.*[30]

As an undergraduate at the University of California, Berkeley, and a law student at the University of California, Davis, Quraishi-Landes began to look critically at issues of Islam and gender and, in particular, Islamic feminism. As one of the few Muslim women in the United States engaging gender issues, she says, she quickly started to receive messages from those in the Muslim community asking for her opinions and expertise on how to navigate between U.S. and Islamic law. As a result, Quraishi-Landes recognized the need to investigate how U.S. Muslims, specifically women, could navigate issues like divorce, child custody, and so forth. So, she says, "I went back and I read everything I could find on Islamic law and women. That was the first time I really put myself in that space. And it wasn't because I naturally was interested in women's issues. It's because I was interested in justice." During this time, in the early 1990s, Quraishi-Landes discovered the work of scholars like Amina Wadud and Leila Ahmed, especially Ahmed's book, *Women and Gender in Islam*, and subsequently began connecting with other women interested in similar issues online.

She found an active community in a Listserv called Sister's Net, which was "a bunch of young Muslim women having conversations across a lot of divides, across racial divides, across national divides, and levels of class." There, she connected with women like Azizah al-Hibri, a Muslim woman law professor in Richmond, Virginia, who asked Quraishi-Landes to serve on her board of KARAMAH: Muslim Women Lawyers for Human Rights, a nonprofit group dedicated to "human rights globally, especially gender equity, religious freedom, and civil rights in the United States."[31] This led to an invitation for her to give a presentation at the upcoming Women's World Conference in Beijing in 1995 on "issues facing Muslim women in the United States," along with Dr. Laila Al-Marayati, attorney Samer Hathout, and Dr. al-Hibri.

To research these issues, Quraishi-Landes wrote to the Sister's Net Listserv and requested that women share their stories and ideas. The response was overwhelming. "Suddenly," she says, "I have woman after woman writing me back with so many stories." Out of those stories, she, along with the other presenters, created composite characters that they hoped reflected the dizzying array of responses they received, from recently arrived immigrants, from second- and third-generation African American Muslim women, from young and old. The most critical question in preparing the presentation was, "How are we going to speak in a way that is not just our own personal agenda, but it's somehow representative of 'American Muslim women'? So, that was the first step."

Once in Beijing, however, Quraishi-Landes realized the fraught nature of discussing feminism and Islam:

> When we got to Beijing, I realized we walked into this whole feminist dialogue that had been going on, this idea that feminism is just a cover for neocolonialism. There is truth to that because, as it often is written, it actually was one of the tools used to justify colonialism, that we're going to save your women from those bad men. So when there is a global UN conference on women, many Muslim countries saw that as a "feminist" attack on Islam. So [certain Muslim countries] sent their representatives, as well as many [nongovernmental organizations], to defend Islam in the face of this "attack." That was a very different motivation than groups like KARAMAH and the Muslim Women's League, which we were connected with. I was interested in Muslim women on the ground. What were their lives like? Was clean water a specific issue for you? Access to leadership in your mosque? We were interested in real-life challenges for Muslim local women. That was our perspective.

Many of the representatives from such "anti-feminist" groups, she shares, even took to personal attacks, dismissing Quraishi-Landes and her colleagues for not properly covering their hair or for how they dressed: "They found every possible reason to discount us about specific local voices. And at the time, I covered my hair, but I covered it in various ways, with a sash sometimes or with a beret. And I wouldn't wear long dresses, I would wear pants and a loose shirt. But these 'representatives,' all men, just dismissed all of us as not covered women. I'm thinking, I've been wearing this thing forever, and you're discounting it. Give me a frickin' break."

Reflecting back on Beijing and her body of work on topics ranging from *sharia* and international rights advocacy, Muslim marriage contract law, Islamic constitutionalism, and rape laws in Pakistan, Quraishi-Landes is slightly wary of how many younger U.S. Muslim women now express discomfort with "feminism." Whereas she understands the colonial, racial, and secular implications of the term quite well, she also believes this sentiment is rooted in a lack of familiarity with the long history of intellectual work and activism by Muslim women, in the United States and beyond. "Sometimes, I feel weird being like this forty-eight-year-old woman telling these young whippersnappers, you don't know how to do this. But when it comes to women's issues, I often think, 'We shouldn't be doing this again. What we did needs building upon. Not re-creation. This time, we need to get this right.'"

Laila Al-Marayati: "I Didn't Really Have a Choice about Becoming an Activist"

Dr. Laila Al-Marayati grew up in the 1970s and 1980s in Southern California, where her parents were instrumental in building and establishing the Islamic Center of Southern California (ICSC).[32] A practicing physician, she is the medical director of women's health at the Eisner Pediatric and Family Medical Center in downtown Los Angeles and a faculty member of the Keck School of Medicine at the University of Southern California. A longtime activist for Palestinian rights as well as Muslim women's issues, Al-Marayati explains that engaging in activism was never a choice but an integral part of her identity as a Muslim.[33] In 1995,

Figure 5.3. Laila Al-Marayati

she was a member of the official U.S. delegation to the UN Fourth World Conference on Women in Beijing, China, which she attended with Dr. Asifa Quraishi-Landes.

Growing up in the mosque, she recalls that "there were no strict rules, nothing related to separating men and women, or women having to cover their hair." Her Palestinian American father was not particularly religious, although religious identity was very important to him, which led him to establish the ICSC. She laughs that she always preferred going to church with her white American Catholic mother rather than the mosque, since "they [the church] had activities and fun things for kids to do there. And Muslims didn't know how to do that, you know? They just threw us in the back and told us to play." Unlike many mosque communities today, which she notes are very racially and ethnically divided, Al-Marayati says that the ICSC community was very racially and ethnically diverse, "people were from Africa, the Middle East, Arab countries, Afghanistan."

Despite her mosque attendance and her father's commitment to an Islamic identity, Al-Marayati also says that she and her family weren't particularly religious—for example, they didn't pray or fast during Ramadan—until her teen years, when she realized she "wanted to understand myself spiritually." It was around the age of fifteen that she, along with her siblings, began reading the Qur'an, as well as praying and fasting. Her mother eventually converted to Islam when Al-Marayati was eighteen. Thus, even though she was "born" Muslim, she makes clear that "being Muslim evolved out of my own desires as a person. Sometimes, when I tell my story, people think I'm a convert because I made a conscious commitment to be Muslim."

When she began college at the University of California, Los Angeles, in the 1980s, she encountered immigrant Muslims who had very different conceptions of Islamic practices and gender norms. For example, she recalls being told she could not wear pants and a long-sleeved shirt to attend *jummah* (Friday prayers), even though that was what she had done her entire life. Such incidents were "really disorienting," as she came to understand that there were highly varied, and often contradictory, interpretations of Islam. While she decided to stop attending *jummah* in college because she simply "didn't want to fight," she acknowledges that such interactions play a daily part of being a Muslim woman in the

United States: "The struggle ever since has been to say what Islam actually is. . . . Those are struggles we face as women because, if you stand up—this just happened to me at work the other day—people will say, 'Oh, she has a reputation [for anger]'. And I think, What? Because I want to pray? Or stand up for my patients?"

During her residency, Al-Marayati began reading works of Islamic feminism, such as works by Leila Ahmed, Amina Wadud, and Fatima Mernissi. At the same time, she was figuring out how to be a female Muslim doctor at one of the busiest hospitals in the United States, County/ USC Medical Center.[34] "We would do 30,000 deliveries a year. That would mean like forty to fifty babies being born in a twenty-four-hour period. We worked one hundred to one hundred twenty hours a week. Fasting at Ramadan was just figuring out, How do I get through the day? And you know, I just did it." Toward the end of her residency, in 1992, war broke out in Bosnia. It was then, Al-Marayati says, that she realized that, as a Muslim, she didn't really have a choice about becoming an activist—"People would say to me, Muslim women are being raped and killed and what are you doing about it, you, the Muslim community? And I thought, what are we doing? Nothing. So we started the Women's Coalition Against Ethnic Cleansing, which was an interfaith group, and I organized a trip where we went to Croatia. Out of that endeavor grew the Muslim Women's League, which started in 1992." She would realize that her activism was an integral component of her religious practice, a notion that is rooted in her family's history: "Why religion and activism go together for me is [that] my father was from Gaza. And you know, his heart never left there, and he was always an activist for Palestine from the minute he got to this country. So that just was always in the background of our family life: activism, our educations, and gaining knowledge. So I grew up being able to say [that] activism is not incompatible with who we are as Muslims, with being Muslim. And so here we are."[35]

A *Los Angeles Times* reporter and family friend named Kathy Hendricks, who was part of then First Lady Hillary Clinton's staff, invited Al-Marayati to the 1995 World Conference on Women in Beijing as a private-sector advisor to the U.S. delegation. Al-Marayati knew, she says, that she was "the token Muslim woman," a position she's become accustomed to over time. When she, along with Quraishi-Landes, learned that they would be asked to represent American Muslim women at the conference, they wanted to create something that was reflective of the community's diversity, including the experiences of African American Muslim women. Al-Marayati reached out to a friend, Dr. Khadijah Lang, who was a part of the African American Muslim community in Los Angeles. Through Lang, she saw that each community had "internal rules," different interpretations and engagements with Islam that shaped their practices. For example, Al-Marayati says, Lang discussed the presence of polygyny in African American Muslim communities, which was critical to thinking through how to engage U.S. women's issues in the law. Al-Marayati acknowledges the anti-Black racism of many non-Black Muslims: "There's always been the issue of race in the Muslim community that nobody wants to talk about. We all know that." Through many conversations with women such as Lang, however, Al-Marayati and Quraishi-Landes tried to put together case studies that at least "gave a taste of what some of the issues in the American Muslim community are for women." Ultimately, she knew, "that not a single person can get up and give any legitimate presentation that fully represents our community. . . . Our goal was to be able to say *something* because there was no representation. We didn't claim to be authoritative; nobody could claim to represent all Muslim women in America. And nobody can still."

Much of the pushback at the Beijing conference, she says, was "coming from Iranian, Saudi government representatives—men [who] wanted to dictate what Islam was. Especially about women." She tells a story of attending a *jummah* in Beijing:

> I was the only one there [from our group]. . . . It [*jummah*] was in this small room, and this imam was giving this horrible *khutbah* [sermon] about how everything at this conference is *haram* [forbidden], like women's rights, reproductive rights, and how bad it is to challenge things like unequal inheritance laws, etc. And I am there with the other women, we're sitting there in the back. There's a curtain open and one of these *niqabi* women [women wearing face covering] goes up and closes the curtain. Then this African Muslim woman whose hair is in a turban and [wearing] these bright, colorful clothes, she stands up and she opens that curtain. And it's an act of defiance! She doesn't look at anybody, but it's like a challenge. She's like, I dare you to come and close this curtain again

while we're sitting here. That was one of the most important experiences of that whole event for me. Looking at this woman coming from a totally different place, and she's not going take it at all—this idea of women being in the background and being subjugated. That moment has informed a lot of the way I look at what goes on with the Muslim world and what I call "bully Islam." In Beijing, I saw it and experienced it.

She still does not see activism as an option but as part and parcel of American Islam. "I love Islam," she says emphatically. "So when some people say, 'Just keep your religion personal,' the problem for Muslims is [that] we don't have the luxury to do that. Part of what our religion does is call on us to stand for justice, for ourselves and for the people who can't always stand for themselves. . . . God says somebody has to stand for those who can't." Issues of gender rights are central to justice, whatever you choose to call them, Al-Marayati says. But, she states, "Feminism isn't a luxury. I see it every day, even in my work here in downtown Los Angeles, how women's health issues are continually marginalized. It's unfortunate that the term has become so politicized in a way that almost undermined its effectiveness," so that "it became a loaded label that we were better off not using when it came to Islam and Muslims." Still, she continues:

The exact issues we were and are talking about by definition would be feminism, right? But if our goal is to create change, to make things better for people, then we have to do whatever it takes. And if the term "feminism" is going to get in the way of that, then let's leave that term. I also resist anybody labeling me. I mean I don't know [if] that's just me personally—I don't want to be boxed up as "the Muslim feminist." What you call yourself is not the issue. The issue is that women are poor, women are illiterate, women are getting the crap beaten out of them, they don't have access to health care services. . . . So who cares if we call ourselves "feminist" or not? We have lots of work to do.

Hazel Gomez: "Hazel's a Muslim Name"

In 2013, a report on the Florida-based public radio station WLRN reported that Latinos constitute one of the "fastest growing segments of the U.S. Muslim community," making up about 6 percent of U.S. Muslims and a fifth of all new converts to Islam.[36] The report cited numerous cultural and historical ties between Latinos and Islam, such as the large number of words in Spanish (over four thousand) that are derived from Arabic and cultural affinities such the value of family and hospitality to strangers. It also noted that more Latina women convert to Islam than Latino men. During the 2016 presidential campaign and following the election of Donald Trump as the country's forty-fifth president, Latino Muslims confronted a double bind as a community doubly targeted by anti-immigrant hysteria and anti-Muslim racism. As a result of this positioning, however, Latino Muslims themselves have sought to further strengthen their communities, as well as to build alliances between

Figure 5.4. Hazel Gomez

U.S. Muslim and Latino communities, as was the case between Japanese Americans and U.S. Muslims following the 9/11 attacks.

Such domestic contexts critically shape the experiences of Hazel Gomez, a Puerto Rican and Mexican convert to Islam, an aspiring student of the Islamic sciences, and a community activist in Detroit, Michigan. With her husband Mark Crain, Gomez works with Dream of Detroit, a Muslim-led initiative on the west side of Detroit that seeks to combine community organizing with strategic housing and land development in order to build a healthy community and empower a marginalized neighborhood. She also is a student at Rabata, an organization dedicated to promoting positive cultural change through individual empowerment, spiritual upbringing of women by women, and the revival of the female voice in Islamic scholarship.

In her thirties, Gomez is the youngest of the women interviewed in this chapter. Her experiences reflect a post-9/11 engagement with Islam in the United States and a time in which the nation has witnessed a proliferation of both anti-Muslim racism and Islamic institution building and activism on the part of U.S. Muslims. Converting to Islam in her teens, Gomez told me she first met a Muslim at age 13, when she attended Northside College Prep High School in Chicago.[37] Prior to that, she had lived in predominantly Black and Latino neighborhoods, and College Prep "was the first time in my life having white classmates, my first time having Asian classmates, my first time not being solely around Black and Brown folk." The Muslim girl she saw at school was South Asian, and Gomez recalls looking at the young woman, who was wearing a headscarf, and saying to her, "Okay, you're confusing me because you look like a nun, but you're Hindu, so where's your dot?" Laughing, she acknowledges that her words were "completely ignorant," but the other young woman just started laughing and replied that she was Muslim. Though she had no idea what that was at the time, Gomez discovered she had three classes with the young woman, and the two became fast friends.

She was drawn to the South Asian Muslim woman and her friends, Gomez explains, "for social reasons." At the time, she lived with her grandparents, who did not permit her to have boyfriends, in particular, because Gomez's mother had had her at a young age, and her grandparents did not want her to do the same. "So honestly," she says, "I became friends with those [Muslim] girls because they didn't have boy-friends. Because I thought, 'They're not going to get me into trouble.'" But she soon began noticing their faith, mainly owing to how she was struggling with her own. At the time, she shares, her mother was "in and out of my life due to addiction issues and my father because of incarceration.[38] So growing up, I was a very angry child, very angry at God. My grandma would find me crying and punching my pillow while shouting, 'Why me?!' I was mad about my parents not being around, I was mad about my siblings and I almost being taken into foster care." Though she felt blessed to be raised by my grandparents, she says she was still resentful at the perceived happiness of others: "I just thought it wasn't fair."

The same year she met the Muslim girls, she tried to become more religious as a Catholic, fasting during Lent and "sometimes covering my hair like it said to do in the Bible."[39] Around 2000 or 2001, Ramadan and Lent fell close together, and as she watched her friends, she felt, she says,

> for lack of a better word: jealousy. I was jealous at their spiritual experience. They weren't eating or drinking anything yet they were content to go to the library and read Qur'an during lunchtime. The way I was taught to do Lent was to eat half of my meals, essentially to learn to eat very little, and only fish could be consumed on Fridays, not meat. So I'm at school and I'm like, "I have to throw half my lunch away." I was raised to not throw food away, but I had to while at school because I was fasting for Lent. So I would just not eat lunch, and I would go to the library with my friends. I tried to read from the Bible, but I wasn't getting that same light that they seemed to have. I remember making a mental note to myself, "Okay, I'm going to look into this. What makes them so happy? They're not eating [*laughter*], they're reading the Qur'an, and they're so content. They're praying five times a day. Why are these girls like this?

Without telling her friends, Gomez began researching Islam on her own. Soon thereafter, she had a dream, in which she heard the *adhan* (Islamic call to prayer), although, at the time, she was not aware what it was. In it, she was standing against a wall and felt extremely sad when her friend's uncle waved her over and said, "Come, come, come. Allah wants you to pray. Come, come, come." She went and stood in a prayer line and saw her friend standing next to her with a smile. When she woke up, she remembers, her heart was pounding. It was then she decided she wanted to become Muslim. When she went to school that day, she told her friends about the dream, and not long after they took her with them to *salat* (prayers). As the prayers began, Gomez realized she was hearing the "song" from her dream, the *adhan*. In her senior year of high school, she converted to Islam.

Her grandparents were unhappy with her decision but still supportive. Her grandmother stopped cooking pork in their meals, substituting it with beef or chicken. Her family also struggled with her choice to wear the headscarf, in particular Gomez's great-grandmother, Mami Lucy, an Afro-Latina from Puerto Rico. "She sat me down and asked me, 'Are you Arab now? Do you think you're Arab? Why are you covered?' So I answered her, 'Gramma Mami Lucy . . .'—because she always wore headwraps—'you wear headwraps all the time.' And she's like, 'Right. But that comes from our African culture. Everybody does that in Puerto Rico.' So she asked me, 'Why can't you just wear it like this [like an African headwrap]?'" Gomez told her great-grandmother that she might, one day, but that she was comfortable wearing it like this for now, with her hair, neck, and chest covered. Sometimes, when she saw Mami Lucy though, she would "wrap it up" in that way, "and it would just make her happy." Another relative also expressed distaste for Islam, saying she didn't want to be seen in public with Gomez for fear people would think they "were Arabs." Gomez told her, "Look, I still speak Spanish. I am very proud of who I am. I dress all kinds of ways. I'm never going to lose who I am. Really, being Muslim just reinforces who I am, and it enhances all the values I was raised with."

She points out that such examples illustrate how "Latino Muslims are in a unique space because we are so proud of our culture and we want to hold onto it upon accepting Islam":

Girl, you'll see the Puerto Rican flag hanging on my rearview mirror; it's that deep. We are proud of our heritage, but it's not an arrogant pride. It's like, "This is where I'm from. I am a mix of Africa, of Spain, of the indigenous peoples." That's what we are. The thing is, [we Latinos are] just so unique in that we're here despite, or because of, colonialism, imperialism, and slavery. . . . To me, that is so powerful. With any peoples, whether convert or raised Muslim, you pick the beauty of your culture, and you enhance it with Islam. You keep family ties. You maintain good manners and improve your character. Sure, we may not celebrate certain holidays, but we spend that time with our families. We exchange gifts with our families on Eid because as Muslims, we should be giving gifts. As converts, people need to understand that living out our faith includes not shunning our families even if they are of a different faith or of no faith.

Because of this unique space, she continues, "Latino Muslims fill in this much-needed gap where we are a bridge between the various immigrant communities and the African American community." She offers the example of how she can relate to the diasporic affiliations of West Africans, as well as other immigrant communities, while also understanding very well the logics of institutional racism in regard to the targeting of Black and Brown people. "We, as Latinos, can relate to so many different people because we are transnational."

When I spoke to Gomez, she had just returned home from attending two conferences in Houston, Texas, dedicated to the Latino Muslim experience: the First National Latino Muslim Conference and the Texas Dawah Convention in Houston. Participants hailed from a diverse range of Latino backgrounds—"from Guatemala, Puerto Rico, Panama, Argentina, some American-born, and others born in their respective countries." Gomez says she particularly enjoyed a panel called "Latina Muslim Challenges," which featured four women who spoke about common scenarios within the Latina Muslim experience, such as "single motherhood, and women who are taken advantage of for green cards from men from the Middle East and South Asia." The panel was heartening because "you could hear these women share their stories." Such stories reflect how the needs of Latino Muslims are not about "just trying to have their own *masjid* or trying to ethnically separate from the greater Muslim community" but instead to "deal with our issues that we have in our community, [such as] immigration, drug issues, fear of law enforcement. . . . To have conversations that are spoken from a Latino cultural and Muslim perspective are critical for the growth of the community and for the understanding of themselves." She notes that although few people know of it, there are more and more Latina Muslim women trained in Islamic knowledge and who teach others in their homes and communities. She hopes these women will be "out there more" to be mentors for Latina Muslim women and men as well. "It is absolutely critical for this fledgling community [of Latino Muslims] to figure out ways to Islamically address the issues women go through, for example, being used for green cards, immigration issues, etc. We need scholars who understand the unique dynamics of our community."

Gomez herself is a student of the Islamic sciences at Rabata, a women-centered organization of Islamic learning headed by Anse Tamara Gray, a white American convert to Islam who studies Islam in Syria. Gomez says Anse Tamara's guidance was critical "when I truly needed help and guidance as a woman, when I was transitioning from one phase of my life to another—from singlehood to married life and then to motherhood." The teacher highlighted how central issues around gender justice and feminism were to Muslim women's engagements with Islam, and she helped Gomez see the ways women and, specifically for her, Latina women are subjected to oppression and stereotypes. "As my role changed in life," Gomez says, "as I became a wife, a mother, I realized, 'Man, women really get the short end of the stick [laughs]." Anse Tamara also taught her "an Islam that is deeply rooted in the reality of our lives": "She'll say, 'If people ask you, "Why didn't you change your name?" You tell them your name is Hazel.' So Hazel's a Muslim name.[40] That's it. You don't have to change your name to an Arabic name." Finally, she says, Anse Tamara works to convince Muslim women that they should themselves be sources of religious and spiritual knowledge, instead of relying on men for information: "The beauty of Rabata and the female teachers who teach there emphasizes how every single person, especially if you are woman, needs to be knowledgeable and seek sacred knowledge herself. Because of Islam and by being Muslim, I have learned so much. I've seen and been exposed to so many different people and have had so many different experiences."

Muslims "need a liberation theology," Gomez says, and Latino Muslims even more so because so many in their communities "live in urban centers that are predominantly Black and Latino. As Latinos . . . we have this very unique experience where we are immigrants, but we understand issues such as the use of payday loan stores instead of banks or credit unions, lack of access to quality foods, underfunded public schools, etc." Her own family, she points out, has been affected by mass incarceration and deportation and immigration issues. Many South Asian and Arab American Muslims, she thinks, have a lot to learn from Black and Latino Muslims, especially in regard to how to build strong Muslim communities that withstand destructive state practices of racism, profiling, surveillance, and so forth. She says that she's heard first-, second-, and even third-generation South Asian or Arab American Muslims say that in the post-9/11 era, and now the Trump era, this is their first time being marginalized, especially those from middle- and upper-class upbringings. While that "is kind of shocking" for her, she says it also isn't at all, as many South Asian and Arab American Muslims have "this aspiration to whiteness [and hold] the notion of attaining the American Dream." But, "the bubble is busted":

> We are now in this space where many communities are forced to—even if they didn't want to engage or even thought about engaging with the Black or Latino Muslims—they kind of need to now. You are Muslim, you are Brown, and these are the people [Black and Latino Muslims] that are going to help you understand that. We need to come together and build these bridges, or else the rifts will become wider and wider. Allah said in the Qur'an that He made us into nations and tribes so that we may know one another, and if anything, the Trump era has forced us to get to know one another.

Ultimately, Gomez says, "Being Muslim is an inward and outward way of living our lives." By this she means that there is the inner work one must do in regard to her faith, as well as the outward rules and rituals, such as prayer, fasting, and so on. Part of the Islamic tradition, she emphasizes, is that "we are supposed to speak for the oppressed and for people who do not have a voice, be they Muslim or not Muslim." Among U.S. Muslim communities, Gomez knows that "activism may not be for everybody—not everybody wants to be out organizing or participating in protests, and that's fine." But now is a time when everybody needs to have some sort of political engagement: "That may mean being a revolutionary parent, that may mean cooking food for lawyers working around the clock on the Muslim ban—activism looks different for everybody, but it just shows that we cannot live in a Muslim bubble and think that that is okay. We were sent to this earth to be vicegerents of Allah while we're here."

* * *

The voices of the women gathered here reflect the complex and varied relationships U.S. Muslim women hold with "feminism," as well as the way issues of race shape their approaches to gender justice. They also offer context and insight into the ways race and culture have shaped trajectories of Muslim feminism in the United States. In Aisha Al-Adawiya's narrative, she makes clear that women's empowerment was central to her conversion to Islam, although she remains consistently mindful that this empowerment does not mimic the tenets and norms of Western feminism. As the voices of Asifa Quraishi-Landes and Laila Al-Marayati demonstrate, articulations of U.S. Muslim women's activism by South Asian and Arab American Muslim women began to gain far wider purchase in the late 1980s and 1990s, and it was at that time that U.S. Muslim women started to engage more mainstream political forma-tions (such as the 1995 Beijing World Conference on Women) in their capacity as U.S. Muslim women. Their narratives also demonstrate how issues of race and ethnicity consistently challenged efforts to articulate broad notions of who U.S. Muslim women were (and are) and the issues confronting them. Finally, in Hazel Gomez's words, she expresses a dis-tinct and unambiguous position about her identity as a Latina Muslim woman and how her positionality within U.S. racial politics produces her ways of being a U.S. Muslim woman. As these narratives show—as well as the stories of the women given throughout this book—U.S. Mus-lim women's ways of being Muslim and practicing Islam, in private and public space, at various moments in history, and enacted from different racial epistemologies and subjectivities, require constant expressions of *againstness* to power, whether vis-à-vis the state, one's community, one's family, and so on. In the four narratives in this chapter, specifically, we see U.S. Muslim women actively creating their identities through social justice work and political activism, which may not have been the case with the other women discussed. However, I want to argue once more that their experiences may be envisioned through a larger legacy of affective insurgency in U.S. Muslim women's lives, in how they have pursued visions of justice against the realities of race as women of color, as well against Islam's persistent presence as a racial-religious form in the nation's cultural imaginary. This larger legacy of affective insurgency is at the heart of Muslim feminism in the United States, forged in the tensions and contradictions between *'asabiya* and *ummah*, in how women have navigated gender norms and traditions within their racial/ethnic communities in a U.S. context, all the while seeking broader identities and affiliations as Muslim women. Taken together, their voices, alongside the rest of the women's voices in this volume, express what the Syrian American Muslim poet and writer Mohja Kahf describes in this chapter's epigraph as a "third language" of American Islam, which centers the spiritual strivings and perspectives of U.S. Muslim women in all their unwieldy, insurgent, and utterly marvelous forms.

Conclusion

Soul Flower Farm

Soul Flower Farm sits on the edge of a series of rolling hills in California's East Bay, in the city of El Sobrante located about ten miles from Berkeley. Goats graze on the hillside, and one can hear chickens clucking in their coop. On a wooden shed nearby is a painting of a giant golden sunflower with a vibrant magenta center, across from which the farm announces its name to visitors. On a crisp summer day in 2015, the mural almost sparkles, its vivid colors accentuating the green of the trees around it, as well as the pale, brittle yellow of the grass beneath it, the result of a five-year drought in California, which the state eventually declared over in 2017. Soul Flower Farm's website describes it as "a small urban farm . . . striving to incorporate biodynamic farming methods and permaculture design to be self-sustaining." Under a photograph of its proprietors, Maya Blow and her husband, Yasir Cross, the description continues: "Raising goats, chickens, ducks, bees, and boys, homeschooling, sustainable building, and practicing holistic medicine keeps us busy."[1]

I first met Maya Blow in 2003, when we both participated in a weekly women's Qur'an reading circle in Oakland, California, hosted by Dr. Hina Azam, who is now an associate professor in the Middle East Studies Department at the University of Texas at Austin. Our group was primarily made up of U.S.-born converts to Islam, plus myself. At the time I was there to further explore the faith owing to my activist commitments, although I would eventually take my *shahada* (the Muslim declaration of faith) in early 2004. The group was very informal, a space where we would take turns reading portions of the Qur'an and offer our own personal reflections on what each section meant to us, how it resonated in our lives. At times, Hina, who is fluent in Arabic and who was then completing her doctorate in Islamic Studies, would explain the scholarly

Figure C.1. Soul Flower Farm, August 2015. Author's photo.

discourse around a particular verse, and we would also discuss the impact of specific interpretations in contemporary U.S. Muslim communities. We were a racially and ethnically varied group—South Asian, white, Black, Arab, and East Asian (myself)—as well as multigenerational and from varying socioeconomic backgrounds. About half the women wore headscarves, the others did not. Two years after the 9/11 attacks, many of our discussions would at times turn to misperceptions around Islam, gender, and women. As someone encountering many parts of the Qur'an for the first time, which directly contradicted so much of what was being voiced in the media and popular culture about Muslims and their faith, I was oftentimes shocked by the level of distortion and ignorance around the religion and its practitioners. Looking back, I am immensely grateful for this space, which was one of my first safe harbors in my encounters with Islam.

Like many of the other women in our group, Maya was a mother of young children, in her case two boys. Owing to parental obligations, the other mothers in the group and she would sometimes miss a week or two of our meetings. I also recall her saying that she was pursuing some sort of classes in holistic healing and, later, that she hoped to pursue an education in homeopathy full-time. Although our group continued on for another year or so, I saw less of Maya over time, and I assumed she had started her homeopathic training. I later learned she had entered the Institute of Classical Homeopathy in San Francisco for their homeo-pathic medicine program while she also homeschooled her two sons. I would see her from time, at *iftars* (evening meals to break the fast dur-ing Ramadan) or at other community gatherings, until I moved away from the Bay Area with my family in 2012. A story Maya once told to our group left a strong impression on me: As a biracial woman, African American and white, she had hung out with a social group of other bi-racial kids in high school. Of her friends, she found out later in life that five had converted to Islam, completely independently of one another, including herself.

I later heard that Maya and her husband had purchased land to start a farm in the East Bay. By the early 2000s, in the ecologically conscious Bay Area, farmers markets and organic produce were already quite common, as were burgeoning conversations around environmental justice and food justice, in which local activists were highlighting how the poorest neighborhoods—always primarily inhabited by people of color—were also always those who suffered from the highest levels of toxicity in the air and soil, who had issues with their water, and who lacked access to fresh produce and healthy food in their neighborhoods. Yet, as I had come to learn more about Islam and had become Muslim myself, all the while doing the research that would go into this book, I noted in the Bay Area a frequent intersection—and specifically in the lives of Muslim women—of Islam, holistic health, urban gardening and agriculture, homeschooling, and racial justice. The intersection of these elements was not explicit; some Muslim women would perhaps home-school their children and grow a small portion of their own food in the backyard, while others might participate in activist efforts to combat police violence in Oakland and study integrative nutrition, while taking courses in the Islamic sciences at what was at the time called the Zay-tuna Institute in Hayward, California. This school would later go on to become Zaytuna College, the nation's first accredited Muslim liberal arts college. Thus it made sense that Maya would be starting a farm. At the time, there were also a number of other Islamically run preschools and children's programs in the Bay Area, such as Peace Village in Fremont,

California, a preschool and urban farm, and ILM Tree, a Bay Area–based Muslim homeschooling collective that would eventually come to settle into a space as part of the Sienna Ranch, a twenty-two-acre ranch in Lafayette, California.

As a mother to young children myself by this time, I was deeply intrigued by the intermixture of these women's devotion educating their children, growing their own food, and developing their knowledge of Islam, all during a time when anti-Muslim sentiment was palpable throughout the nation. All of the women I met engaged in these types of activities were generally highly politically engaged, too, with strong opinions about U.S. military interventions overseas, as well as the treatment of Muslim and other marginalized groups in the United States. At the same time, I sometimes questioned whether raising one's child in an entirely Muslim environment, with such clearly demarcated gender roles in which women were always the primary caretakers of children, was a viable and effective response to the political realities that U.S. Muslim communities faced on the ground, from surveillance and racial profiling, to violence and harassment directed at women, to social inequality, poverty, and incarceration. Further, I also had concerns that Muslim organizations that engaged in urban farming or educational reform efforts in places like the Bay Area would wind up catering to only more affluent South Asian and Arab American Muslim communities, as opposed to casting a wider net and opening their venues and services up to less economically privileged Muslims and non-Muslim populations of Black and Brown people in the communities around them.

In 2014, I contacted Maya to ask how she was doing and if she might be open to speaking to me about her experiences as a homeopath, healer, urban farmer, and a Muslim woman. By then, Soul Flower Farm was up and running, and she was busy setting up the farm itself, as well as continuing work on her herbal medicine and homeopathy practices. She had also begun offering classes at the farm, with titles such as "All about Nettles," "Food as Medicine," and "Tonic Herbalism," while her husband Yasir offered classes on beekeeping. Because of both of our schedules, we were not able to meet until the summer of 2015, when I was able to visit Maya at the farm, where she showed me the animals, crops, and plants, as well as a beautiful and spacious outdoor canopy/tent space filled with seating, cushions, and rugs, which she said was a space for events such as classes, women's spiritual retreats, and social activist training. Later, when we sat down to talk, she spoke to me about her experiences as a Muslim woman in the post-9/11 United States. In reflecting upon our conversation afterward, I realized that Maya's account reflected a burgeoning structure of feeling within U.S. Muslim communities taking place at the intersections of religion, environment, and racial and social movements in the United States and beyond.

Born in Stamford, Connecticut, in the mid-1980s to a white American mother and an African American father, Maya says she fell in love with the natural world very early in life and was "always very connected to my spirituality." After her parents divorced when she was five, her mother and she moved to Cupertino, California, where she was raised Episcopalian and their church "was white, all white." By high school, she had become friends with a group of biracial kids, she says, who "would go up into the hills and we would like do our drumming and collect sage, little hippie kids you know?" They would also "talk a lot about God, and a lot about spirituality. . . . We were always questioning, always longing." One of her friends began attending Nation of Islam meetings, and although she went along, she "never really felt like it was exactly my thing."

When Maya went to college at Clark Atlanta University in Atlanta, Georgia (a HBCU, historically black college or university), her freshman roommate was a Sunni Muslim whose father was an imam. Her roommate taught her how to pray, and with her, she fasted during Ramadan, although she did not convert until two years later, when she left Clark and returned to the Bay Area. Her conversion took place on a Sunday, she recalls, when she "went to three different *masjids*, just to see which one was open." When she found one, she took her *shahada*. Becoming Muslim, Maya says, was "a clean slate." She got rid of the thousands of CDs she owned, threw out half of her clothing, and started staying up all night praying. Soon she began attending a mosque every Friday for *jummah* and found others who would become her community.

Two years later, she met her husband, Yasir Cross, who was also an African American convert to Islam, and they married after knowing one another for only five months. As converts, she said they set very strict guidelines around their lives. She wore hijab and they "got into this very kind of almost, small-world way of living . . . in this Muslim bubble, like we're in a box." A lot of their life, she recalls, was about what they couldn't do because they were Muslims. After 9/11, however, a lot changed. She says that, even in the supposedly progressive Bay Area, in Berkeley and Oakland, she was spit on and had objects thrown at her because she wore a headscarf. But she also started to realize the racial aspects of such treatment, which did not just manifest in outright hostility but also in the looks and treatment she would get from affluent, white mothers she would encounter at the park with her children, who "were always judging me, treating me like this teenage mom . . . race also has a lot to do with that." She found a group of Muslim mothers in the area with whom she would spend a great deal of time when her children were young. Many of them, like her, would eventually homeschool their children.

When her children got older, Maya was compelled to pursue her passion for nature and began studying at the California School of Herbal Studies, where she completed a two-year program. From there she went on to another two-year program at a four-year homeopathic medical school in San Francisco. Her spirituality, she says, consistently guided her path, and although she says neither program was specifically grounded in Islamic practices, she says that "there is a lot of spiritual energy in homeopathy that ties into Islamic beliefs. In homeopathy, you connect the mind, the body, the spirit, and the emotions. It's not just the physiological treatment, so you're really looking at the whole person." It was also at that time that Maya realized that some of her relationships in the Muslim community had become stifling, and as she developed a fuller sense of self, she knew she had to find a more expansive—and freer—space in which to live her and her family's life.

In 2010, after completing her homeopathy studies, her husband and she purchased Soul Flower Farm. They got to work right away, planting the garden, getting chickens and goats, setting up beehives. Two years later, they got a cow. The first year, they produced 30 percent of what they ate; by now they produce 99 percent. In considering the farm's relationship with the community around it, Maya says she definitely wanted to get Muslims involved "because, as Muslims, we are supposed to be living close to the earth, being in touch with where our food comes from, understanding these things on an innate level." But she also started reaching out to local activist and justice organizations in the Bay Area, such as Pathways to Resilience, an organization that works with formerly incarcerated individuals from San Quentin State Prison, afterschool programs for urban youth in Richmond, and a black farmer's group in Oakland. On the farm, individuals from these organizations can learn farming and sustainability practices, as well as engaging the land as means to work through and heal trauma.

Maya herself says that opening and running the farm has been a healing practice for her as well and that she "went through a lot of personal hardship and trauma before I got to the point of living at this location." Soul Flower Farm was, and is, "a complete and total gift . . . a space to heal and to rejuvenate myself . . . [by having] my hands in the ground." As the farm further evolves and grows, she has also come to understand that her engagement with Islam is changing as well. While she says she "definitely considers [herself] a Muslim [and] definitely love[s] Islam," she is also trying to integrate her religious practices with "a lot of new information . . . about myself, about the world, about my purpose," and to figure out how "Islam fits in to my life now." She realizes, she says, that she is in a new phase of "being Muslim," and although her engagement with Islam changes, it continues to be "the backbone, that sounding board to go back to, whether in my marriage, within my relationships, decisions, etc. It is a place to go back to, where I have a foundation."

* * *

I view Soul Flower Farm, and other spaces like it, as critical sites in which spiritual and religious life and social justice intersect and, I hope, take root (quite literally) on the ground. I also view the farm, and how Maya Blow has come to envision its purpose, as a vibrant reflection of how Islam continues to evolve as a lived religion in U.S. Muslim women's lives. As her journey reveals, Islam's affective insurgencies do not remain static; they shift and change in response not only to the world around us but in response to the worlds within us as well. Maya's practices of holistic health and healing, of putting one's hands in the earth, of producing one's own food, and of connecting disenfranchised communities through food production and preparation seem to me to continue the legacies of improvisation, insurgent critique, and the search for safe harbor that have been at the heart of U.S. Muslim women's lived experiences of Islam throughout the last century. In the age of the Anthropocene, U.S. Muslim women such as Maya and the other women I have interviewed and discussed in the Bay Area and beyond are once again responding to the political and social exigencies of the world around them by considering how Islam enjoins them to confront the realities of ecological emergency, of food instability, of events like the water crisis in Flint, Michigan, or the devastating drought in California—calamities that always disproportionately affect women, the poor, and people of color.

In this book, I have attempted to demonstrate how women of color in the United states have adopted and enacted forms of Islamic engagement to respond to forms of crisis on various scales. In chorus, their voices, experiences, perspectives, and images intone the affective insurgencies of U.S. American Islam, those embodied and lived practices of being U.S. Muslim women that consistently envision, enact, and cultivate the rhythms of U.S. Muslim life. Black American Muslim women are historically at the heart of these rhythms, and it is imperative to look to their stories and experiences to better chart a path for the future. From the transnational dreams of Black American women of the Ahmadiyya Movement in Islam after the Great Migration, to the insurgent domesticity of women in the Nation of Islam, to the merging of marriage and spirituality in the lives of Betty Shabazz and Dakota Staton and the voices of Latina, South Asian, Arab, multiracial, and white Muslim women activists and scholars, and finally to the healing spaces of sites like Soul Flower Farm, "Islam" has functioned as the prism through which the lived experiences of U.S. Muslim women are, and will continue to be, channeled into insurgent visions of culture, politics, religion, and social change.

ACKNOWLEDGMENTS

Bismillah ar-Rahman ar-Raheem.

In the name of God, the most gracious, the most merciful.

This book is the culmination of efforts far beyond my own. There are so many to thank, as well as, I realize, so many to ask for forgiveness, owing to various states of disarray I have inhabited while completing this volume. For all those who have guided, supported, and encouraged me, as well as those who just put up with me, I am deeply, wholly, and forever grateful. For all those I name here, and for any I may neglect, I pray for the opportunity to extend my gratitude in person soon, *insh'Allah.*

As I discovered quite early on, the stories of U.S. Muslim women have just begun to be told. It was an honor and privilege to be able to sit with the fascinating women whose images, writings, words, labors, legacies, and personhood fill this volume. In particular, I extend heartfelt thanks to Sister Aisha Al-Adawiya, Dr. Laila Al-Marayati, Maya Blow, Hazel Gomez, Dr. Asifa Quraishi-Landes, and Dr. Amina Wadud for taking the time to speak with me and allowing their words to be shared here. As this is a book about legacies and inheritances, I owe a debt of gratitude to the elders in my life who continually demonstrate the richness and complexity of being U.S. Muslim women: *jazak'Allah khair* to Aunties Aziza Ahmad, Jameela Hamid, and Noor Jawad, and to my mother-in-law, Khadija Malik, for her patience, wisdom, and care. Through the years, a number of amazing women in the academy have nurtured and supported this project with their comments and feedback—thank you to Evelyn Alsultany, Juliane Hammer, Sunaina Maira, Zareena Grewal, and Su'ad Abdul Khabeer, for your generosity and support and for laying the groundwork on which this work builds.

This book could not have been written without the friendship and intellectual companionship of Iyko Day, who has been listening to me go on about everything under the sun since forever. She is a true sister-friend who has generously read draft after draft, provided constant encouragement, and rearranged my furniture in the most amazing ways. I have also been buoyed over the years by the friendship of dear University of California comrades like Danika Medak-Saltzman (blanket maker extraordinaire), David Hernandez, Setsu Shigematsu, Dory Nason, Mercy Romero, Irum Sheikh, Rickey Vincent, and Jodi Kim. At UC Berkeley, as an undergraduate and graduate student, and at Mills College during my MFA, I was, and continue to be, inspired by the brilliance of Professors Sau-ling Wong, Ruth Wilson Gilmore, Michael Omi, Patricia Penn Hilden, Elmaz Abinader, June Jordan, Barbara Christian, Mitchell Breitwieser, Ishmael Reed, and Ronald Takaki, each of whom taught me more than they'll ever know. I continually stand in awe of my advisors: Colleen Lye, who challenged and sharpened my thinking at every turn; Jose David Saldivar, who explained "culture" and showed me the power of close reading; and Robin D. G. Kelley, for his continued confidence and unwavering integrity. A special shout-out to my chair, the inimitable Elaine H. Kim, who encouraged me to explore a topic few were working on and believed in me every step of the way. She is a model of engaged scholarship and activism and has literally saved my life time and time again.

This book has benefited immensely from conversations with amazing writers, scholars, and thinkers across many fields. Before entering academe, I had already worked with the best writing teacher around, J. H. "Tommy" Tompkins, my indefatigable editor during my days as a journalist at the *San Francisco Bay Guardian*. In my PhD program in ethnic studies at the University of California, Berkeley, I could not have asked for a more fabulous cohort, who, in addition to some named above, included Gerardo Arellano, Francisco Casique, Vina Ha, Navin Moul, Lilia Soto, Ananda Sattwa, and Daphne Taylor-Garcia. Through the Asian Pacific American Religions Research Initiative (APARRI), I was exposed to the generous minds of David Kyuman Kim, Sharon Suh, Khyati Joshi, Jane Iwamura, Chris Chua, Russell Jeong, Joe Cheah, David Yoo, Jaideep Singh, Janelle Wong, and Carolyn Chen, who pushed my thinking about race and "lived religion." It has been a true blessing to work on the intersections of race, gender, and Islam in the United States over the years in the company of committed and passionately invested scholars who are changing the conversation, such as Zaheer Ali, Arshad Ali, Donna Auston, Moustafa Bayoumi, Sohail Daulatzai, Fatimah Fanusie, Maryam Kashani, Debra Majeed, Shabana Mir, and Junaid Rana. A number of chapters received wonderful comments and suggestions during my time as a fellow at the Institute for Research on Women (IRW) at Rutgers in 2014–2015, led so dynamically by my colleague and friend, Nicole Fleetwood. Finally, *Being Muslim* simply would not *be* without the life-changing experience of the Scholars-in-Residence Program at the Schomburg Center for Research in Black Culture in 2015–2016, where I can say without pretense that I encountered the most nurturing and generative space for my ideas in the academy that I have ever known. This was wholly due to the shining spirits and luminous minds of fellow scholars C. Riley Snorton, Caree Banton, Soyica Colbert, Jeff Diamant, Tsitsi Jaji, Nicole Wright, Tanisha Ford, Kaima Glover, and Andrianna Campbell. *And* Sister Sonia Sanchez (yes, THE Sonia Sanchez), who shared with us visions of freedom with a generosity I will never forget. All of this happened because of the remarkable efforts of Sister Aisha Al-Adawiya and the peerless leadership of Farah Jasmine Griffin, who radiates brilliance and compassion wherever she goes.

I have been blessed throughout my career to be supported by additional fellowships from the Ford Foundation; the University of California, Berkeley, Graduate Opportunity Program; the University of California, Berkeley, Ethnic Studies Department; and the University of California President's Postdoctoral Program. During my time as a University of California President's Postdoctoral scholar at the University of California, Santa Cruz, from 2009 to 2011, I was guided by the mentorship of Eric Porter, supported by colleagues Catherine Ramirez, Sylvanna Falcon, Amy Lonetree, and Christine Hong, and friends Chiung-Chi Chen and Nameera Akhtar. Since arriving at to the Departments of American and Women's and Gender Studies at Rutgers–New Brunswick in 2012, I have realized that I truly have the best colleagues in the world, who have facilitated my transition to East Coast winters with a good humor that makes the weather (slightly) easier to bear. In American Studies, I am grateful for the camaraderie of Louise Barnett, Jeff Decker, Leslie Fishbein, Nicole Fleetwood, Angus Gillespie, Louis Prisock, Michael Rockland, Ben Sifuentes-Jauregui, Andy Urban, and Caroline Wigginton (we miss you!), with special thanks to my departmental mentor, Lou Masur, and my truly fabulous chair, Allan Isaac, for their wisdom, friendship, and for being constant streams of invaluable advice. I also want to thank the American Studies departmental administrators Stephanie East and Olga Lozano, and before them, Helene Grynberg, who have always had my back. In Women's and Gender Studies, my appreciation goes out to Nikol Alexander-Floyd, Radhika Balakrishnan, Ethel Brooks, Charlotte Bunch, Sue Carroll, Ed Cohen, Harriet Davidson, Carlos Decena, Judy Gerson, Mary Gossey, Mary Hawkseworth, Jasbir Puar, Julie Rajan, Yana Rodgers, Zakia Salime, and Louisa Schein, and especially to my departmental chairs, Abena Busia, who has offered steadfast support and kindness from Day 1, and Mary Trigg, who has guided me so deftly through the end stages of this manuscript. Finally, an extra shout-out to the junior faculty crew: Brittney Cooper, Marisa Fuentes, Maya Mikdashi, and Kyla Schuller. What an honor to work with each and every one of you.

It is in the classroom that so many of my ideas find voice. It is not an exaggeration to say, as I tell people all the time, that I have best students in the world at Rutgers. To each of my undergraduate and graduate students—you teach me more than you know. In the development of this project, I would particularly like to thank the undergraduate students in my Fall 2016 "Islam in/and America" class for their careful feedback on my introduction to this book. At Rutgers, I have had the privilege of working with undergraduate students who I am now proud to call peers and friends in Sophia Albanaa, Anna Achampong, Trefina Dixon, Rashmee Kumar, and Lai Wo. Thanks to my graduate students for the privilege on serving on your MA and PhD committees: Intimaa Al-Saldudi, Donna Auston, JB Brager, Che Gossett, Joss Taylor, Louis Tam, and Lindsay Whitmore—your ideas continually inspire my own.

At NYU Press, I am grateful for the keen eye of my editor Eric Zinner, who showed an interest in this project long before I knew what it was, and to Alicia Nadkarni, who has guided me through the publishing process with patience and care. My deepest thanks to my anonymous readers, whose feedback and comments were invaluable in refining my thoughts and strengthening the manuscript. I would also like to thank Danielle Kasparak at the University of Minnesota Press and Courtney Berger at Duke University, each of whom gave me excellent feedback and suggestions on portions of the manuscript, and Zoë Ruiz, for her sharp and insightful editing skills. For helping me get through countless hours of research, thanks to librarian Kayo Denda at Rutgers and Schomburg archivists Stephen Fullwood and Shola Lynch for leading me to answers just when I needed them. At Rutgers, I was thrilled to encounter, and eventually lead, between 2013 and 2014, the Women of Color Scholars Initiative, through which I was blessed to meet amazing WOC scholars in other departments, especially Preetha Mani, Chie Ikeya, and Suzy Kim, who are a constant source of laughter and good cheer.

Beyond the academy, we often forget, there is life. This book, and the journey I've traveled while writing it, have been made worth the while by many beautiful souls who have grounded me in reality and elevated my spirit. Thanks to Hina Azam, Moina Noor, Habiba Noor, Lynn Jehle, Jessica Livingston, Ruxana Meer, Jeff Chang, Vijay Iyer, Jenna Mammina, and Jennifer Maytorena Taylor for your friendship throughout the years. To Rick Lee—you are my best Chinese food friend, and to my cousin Amy Hou, thank goodness for family on the East (and now West) Coast. Also, much love to all of my extended family in Milwaukee and California, especially to my sisters-in-law Tahira Malik and Raqiba Malik and all of my aunties, uncles, cousins, nieces and nephews in the Bay. Three specific individuals have put up with my rabbit brain for far too long. To Karen Dere, your kindness knows no bounds, and you have held me up time and time again. Not only are you one of the best people on this planet, but you have way cool T-shirts. To Susan Ku, Auntie Sue-Sue, who knows everything about me and still likes me, who has brought bags of In-and-Out and waited through countless bedtimes so we could keep talking, I am eternally grateful for your presence in my life. Finally, to Jill Denyes, thank you for sharing Ethiopian food, from Oakland to Jersey, and being a sister. You have no idea how much it means to me to have you near.

Through it all, there are those who do the hard work of loving you. I owe many lifetimes of gratitude to my parents, Ting Chung and Sheila Chan, for their hard work, their sacrifices, and for allowing me to pursue my goals. Thank you, Mom and Dad, for the countless hours of child-care, cooked meals, and all the ways you make your grandchildren smile. To my beautiful stepdaughter, Sareyah Malik, I am proud to watch you becoming the woman you told me you wanted to be. I love you fiercely and am grateful to be a part of your life.

To Sumaiyya Noor and Safiyyah Jihan, being your mother is delightful, hilarious, exhilarating, revelatory, and totally awesome. Thank you for all your cuddles, smiles, jokes, and hugs, and for always reminding me that I could do it. This book is for you, so you may see the footsteps that are already there. Mommy loves you infinity forever.

Finally, to Badi Malik, the best husband, father, and friend there is, who has loved me through every word, shared my struggles, and nurtured my dreams. None of this would have been possible without you, and life is possible with you. We did it.

NOTES

INTRODUCTION

1 Some scholars have named this distinction through the terms "indigenous" and "immigrant," although I choose not to employ that terminology here, primarily owing to how I view it as effacing the racial, class, and generational complexity of U.S. Muslim communities.

2 For example, in *Muslim Women in America*, Haddad, Smith, and Moore write in the early pages of their introduction, in a section titled "Where Did They Come From?" that "the first Muslims to begin the process of becoming American, aside from a very few African Muslim slaves who managed to retain their faith, were those who arrived in the West in the late nineteenth and early twentieth century. They came from the rural areas of what was known as Greater Syria, which include the current states of Jordan, Lebanon, Palestine, and Syria, then part of the Ottoman Empire" (5). Also see Wadud, "American Muslim Identity."

3 See Daulatzai, *Black Star, Crescent Moon*; Jackson, *Islam and the Blackamerican*; Aidi, *Rebel Music*; and Curtis, *Islam in Black America*.

4 Crenshaw, "Mapping the Margins," 1243–1244.

5 See Jackson, *Islam and the Blackamerican*.

6 For an excellent study of these complexities, see Abdullah, *Black Mecca*.

7 Khabeer takes a similar position in her book, *Muslim Cool*, in which she argues for "the critical importance of Blackness to all U.S. Muslim self-making, including those who move away from Blackness as well as those who . . . move toward Blackness as a way of being Muslim" (23).

8 See Sanchez, Interview.

9 Taylor, "Elijah Muhammad's Nation of Islam, 178.

10 Formerly known as the *Negro Digest, Black World* magazine emerged the early 1970s as an important platform for writers in the Black Arts movement, often called the cultural voice of the Black Power movement. Islam—via the Nation of Islam as well as Sunni Islam—powerfully influenced many Black Arts writers and artists, including Amiri Baraka, often called the "father" of Black Arts. In a 1968 interview, Baraka (still using the name LeRoi Jones at the time) said Islam's "unifying principle and its high moral principle are what the Black man needs . . . to withstand the degeneracy that America represents" (Marvin X and Faruk, "Islam and Black Art," 52), and he himself was a member of the Nation of Islam, later becoming a Sunni Muslim. Also see Sanchez, *A Blues Book*.

11 Elsayed, "Feeling Muslim."

12 In January 2015, Duke University officials canceled their decision to have weekly Islamic Friday prayer services begin with an amplified call to prayer from the campus chapel's bell tower. They said they did so owing to intense backlash, including death threats.

13 Deah was the son of Syrian Muslims of Palestinian origin, and Yusor and Razan were the children of Jordanian immigrants who were also of Palestinian descent.

14 Deah had lived in the complex alone prior to marriage and had not been reported to have had conflicts with Hicks. It was only after he married Yusor, who, because of her headscarf, was visibly Muslim, that Hicks began to behave aggressively toward the couple and their friends, often becoming belligerent over their use of a shared parking space in the complex's lot. For an excellent review of the case, see Talbot, "The Story of a Hate Crime."

15 Elsayed, "Feeling Muslim."

16 Ibid.

17 See Pew Research Center, "A Demographic Portrait of Muslim Americans."

18 I adapt the concept of "againstness" from the work of the feminist scholar Sara Ahmed. As Ahmed writes in regard to feminism, it is "when feminism is no longer directed towards a critique of patriarchy, or secured by the categories of 'women' or 'gender,' that is doing the most 'moving' work. *The loss of such an object is not the failure of feminist activism, but is indicative of its capacity to move, or to become a movement*" (italics in original). See Sara Ahmed, *The Cultural Politics of Emotion*, 177.

19 See McGuire, *Lived Religion*; Orsi, *Between Heaven and Earth*; David Hall, *Lived Religion in America*; and Ammerman, *Everyday Religion*.

20 Orsi, "Everyday Miracles," 8.

21 There are increasingly more titles that examine the intersections of race and religion. See Prentiss, *Religion and the Creation of Race and Ethnicity*; and Goldschmidt and McAlister, *Race, Nation, and Religion*.

22 Jackson, *Islam and the Blackamerican*, 3–4. See also Curtis, *Islam in Black America*; Daulatzai, *Black Star, Crescent Moon*; Aidi, *Rebel Music*; and Dannin, *Black Pilgrimage to Islam*.

23 Amina Wadud, *Inside the Gender Jihad*, 59.

24 Zareena Grewal notes the differing narratives that characterize white women's conversions to Islam as opposed to Black and Latino women. She writes: "Women of color who become Muslim . . . identify the appeal of Islam in terms of the same racial, political, and social factors as their male counterparts, such as Islam's historical relationship to social justice movements in the U.S. . . . In contrast, when these authors turn to explaining Islam's appeal to white Americans . . . they offer a gender-specific, spiritual explanation." See Zareena Grewal, *Islam Is a Foreign Country*, 222.

25 Rouse, *Engaged Surrender*, 20.

26 See Leila Ahmed, *Women and Gender in Islam*; Abu-Lughod, "Do Muslim Women Need Saving?"; Hoodfar, "The Veil"; and Kahf, *Western Representations of Muslim Women*.

27 Lye, *America's Asia*, 5. I am mindful that Lye advances the term in a Marxist analysis that seeks to investigate how Asians operate within the racializing logics of capitalism, and I realize that it does not neatly transpose onto categories of race and religion.

28 Ibid.

29 Ibid.

30 Rana, *Terrifying Muslims*.

31 Day, *Alien Capital*.

32 Rana, "The Story of Islamophobia," 148.

33 Arjana, *Muslims in the Western Imagination*, 1.

34 Ibid., 2.

35 Ibid., 3.

36 Perhaps the most obvious example of this is the notion of *taqiyya*, which is regularly used by Islamophobes as proof of Muslim monstrosity. Although *taqiyya* is defined in Islam as the permission for Muslims to keep silent about their religious identity if under threat of harm—for example, if they are prisoners of war—Islamophobes incorrectly believe the term means that Muslims are inherently deceptive, specifically that no matter what they say or do, they harbor the desire to harm and destroy all non-Muslim societies and individuals.

37 In the years since 9/11, and in particular in conjunction with the rise of ISIS, the figure of the Muslim Female Suicide Bomber has also entered the lexicon of anti-Muslim tropes. However, according to a 2017 article in the *Atlantic*, the trope is "almost entirely fictitious, conjured by ISIS's foes to amplify the group's demonic extremity and desperate unraveling." See Cottee and Bloom, "The Myth of the ISIS Female Suicide Bomber."

38 Mahmood, *Politics of Piety*, 167.

39 Pratt, "Arts of the Contact Zone."

40 For more on how the trope of the Poor Muslim Woman is used to justify Western imperialism and military aggression, see Hirschkind and Mahmood, "Feminism, the Taliban, and the Politics of Couterinsurgency"; Hoodfar, "The Veil"; Viner, "Feminism as Imperialism"; and Leila Ahmed, *Women and Gender in Islam*.

41 Abu-Lughod, "Do Muslim Women Need Saving?"

42 Leila Ahmed, *Women and Gender in Islam*.

43 Kahf, *The Girl in the Tangerine Scarf*, 361–362. Other rebukes to such male authority often cite the example of Khadijah, the first wife of the Prophet Muhammad, who was a successful and esteemed businesswoman before her marriage to the Prophet. Khadijah herself proposed to the Prophet, who was fifteen years her junior.

44 Simmons, "Are We Up to the Challenge?" 240.

45 Rouse, *Engaged Surrender*, 142–143.

46 See Wadud, *Qur'an and Woman*.

47 Wadud is perhaps most well known for leading a 2005 mixed-gender Islamic *jummah* prayer service in Manhattan, New York. Many Islamic scholars argue that it is impermissible within Islam's dictates for a woman to lead a mixed congregation

in prayer. Progressive scholars such as Wadud and others counter that there is no such ruling in Islam and that such conclusions are derived from patriarchal interpretations of the Qur'an and hadith.

48 Wadud, *Inside the Gender Jihad*, 79–80.

49 Combahee River Collective, "A Black Feminist Statement," 212.

50 Collins, *Black Feminist Thought*, 17.

51 Walker, "Coming Apart," 329.

52 Walker, *In Search of Our Mothers' Gardens*, xi.

53 Ibid.

54 Ibid.

55 Collins, "What's in a Name?," 11.

56 Ibid.

57 Mitchem, "Womanist Theology," 52.

58 Ibid., 53.

59 Moraga and Anzaldúa, *This Bridge Called My Back*, liii.

60 Ibid., 217; italics and boldface in original.

61 Badran, *Feminism in Islam*, 242.

62 Ibid.

63 Ibid.

64 cooke, "Multiple Critique," 100.

65 Majeed, *Polygyny*, 20.

66 Ibid.

67 See Moraga and Anzaldúa, *This Bridge Called My Back*, liii.

68 Karim, *American Muslim Women*, 96.

69 Ibid.

70 Morrison, *Sula*, 55.

71 Ibid.

72 For example, see Hammer and Safi, *The Cambridge Companion to American Islam*.

73 Stuart Hall, "New Ethnicities."

74 Morrison, *Playing in the Dark*.

CHAPTER 1. "FOUR AMERICAN MOSLEM LADIES"

1 Sadiq's report mentioned a lecture at the Exchange Club of Grand Haven, Michigan, on November 27 and a talk in Crookston, Minnesota, where Sadiq was "invited by the Superintendent of the State Farm School to give a talk on Islam." See Sadiq, "Brief Report," January 1923.

2 "Moslem" was the common spelling of the term used to describe followers of Islam until the 1980s in the United States. The term "Mohammedan" was also used, but it was always deemed incorrect and offensive, as Muslims do not worship the Prophet Muhammad. In the 1990s, "Muslim" largely replaced the earlier term, which has now come to be viewed as derogatory and offensive owing to its antiquated nature.

3 For example, the image accompanies an extensive entry on African American Muslims in the *Encyclopedia of Muslim-American History* with this caption:

> Ahmadi missionary Muhammad Sadiq found that men and women were attracted to his message that Islam could be a source of black pride and racial equality. In this 1923 photograph titled "Four American Moslem Ladies," these African American women are wearing clothes that combine South Asian and American styles of dress.

The author of the encyclopedia entry, Lawrence Mamiya, does not explain why, for example, the image of these four women might reflect Islam's relationship with "black pride and racial equality" or why it might be significant for these women to "combine South Asian and American styles of dress." The entry also does not explain that the women featured in the photo were part of a multiracial congregation that also included many whites, as well as South Asian members. See Mamiya, "African-American Muslims."

4 For example, Edward Curtis writes of Mary Juma, a female Muslim immigrant from Syria, who arrived in Ross, North Dakota, in 1902. With her husband and children, she was part of a Muslim community that built a small mosque and where they had a farm. Juma's community was unique in that, although "most of the Ottoman emigrants who arrived in the United States from the 1880s through World War I were Christian . . . North Dakota was different [as] approximately one-third of all Syrian and Lebanese North Dakotans during this time was Muslim, and more than one hundred lived in Ross alone." See Curtis, *Muslims in America*, 49.

5 See Turner, *Islam in the African American Experience*; McCloud, *African American Islam*; Gomez, *Black Crescent*; and Curtis, *Islam in Black America*.

6 An extensive treatment of the AMI's role in development of Black American Islam can be found in Turner's *Islam and the African American Experience*.

7 Such labels stem from the claims—discussed further later on—of the AMI's founder, Hazrat Mirza Ghulam Ahmad, who in 1889 declared himself the Mahdi, or the Promised Messiah of Islam and Christianity. In Sunni theological doctrine, this contradicts the idea of the *al-nabi al-khatm*, or the seal of the prophets—e.g., that the Prophet Muhammad was the final and last of God's prophets and, thus, none may follow him.

8 For example, Ahmadi Muslims bear the legal status of "non-Muslim" (indicated in identity cards and stamped on passports) in Pakistan and are prohibited from performing any Islamic rituals, such as speaking the Islamic greeting, "Assalaamu Alaikum," or praying in mosques.

9 Kelley, *Freedom Dreams*, 10.

10 Davis, *Blues Legacies*, 20.

11 Census and vital record information comes from both the *FamilySearch* (https://familysearch.org) and *Ancestry* (www.ancestry.com) databases.

12 The Quaker brothers John, Andrew, and Joseph Ellicott founded the eponymous city in the late eighteenth century, first naming it Ellicott Mills.

13 Such polarization marked Ellicott City as well. According to the *New York Times*, on November 4, 1879, a group of about one hundred white Democrats from Baltimore tore through Howard County, firing at Black voters in order to prevent the election of the Republican candidate for governor, James Albert Gary. (He lost to Democrat William Thomas Hamilton.) Beginning in Elkridge, they then proceeded to Sykesville, where "the roughs fired upon and scattered another crowd of colored voters," then moved on to Ellicott. As a result, the *Times* reported, "a large number of Negroes were disenfranchised and the Democrats carried the county by the grossest frauds." See "Colored Voters Shot Down and Driven Away from the Polls," *New York Times*, November 5, 1879, 5.

14 Quote from Ellicott City, "Civil War."

15 The one-room schoolhouse operated through the 1950s, accepting students from grades 1–7. Although a product of segregation, the school also offered the small but active Black community in Ellicott the opportunity for leadership in their community—in 1895, the school's white leadership was turned over to a board of Black trustees.

16 Spear, *Black Chicago*, 129.

17 Best, *Passionately Human*, 19.

18 The riots were sparked by the drowning of a Black American teen in Lake Michigan after he was stoned by white youths. The Black youth was said to be violating the unofficial segregation of Chicago's beaches, and tensions erupted after police refused to arrest the white man who initiated the boy's attack. Concentrated in the city's South Side, the riots lasted a week; they finally ended on August 3, 1919. By then, over one thousand Black families lost their homes in fires set by rioters.

19 Ibid., 75.

20 Ibid., 147.

21 Ibid., 132.

22 Jones, *Labor of Love*.

23 Ibid.

24 Ibid., 138.

25 Ibid., 137.

26 DuBois, *The Souls of Black Folk*.

27 Best, *Passionately Human*, 23–24.

28 Higginbotham, *Righteous Discontent*, 185.

29 Ibid., 187.

30 Ibid., 196.

31 Jones, *Labor of Love*, 160.

32 See Domosh, "A 'Civilized' Commerce," 244. Commemorating the four hundredth anniversary of Columbus's "discovery" of America, the exposition brought more than twenty-seven million people to see the exhibits of the forty-six nations that participated, including "native villages" in which indigenous

peoples from around the world were displayed in their "natural habitats." Owing to the unprecedented nature of the gathering, organizers convened various congresses to discuss topics with international representatives, such as medicine, philosophy, and literature.

33 The white American convert Muhammad Russell Alexander Webb was the representative of Islam at the fair. For more on Webb, see Abd-Allah, *A Muslim in Victorian America*. It is of interest that Webb corresponded with Mirza Ghulam Ahmad prior to his conversion to Islam, which Abd-Allah discusses in his book (60–66). Although Webb did not convert to Ahmadiyya Islam, Abd-Allah notes that "the Ahmadiyya maintain that Mirza Ahmad was instrumental in Webb's conversion" and "attach considerable importance to the Webb-Mirza Ahmad correspondence, especially as an indication of the role Mirza Ahmad played in calling Westerners to Islam" (244).

34 Tchen, *New York before Chinatown*, 22.

35 Kidd, *American Christians and Islam*, 59.

36 The best-known of the anti-Asian exclusion laws was the 1882 Chinese Exclusion Act, which banned Chinese migration for ten years. Yet Asians were already banned from citizenship prior to that, through the 1870 Naturalization Act, which limited naturalization to whites and "aliens of African nativity and to persons of African descent," thus excluding all Asians from citizenship. The Naturalization Act of 1906 upheld and reinforced the exclusion of Asians, still restricting citizenship to "free white persons" and "persons of African descent" and adding clauses requiring that all immigrants be required to learn English before becoming citizens.

37 At the close of the nineteenth century, however, the Black Presbyterian minister and Liberian nationalist Edward Wilmot Blyden (who eventually became the Liberian secretary of state and presidential candidate) expressed respect and admiration for Islam as a tradition that could foster African nationalism. Later in the 1910s, Marcus Garvey popularized the struggle for Pan-Africanism and Black nationalism through the work of the United Negro Improvement Association. In Garvey's speeches and writing, Islam was often portrayed as a religious tradition that had roots in Africa and thus challenged and rejected Western and white supremacist devaluations of blackness and Black culture. For more on Blyden and Garvey's thoughts on Islam, see Curtis, *Islam in Black America*; Gomez, *Black Crescent*; and Turner, *Islam in the African American Experience*.

38 Although Drew Ali's movement adapted more of its Islamic imagery from the Freemasons (in particular, the Shriners) than from actual Islamic traditions or practices, the critical importance of Drew Ali and the Moorish Science Temple in the history of American Islam came from how they linked Black liberation to a sense of national and moral renewal—in similar fashion, one should note, to the ways Black church women viewed respectability and morality as critical

to the quest for Black freedom. For Drew Ali, however, this came from reimagining Blacks as "Moors," constructing an origin narrative and ancestral lineage that rendered Black men "Asiatic" and thus able to eschew the category of blackness. Drew Ali taught his followers that, owing to their Moorish history, they "shared a common religion, Islam, with all nations of Asiatic descent." For more on Noble Drew Ali, see Curtis, *Muslims in America*, 50–51, and *Islam in Black America*; and Turner, *Islam in the African American Experience*.

39 Didier, "Those Who're Missionaries to Christians."

40 Ibid.

41 Ibid.

42 Bayoumi, "East of the Sun," 256.

43 Indeed, many of Sadiq's writings are marked with wry observations about American life and culture. While indignant about his treatment, he was clear-eyed about the violence of racist bigotry against non-whites and lampooned the U.S. immigration policies in his essay, "If Jesus Comes to America," in which he imagined a conversation between Jesus and a U.S. immigration official:

> IMMIGRATION OFFICER: WHAT IS YOUR NAME?"
> JESUS: JESUS.
> IMMIGRATION OFFICER: WHAT IS YOUR FIRST NAME?
> JESUS: THIS IS MY FIRST NAME.
> IMMIGRATION OFFICER: WHAT IS YOUR SECOND NAME?
> JESUS: I HAVE NO SECOND NAME. THIS IS MY ONLY NAME.
> IMMIGRATION OFFICER: FUNNY, WHAT IS YOUR FATHER'S NAME?
> JESUS: I HAVE NO FATHER.

The immigration officer concludes that "Jesus cannot be allowed to enter this country." See Sadiq, "If Jesus Comes to America."

44 For more on Karoub and the Muslim community in Detroit, see Howell, *Old Islam in Detroit*.

45 Mirza Ghulam Ahmad (1835?–1908), the son of a middle-class Muslim landowner in Qadian, Punjab, lived a life of religious study and seclusion and claimed to begin receiving revelations from God in 1879. He published his first book the following year, *Al-Barahin-al-Ahmadiyya* (1880), "in which he sought to rejuvenate Islam by arguing for the validity of its principles in the context of the increasing threat posed by the Hindu majority and Christian missionaries in the Punjab" (Turner, *Islam in the African American Experience*, 111). While the text was generally well received, Ahmad's views became more controversial in his following books, *Fath-i Islam, Izala-y Awham,* and *Tawzih-I Maram*, published in 1890 and 1891, in which he spoke explicitly of his revelations and stated that he was the *mujadid* (renewer) and *masih-maw'ud*, or Promised Messiah, of Christianity and Islam. Finally, in his 1899 text *Masih Hindustan Men*, Ahmad "said that Jesus had not died on the cross, but instead had gone to India, died

there, and had ascended physically to heaven" (ibid., 112). These claims led to Ahmad being labeled a heretic by orthodox Sunni Muslims.

46 Sadiq, "Brief Report," *Moslem Sunrise*, July 1922.

47 WTTW, "From Riots to Renaissance."

48 See Deutsch, "The Asiatic Black Man."

49 Sadiq, "The Only Solution," 41–42. In Sadiq's and the AMI's early work, as documented in the *Moslem Sunrise*, one notes the articulation of what Edward Curtis in *Islam in Black America* has called "the tension between universalism and particularism in African American Islam . . . a tension between Islamic universalism and black particularism" (12). Whereas Sadiq acknowledged and attempted to address the ills of anti-Black racism in the United States, his prescription of Ahmadiyya Islam as a universal antidote for racism was naïve and simplistic at best, and hollow and manipulative at its worst. For example, Black Americans who joined the AMI could not possibly understand the extent of the animosity toward Ahmadi Muslims from Sunnis, an animus that would increase as more Sunni immigrants entered the United States in the latter half of the twentieth century. Furthermore, while Sadiq and subsequent missionaries encouraged their followers to take on major responsibilities and assume leadership roles, the position of missionary, which held the most power in the organization, was always reserved for and filled by South Asian Ahmadi Muslims, rendering a caste system within the organization that remains to this day.

50 See Turner, *Islam in the African American Experience*; and McCloud, *African American Islam*.

51 See Rouse, *Engaged Surrender*.

52 Kazi, *Muslim Women in India*, 7. See also Rouse, *Engaged Surrender*; Taylor, "As-Salaam Alaikum"; and Gibson and Karim, *Women of the Nation*.

53 Sadiq, "One Year's Moslem Missionary Work," 13.

54 See Thaha, "Islam My Savior."

55 Ibid.

56 In addition to Rahatullah, Sadiq collaborated with a number of other white women in his work prior to arrival in Bronzeville. For example, he frequently included the writings and poetry of one Lady Mary Amelia Hunt, whom he called "the Aurora Poet-Laureate" (presumably the poet laureate of the city of Aurora, Illinois). Hunt's words first appear in the *Moslem Sunrise*'s inaugural issue in the form of a letter she addresses to "The Editor Review of Religions, Qadian, India [*sic*]." In the following issue, Hunt is mentioned as working with Sadiq to translate "some couplets from the Great Teacher Ahmad's Poems," with the title, "I and My Love." She is not, however, listed in the conversion rolls that are included in the publication each month, revealing that, while she must have deeply admired Sadiq and his work, she ultimately decided not to convert to Ahmadiyya Islam.

57 Sadiq, "A Verse from the Holy Book" (italics added).

58 Ibid.

CHAPTER 2. INSURGENT DOMESTICITY

1 Berger, "Malcolm X."

2 As the work of American studies scholar Amy Kaplan demonstrates, notions of "separate spheres" in regard to women's lives are completely arbitrary, and the very construction of what is "domestic" is always linked to notions of the nation and citizenship, of belonging and otherness. Kaplan writes that what is "domestic" wholly depends upon the "explicit or implicit contrast with the foreign." See Kaplan, "Manifest Domesticity," 581.

3 See Gibson and Karim, *Women of the Nation*; Jeffries, *A Nation Can Rise No Higher*; and Taylor, "As-Salaam Alaikum."

4 Turman, "The Greatest Tool," 131.

5 Ibid., 133.

6 See Mike Wallace and Louis Lomax, *The Hate That Hate Produced*.

7 Curtis, *Black Muslim Religion*, 5.

8 The Honorable Elijah Muhmmad makes this clear in his writing and teachings. See Muhammad, *Message to the Blackman*, 13.

9 In 2014 alone, two full-length manuscripts—Gibson and Karim's *Women of the Nation* and Jeffries's *A Nation Can Rise No Higher*—were published. Both offer analysis of primary documents, such as *Muhammad Speaks*, the Nation of Islam's official newspaper, and the group's internal literature, as well as offering firsthand accounts of NOI women themselves relaying their experiences in the organizations. Other scholars, such as the historian Ula Y. Taylor, the religious studies scholar Rosetta E. Ross, and the anthropologist Carolyn Moxley Rouse, have written on the women of the Nation. See Gibson and Karim, *Women of the Nation*; Jeffries, *A Nation Can Rise No Higher*; Taylor, "As-Salaam Alaikum"; and Ross, *Witnessing and Testifying*.

10 See Wolcott, *Remaking Respectability*.

11 Ibid.

12 Curtis, *Islam in Black America*, 68.

13 Fard Muhammad is also referred to Mr. Farrad Muhammad, Mr. F. M. Ali, Professor Fard, Mr. Wali Fard, Wallace D. Fard, and W. D. Fard.

14 Berg, *Elijah Muhammad and the Nation of Islam*, 25.

15 Ibid., 33.

16 Lincoln, *The Black Muslims in America*, 17.

17 Ibid. For more on the NOI, see Berg, *Elijah Muhammad and the Nation of Islam*; Curtis, *Islam in Black America*; Turner, *Islam in the African American Experience*; Taylor, "Elijah Muhammad's Nation of Islam"; McCloud, *African American Islam*; and Gomez, *Black Crescent*.

18 Muhammad, *Message to the Blackman*, 58.

19 Ibid., 59.

20 Taylor, "As-Salaam Alaikum," 179.

21 Tate, *Little X*, 3.

22 Griffin, "Ironies of the Saint."

23 Ibid., 216.

24 Taylor, "As-Salaam Alaikum."

25 Gibson and Karim, *Women of the Nation*, 23.

26 Ibid.

27 Collins, "Learning to Think," 60.

28 May, *Homeward Bound*, 11.

29 Ibid., 5

30 Ibid., 4.

31 Lipsitz, *The Possessive Investment*, 5.

32 Field, "Introduction," 17.

33 Schlesinger, "The Crisis," 293.

34 Ibid., 301.

35 See Corber, *Homosexuality*; Cuordileone, "Politics"; and May, *Homeward Bound*.

36 Dudziak, *Cold War Civil Rights*, 250.

37 Ibid.

38 Ibid.

39 Ibid.

40 Lomax was the reporter who brought the story of the NOI to Wallace and CBS, due to how the NOI would talk only to Black reporters. In a 1988 interview, Wallace described how he came to know of the group: "Lou Lomax, a reporter I'd never heard of, came to my office, told me about something called the Black Muslims. I'd never heard of them. . . . He told me at great length about an organization called the Black Muslims. He didn't tell me how many people they were or how strong they were. What he suggested to me was that they were not a particularly well-known organization. They had never been written about in the White press." See Mike Wallace, Interview.

41 Lincoln, *The Black Muslims in America*, 128.

42 See Griffin, "Ironies of the Saint"; Taylor, "Elijah Muhammad's Nation of Islam"; and Turman, "The Greatest Tool."

43 Leak, "Malcolm X," 51.

44 Ibid., 52.

45 Mike Wallace, Interview.

46 Berger, "Malcolm X."

47 Tulloch, *The Birth of Cool*, 148.

48 Malcolm X, ed., *The Messenger* magazine, vol. 1, no. 1 (East Elmhurst, NY: Muhammad's Temple of Islam, 1959), Beinecke Rare Book and Manuscript Library, Yale University, call no. JWJ A +M564.

49 Malcolm X to Betty Shabazz, April 1, 1959, "Letters Sent, 1955–1964," Malcolm X Collection, Papers, Schomburg Center for Research in Black Culture, Manuscripts, Archives and Rare Books Division, New York Public Library, R.2 B.2 F.1.

50 Radford-Hill, "Womanizing Malcolm X." Throughout the 1980s and 1990s, as Radford-Hill discusses, black feminists and womanists such as Michele Wallace,

Audre Lorde, bell hooks, Angela Davis, Patricia Hill Collins, Barbara Ransby, Maya Angelou, Alice Walker, Sonia Sanchez, and Farah Jasmine Griffin engaged critically with X's legacy in a series of writings.

51 Gordon Parks, "What Their Cry Means to Me," 31.

52 Ibid.

53 Ibid., 32.

54 Ibid., 79.

55 Field, "Baldwin's FBI Files," 202.

56 Pinckney, "The Magic of James Baldwin." For more on Baldwin's relationship with Elijah Muhammad, see Balfour, "Finding the Words"; Shulman, "Baldwin, Prophecy, and Politics"; and Murray, *Our Living Manhood.*

57 Baldwin, *The Fire Next Time*, 57.

58 Ibid., 56.

59 Ibid., 71.

60 Ibid., 62.

61 Ibid.

62 Majeed, *Polygyny*, 23.

CHAPTER 3. GARMENTS FOR ONE ANOTHER

1 Shaikh, "We Have a Marriage Crisis."

2 This has been contested by some Muslim religious scholars but remains the general consensus among most Muslims.

3 Zuberi, "The Muslim Marriage Crisis."

4 High divorce rates have also become an oft-discussed issue in U.S. Muslim communities. An August 2016 article on the Islamic website *Sound Vision* stated that the most recent study of Muslim marriage in the United States was conducted in the early 1990s and found that the Muslim divorce rate was 31.14 percent. (The highest divorce rates in Muslim-majority countries is 10 percent, in Turkey and Egypt). The article quoted Imam Mohamed Magid, vice president of the Islamic Society of North America, saying that divorce was undoubtedly on the rise in U.S. Muslim communities, while another leader, Imam Ziya Kavakci of the Islamic Association of North Texas, said divorce was a "rampant problem" and that "the *ummah* is a mess when it comes to marriage." See Siddiqui, "Divorce among American Muslims."

5 Hammer, "Marriage in American Muslim Communities," 35.

6 Ibid., 37.

7 Hassan, "Marriage."

8 Friedan, *The Feminine Mystique.*

9 hooks, *Feminist Theory*, 3.

10 See Bayoumi, "East of the Sun."

11 See Rickford, *Betty Shabazz.*

12 Freeman, "Marriage," 152.

13 Ibid., 153.

14 Goodell, *The American Slave Code*, 105.

15 Goring, "The History of Slave Marriage," 305.

16 Freeman, "Marriage."

17 Billingsley and Morrison-Rodriguez, "The Black Family," 33.

18 Curwood, *Stormy Weather*, 15.

19 Ibid.

20 Frazier, *The Negro Family in the United States*.

21 Ibid. It is interesting to note the similarities between Frazier's arguments and that made by Schlesinger, "The Crisis," as discussed in chapter 2.

22 Lindsey and Evans, *The Companionate Marriage*.

23 Curwood, *Stormy Weather*.

24 Tucker, *Women, Family, and Gender*, 38.

25 Quraishi, "Understanding Sharia."

26 Ibid.

27 It is important to note that these schools are particular to Sunni Islam, in which there are four major schools of Islamic thought that produce different *fiqh* rulings: Hanafi, Maliki, Shafi'i, and Hanbali.

28 In Christian and Jewish traditions, Hajar is spelled "Hagar." However, as Amina Wadud points out, there is no letter "g" in Arabic, nor are any words pronounced with a hard "g" sound. As such, I use "Hajar" as the preferred spelling here.

29 Rickford, *Betty Shabazz*, xiv.

30 Ibid., 283.

31 In her book, *Inside the Gender Jihad*, Amina Wadud proposes what she calls "a new Hajar paradigm" that rereads the story with deep considerations of Hajar's suffering and sacrifice in the desert in order to reframe calls for gender justice for Muslim women beyond patriarchal framings. Citing the experiences of African American female heads of household, Wadud argues that Islamic law should "accommodate the reality" of single motherhood "instead of turn[ing] a blind eye to it." She proposes legal accommodations that "include mechanisms to help ensure the safety and well-being of families with single women as head of household, to prevent the double burden of the negative stigma of fixed ideals of family, mother, and female, as well as of the public sphere." See Wadud, *Inside the Gender Jihad*, 148–49.

32 The most referenced account of Malcolm X's life remains *The Autobiography of Malcolm X*, as written by Malcolm X with Alex Haley. In 2011, the late historian Manning Marable published what he stated was a definitive biography of the leader's life, *Malcolm X: A Life of Reinvention*, although X's daughters and many who knew him, as well as other scholars, disputed Marable's claims, prompting an entire scholarly volume in response; see Bell and Burroughs, *A Lie of Reinvention: Correcting Manning Marable's Malcolm X*. There have also been numerous volumes written on Elijah Muhammad and the Nation of Islam that discuss Malcolm X extensively, including the Nation of Islam's role in his death; see Evanzz, *The Judas Factor* and *The Messenger*; Clegg, *An Original Man*; Gardell, *In the Name*

of Elijah Muhammad; and Curtis, *Islam in Black America*. A number of works emerged following the release of Spike Lee's 1992 film, *Malcolm X*, exploring his legacy and impact on a new generation of Black youth and on hip hop culture; see, e.g., Dyson, *Making Malcolm*.

33 See Breitman, *Malcolm X Speaks*; and Perry, *Malcolm X: The Last Speeches*.

34 In this section, I refer to Betty Shabazz as "Betty" and not by her last name for the sake of clarity, as her last name changes at different periods in her life, and to distinguish her from her husband.

35 Author interview with Sister Aisha Al-Adawiya, at the Schomburg Center for Research in Black Culture, New York Public Library, New York, November 23, 2015.

36 All information is drawn from Rickford, *Betty Shabazz*.

37 Ibid., 52.

38 Ibid.

39 Ibid., 159.

40 Betty Shabazz to Elijah Muhammad, February 19, 1963, Malcolm X Collection, Papers, Schomburg Center for Research in Black Culture, Manuscripts, Archives and Rare Books Division, New York Public Library, box 2, folder 1.

41 Ibid.

42 Ibid.

43 Ibid.

44 Ibid.

45 Betty Shabazz to Elijah Muhammad, January 5, 1964, Malcolm X Collection, Papers, Schomburg Center for Research in Black Culture, Manuscripts, Archives and Rare Books Division, New York Public Library, box 2, folder 1.

46 Ibid.

47 Ibid.

48 Malcolm X discusses the hardship his work places upon Betty in his autobiography, saying, "I don't imagine many other women might put up with the way I am. Awakening this brainwashed black man and telling this arrogant, devilish white man the truth about himself, Betty understands, is a full-time job. If I have work to do when I am home, the little time I am home, she lets me have the quiet I need to work in. I'm rarely at home more than half of any week; I have been away as much as five months. I never get much chance to take her anywhere, and I know she likes to be with her husband." See Malcolm X and Haley, *The Autobiography of Malcolm X*, 268.

49 Betty Shabazz to Elijah Muhammad, March 5, 1964, Malcolm X Collection, Papers, Schomburg Center for Research in Black Culture, Manuscripts, Archives and Rare Books Division, New York Public Library, box 2, folder 1.; italics added.

50 Ibid.

51 Malcolm X and Haley, *The Autobiography of Malcolm X*, 316.

52 Spoken by Dr. Yosef ben-Jochannan in Rickford, *Betty Shabazz*, 32.

53 Ibid.

54 Ilyasah Shabazz, *Growing up X*, 42.

55 Ibid.

56 Ibid.

57 Betty Shabazz, "The Legacy of My Husband, Malcolm X." *Ebony*, along with its sister publication *Jet* magazine, was the most widely circulating African American publication in the nation at that time.

58 Ibid., 173.

59 Ibid.

60 Ibid.; italics added.

61 Ibid., 176.

62 Ibid.

63 That is, *sharia*. See Rickford, *Betty Shabazz*, 340.

64 Betty Shabazz, "The Legacy of My Husband, Malcolm X," 176.

65 Ibid.

66 Ibid., 178.

67 Ibid., 180.

68 Ibid.

69 Ibid., 182.

70 Shabazz was badly burned in a fire in her apartment, allegedly set by her grandson, Malcolm Shabazz, on June 1, 1997. She died in the hospital three weeks later on June 23, 1997.

71 Still, "Why Singer Believes in Four Wives," 18.

72 Ibid.

73 Robinson, "New York Beat."

74 "Dance Nights Set for Smalls," *New York Amsterdam News*, July 12, 1957, 17.

75 Still, "Why Singer Believes in Four Wives,"19.

76 Ibid. Staton's views actually correspond with those of some contemporary Black Muslim women regarding polygamy, or polygyny, as Debra Majeed discusses in her book on the topic. As Majeed writes, "African American women may choose polygyny because they believe it to be the only way they can retain their cultural heritage, authentically practice a significant aspect of their faith, and enjoy the status afforded to married women. Yes, for some women living polygyny *is* living Islam." See Majeed, *Polygyny*, 24; italics in original.

77 Ibid.

78 Ibid., 20.

79 Turner, *Islam in the African American Experience.*

80 Friedwald, *A Biographical Guide*, 448.

81 Dannin, *Black Pilgrimage to Islam*, 58.

82 Ibid.

83 In his autobiography, Dizzy Gillespie speculated that Islam operated as a means for Black men to escape the dangers of racism. Many of the musicians he knew believed, he wrote, that, "if you join the Muslim faith, you ain't colored no more, you'll be white. . . . You get a new name and you don't have to be a nigger no more." He concludes that he thinks that "everybody started joining because they

considered it a big advantage to not be black during the time of segregation."
See Gillespie and Fraser, *To Be, or Not . . . to Bop*, 291.

84 *Chicago Defender*, June 6, 1959, 22, photo caption.
85 DeCaro, *On the Side of My People*, 147.
86 "Dakota Staton, Ahmad Jamal Disavow 'New Muslims,'" *Jet* magazine, September 10, 1959, 61.
87 Ibid.
88 Touré, a committed anticolonialist and the leader of the Democratic Party, had spearheaded the independence effort, and thus became the nation's president.
89 Booker, "Lawson Hits Press; Defends His Role," 1.
90 "Fete for Touré Noisy, Booing Fiasco," *Pittsburgh Courier*, November 21, 1959.
91 "She Likes the Simple Life: Need No Glamor Tag, Dakota Says," *New Pittsburgh Courier*, December 10, 1960, 23.
92 "Dakota Staton Won Fame the Hard Way," *New York Amsterdam News*, January 7, 1961, 10.
93 "She Likes the Simple Life: Need No Glamor Tag, Dakota Says," *New Pittsburgh Courier*, December 10, 1960, 23.
94 Graham, "Dakota Staton Sues Muhammad," 1.
95 "Dakota Staton, Hubby File Suit against Muhammad," *New Pittsburgh Courier*, June 9, 1962, 1.
96 Sokolsky, "These Days," A15.
97 Malcolm X, "Pulse of the Public," column, *New York Amsterdam News*, December 1, 1962.
98 Graham, "Suit against Muhammad Ridiculous."
99 It is not clear whether Staton was referring to the headquarters of her husband's Islamic and African Information Center or to the Ahmadiyya mosque in Philadelphia.
100 Sherman, "MUSIC; Ending a Recital Year."

CHAPTER 4. CHADORS, FEMINISTS, TERROR
1 Asadullah, "Rap Music Mogul Disrespects Muslims."
2 "Lil' Kim's Muslim Insulting One World Cover under Fire," *rapdirt.com* (blog), December 27, 2002, http://rapdirt.com.
3 Leila Ahmed, *Woman and Gender in Islam*.
4 Ibid., 151.
5 Ibid.
6 Ibid., 152.
7 In the United States, *hijab* is the term for the headscarf primarily used by more recent immigrants to the United States from South and West Asia, where it has come to be used more in Black American Muslim communities. The word *khimar* has a more practical connotation, literally meaning a scarf or head covering in Arabic, whereas *hijab* holds religious connotations, in that it may also refer to the "curtain" that should separate women from men.

8 Huntington, *The Clash of Civilizations*.

9 Anne H. Betteridge notes in an early account of the protests, "Wearing the veil represented a particular moral stance—morality defined positively by Islamic law or negatively by opposition to the immorality of the Shah's regime and to the West in general." See Betteridge, "To Veil or Not to Veil," 130.

10 Hoffman, "However Slight."

11 Ibid.

12 See Dorman and Farhang, *The U.S. Press and Iran*, 147.

13 Apple, "Iran."

14 Jack Smith, correspondent on *ABC World News Tonight*, March 8, 1979.

15 Mike Lee, correspondent on *CBS Evening News*, March 8, 1979.

16 David Brinkley, news anchor on *NBC Nightly News*, March 8, 1979.

17 Powers, "Veiled Warning."

18 Ibrahim, "Iran's 'New' Women."

19 Associated Press, "Iran's Women Protest."

20 See Powers, "Veiled Warning"; Randal, "Women Protest in Iran"; Associated Press, "Iranian Women March against Khomeini"; Tribune Wire Service, "Mob of Men Attacks Women"; and Jaynes, "Iran Women March."

21 See Editorial, "Iran's Women Talk Back"; Associated Press, "Iranian Women March against Khomeini"; Ibrahim, "Iran's 'New' Women"; and Randal, "Women Protest in Iran."

22 Editorial, "Iran's Women Talk Back."

23 Yuenger, "New Revolt in Iran."

24 Powers, "Veiled Warning."

25 Said, *Orientalism*.

26 See Editorial, "Iran's Women Talk Back"; Associated Press, "Iran's Women Protest"; Randal, "Militant Women Demonstrators"; and "Women Claim Iran Veil Victory," *Los Angeles Times*, March 13, 1979.

27 The Associated Press, "Iran's Women Protest," reported on "Moslem zealots enraged by the unveiled protestors," while Randal, "Militant Women Demonstrators," described harassments from "nastier, jeering, and taunting Moslem men boasting allegiance to Khomeini," and the Tribune Wire Service, "Mob of Men Attacks Women," spoke of mobs of "male revolutionaries [who] hurled stones and curses, brandished knives, and fired rifles at the women, who, despite these threats, stood their ground and persisted with their protests, steadfast in their efforts to reject the chador."

28 *ABC World News Tonight*, March 8, 1979.

29 *CBS Evening News*, March 8, 1979.

30 *ABC World News Tonight*, March 11, 1979.

31 Jaynes, "Iranian Women."

32 Ibrahim, "Iran's 'New' Women."

33 Jaynes, "Iran Women March."

34 Randal, "Sexual Politics."

35 For further reading, see Moallem, *Between Warrior Brother and Veiled Sister*; Nashat, *Women and Revolution in Iran*; and Tabari, "The Enigma" and "The Women's Movement."

36 Randal, "Women Protest in Iran."

37 Associated Press, "Iran's Women Protest."

38 See Millett, *Sexual Politics*, 12. Millett's text has often been criticized for its studied ignorance of issues of race. Margaret Simons has criticized Millett's comparison of slavery and racism to her analysis of sexual politics, saying that Millett "both misrepresents the slavery experience and ignores the experiences of minority women in the analysis as well as masks the differences between the situations of white and minority women. Her theory relies on an ethnocentric view of women's power, of the character of sex roles, and the meaning of family"; see Simons, "Racism and Feminism," 12. In a piece exploring Western perceptions of the Islamic veil, Homa Hoodfar writes that *Sexual Politics* indicated Millett's "lack of commitment to and understanding of issues of race, ethnicity, and class"; see Hoodfar, "The Veil" 12.

39 Millett herself later catalogued her journey in her 1982 autobiography, *Going to Iran*, in which she describes the events leading up to her trip to Tehran and her time there, including her detention in an Iranian prison. The account provides a clear idea of the orientalist, and often racist, assumptions, Millett held of Iran and Islam, as in this passage, in which she describes her first impressions of Tehran: "The first sight of them was terrible. Like black birds, like death, like fate, like everything alien. Foreign, dangerous, unfriendly. There were hundreds of them, specters crowding the barrier, waiting their own, a sea of chadors, the long terrible veil, the full length of it, like a dress descending to the floor, ancient, powerful, annihilating us." See Millett, *Going to Iran*, 49.

40 Bender, "Some Call Her the 'Karl Marx' of New Feminism."

41 Prial, "Feminist Philosopher."

42 Ibid.

43 Bender, "Some Call Her the 'Karl Marx' of New Feminism."

44 Prial, "Feminist Philosopher."

45 "Who's Come a Long Way Baby?," *Time*, August 31, 1970.

46 Ibid.

47 "The Liberation of Kate Millett," *Time*, August 31, 1970.

48 Reuters, "U.S. Feminist Calls Khomeini 'Chauvinist.'"

49 Randal, "Sexual Politics."

50 Reuters, "U.S. Feminist Calls Khomeini 'Chauvinist.'"

51 Kifner, "Iran's Women Fought."

52 Randal, "Sexual Politics."

53 Ibid.; italics added.

54 Associated Press, "Hassled, Heckled."

55 Ibid.

56 Tribune Wire Service, "Millett, Friend Arrested."

57 Pabst, "Iran Expulsion Terrifying."

58 Rivera, "Feminist Fears."

59 Another fascinating aspect of the press coverage of Kate Millett not discussed here is the portrayal of Millett's relationship with her "partner," the photographer Sophie Kier. Millett was open about her homosexual relationship with Kier and had once lamented how the mainstream feminist movement had shunned her after discovering that she was, as she called it, a "queero." Called Millett's "companion" throughout most of the press coverage, Kier was featured prominently in the press photo that accompanied the story of Millett's ouster from Iran, a picture of her with Millett at Tehran's airport as they waited for a plane to take them out of the country.

60 COINTELPRO is an acronym for Counterintelligence Program, run by the Federal Bureau of Investigation (FBI). According to the FBI's website, *The Vault*, it began COINTELPRO in 1956 "to disrupt the activities of the Communist Party of the United States." In the 1960s, the program "expanded to include a number of other domestic groups, such as the Ku Klux Klan, the Socialist Workers Party, and the Black Panther Party," as well as the Nation of Islam. See Federal Bureau of Investigation, "COINTELPRO."

61 In 1974, a thirty-five-year-old white man named Allan Bakke sued the University of California Medical School at Davis for violating his constitutional rights under the Fourteenth Amendment's equal protection clause. Bakke had applied twice for admission to the medical school at Davis and been rejected both times. As part of the university's affirmative action program, the medical school had reserved sixteen spaces each year for qualified minorities. Bakke argued that, since his college grade point average and test scores were highter than those of the minority students who were admitted to the medical school, he had been excluded from admission solely on the basis of race. The case was heard before the Supreme Court as *Regents of the University of California v. Bakke*, 438 U.S. 265 (1978), which ultimately ruled to uphold affirmative action and allow race to be considered as one of several factors in college admission decisions. At the same time, the Court disallowed specific racial quotas, such as the ones in place at the University of California, Davis, medical school, to whose program Bakke was then admitted.

62 Editorial, "Who Will Follow the Chador?"

63 Combahee River Collective, "A Black Feminist Statement."

64 Zinn and Dill, "Theorizing Difference," 321.

65 See Michele Wallace, *Black Macho*.

66 Editors, *Ms.* magazine, January 1979, table of contents.

67 Ibid.

68 Jordan, "To Be Black and Female."

69 Ibid.

70 California's Proposition 13 was passed by nearly two-thirds of the state's voters in 1978. The law reduced property taxes on homes, businesses, and farms by about 57 percent. Many view the proposition as the cause of the decline of public education and social services in California, which has produced, as *Time* magazine writer

Kevin O'Leary wrote, "direct democracy run amok, timid governors, partisan gridlock and a flawed constitution." See O'Leary, "The Legacy of Proposition 13."

71 Ibid.

72 Ibid.

73 Walker, "One Child of One's Own."

74 Morrison, "Toni Morrison on Cinderella's Stepsisters."

75 Kelber, "Iran: Five Days in March."

76 Ibid., 90.

77 Ibid.

78 Ibid., 96.

79 Jaynes, "Iran Women March."

80 Cummings, "Demonstrators in City."

81 Faludi, *Backlash*.

82 Steinem, "The Way We Were," 61.

83 Ibid., 94; italics added.

84 Smith, "Racism and Women's Studies," 49.

85 Simons, "Racism and Feminism."

86 Omi and Winant, *Racial Formation*, 117.

87 See Mahmoody, *Not without My Daughter*.

88 See Brooks, *Nine Parts of Desire*; Goodwin, *Price of Honor*; and Latifa, *My Forbidden Face*.

89 For example, see Sasson, *The Princess Trilogy*.

90 Perhaps the best-known of these post-9/11 publications is Azar Nafisi's *Reading Lolita in Tehran*. For a critique of the memoir, see Donadey and Ahmed-Ghosh, "Why Americans Love Azar Nafisi's *Reading Lolita in Tehran*."

CHAPTER 5. A THIRD LANGUAGE

1 Kahf, "The Marvelous Women."

2 Fernea, *In Search of Islamic Feminism*.

3 Ibid., xi.

4 Ibid., ix.

5 Ibid., 364.

6 Zareena Grewal, *Islam is a Foreign Country*, 6.

7 Ibid., 6–7; italics in original.

8 McCloud, *African American Islam*, 4.

9 Ibid.

10 Ibid.

11 Ibid., 5.

12 See Majeed, *Polygyny*.

13 Walker, *In Search of Our Mothers' Gardens*.

14 See Badran, *Feminism in Islam*; and cooke, "Multiple Critique."

15 Fernea, *In Search of Islamic Feminism*, 402–403.

16 Wadud, *Inside the Gender Jihad*, 79–80.

17 See Wadud, *Qur'an and Woman.*

18 The Quranic verse that has been the subject of most controversy is 4:34, which is verse 34 of Surah an-Nisa (The Women), which reads, "Men shall take full care of women with the bounties which God has bestowed more abundantly on the former than the latter, and with what they may spend out of their possessions. And the righteous women are the truly devout ones, who guard the intimacy which God has [ordained to be] guarded. And as for the women whose ill-will you have reason to fear, admonish them [first]; then leave them alone in bed; then beat them; and if, thereupon they pay you heed, do not seek to harm them. Behold, God is indeed most high, great!" In his commentary on the verse, the translator Muhammad Asad summarizes the interpretations of numerous (male) scholars who state that the verse is primarily symbolic. He further states that "some of the greatest Muslim scholars are of the opinion that it is just barely permissible, and should preferably be avoided" and that the Prophet Muhammad himself "intensely detested the idea of beating one's wife." See *The Message of the Qur'an,* translated and edited by Muhammad Asad.

19 Hidayatullah, *Feminist Edges of the Quran,* 14.

20 For an excellent discussion of the female-led prayer and the debates that surrounded it, see Hammer, *American Muslim Women.*

21 Author interview with Amina Wadud, East Bay, California, August 24, 2016.

22 "About Musawah," Musawah, n.d., www.musawah.org.

23 Wadud, *Inside the Gender Jihad,* 254.

24 Author interview with Sister Aisha Al-Adawiya, at the Schomburg Center for Research in Black Culture, New York Public Library, New York, November 23, 2015.

25 Idries Shah was a Sufi author and scholar of Afghani descent who was primarily raised in England. In 1964, he published *The Sufis,* a landmark text that introduced Sufism to the West as a part of Islam.

26 See Helminski, *Women of Sufism.*

27 See Women in Islam, "Dr. Betty Shabazz Award Ceremony."

28 Italics added.

29 Author interview with Asifa Quraishi-Landes, by phone, October 15, 2015.

30 Italics added. Within a community that was largely made up of visiting students and immigrants, Quraishi-Landes said she had little interaction with African American Muslims until college.

31 See KARAMAH: Muslim Women Lawyers for Human Rights, "About."

32 The Islamic Center of Southern California, Los Angeles, is one of the largest mosques in Southern California. It was founded in 1952, and for a long time, it was only mosque in the region.

33 Author interview with Laila Al-Marayati, by Skype, November 23, 2015.

34 Los Angeles County + University of Southern California Medical Center (LAC+USC) in Los Angeles, California. It is also known as Los Angeles County General.

35 For more on the role of the Palestinian struggle in U.S. activist movements and its impact on U.S Arab and Muslim communities, see Feldman, *A Shadow over Palestine*; and Pennock, *The Rise of the Arab American Left*.

36 See Padgett, "Why So Many Latinos Are Becoming Muslims."

37 Author interview with Hazel Gomez, by Skype, December 29, 2016.

38 Gomez's father would later be deported to Mexico because of his criminal record in addition to being undocumented, although he had lived in the United States since he was a one-year-old.

39 See Corinthians 11:2–16.

40 Italics added by author for emphasis.

CONCLUSION

1 Soul Flower Farm website, n.d., http://soulflowerfarm.blogspot.com.

BIBLIOGRAPHY

Abd-Allah, Umar F. *A Muslim in Victorian America: The Life of Alexander Russell Webb*. New York: Oxford University Press, 2006.

Abdullah, Zain. *Black Mecca: The African Muslims of Harlem*. Oxford: Oxford University Press, 2010.

Abu-Lughod, Lila. "Do Muslim Women Need Saving?" *Time* magazine, November 1, 2013.

Ahmed, Leila. *Women and Gender in Islam: Historical Roots of a Modern Debate*. New Haven, CT: Yale University Press, 1992.

Ahmed, Sara. *The Cultural Politics of Emotion*. New York: Routledge, 2004.

Aidi, Hisham. *Rebel Music: Race, Empire, and the New Muslim Youth Culture*. New York: Vintage, 2014.

Ammerman, Nancy T., ed. *Everyday Religion: Observing Modern Religious Lives*. Oxford: Oxford University Press, 2006.

Apple, R.W., Jr. "Iran: The Heart of the Matter." *New York Times Magazine*, March 11, 1979.

Arjana, Sophia Rose. *Muslims in the Western Imagination*. Oxford: Oxford University Press, 2015.

Asadullah, Ali. "Rap Music Mogul Disrespects Muslims with Magazine Cover." *Arabia. com*, 2002. www.arabia.com.

Associated Press. "Hassled, Heckled Kate Millett Not Leaving Iran, Yet." *Los Angeles Times*, March 16, 1979.

———. "Iranian Women March against Khomeini." *San Francisco Chronicle*, March 9, 1979.

———. "Iran's Women Protest: An Unveiled Threat." *San Francisco Sunday Examiner and Chronicle*, March 11, 1979.

Badran, Margot *Feminism in Islam: Secular and Religious Convergences*. Oxford: Oneworld Publications, 2009.

Baldwin, James. *The Fire Next Time*. 1st ed. 1962; reprint, New York: Vintage International, 1993.

Balfour, Lawrie. "Finding the Words: Baldwin, Race Consciousness, and Democratic Theory." In *Jame Baldwin Now*, edited by Dwight McBride, 75–102. New York: New York University Press, 1999.

Bayoumi, Moustafa. "East of the Sun (West of the Moon): Islam, the Ahmadis, and African America." *Journal of Asian American Studies* 4, no. 3 (2001): 251–263.

Bell, Jared, and Todd Steven Burroughs, eds. *A Lie of Reinvention: Correcting Manning Marable's Malcolm X*. Baltimore: Black Classic Press, 2015.

Bender, Marilyn. "Some Call Her the 'Karl Marx' of New Feminism." *New York Times*, July 20, 1970.

Berg, Herbert. *Elijah Muhammad and the Nation of Islam*. New York: New York University Press, 2009.

Berger, John. "Malcolm X as Visual Strategist." *New York Times*, September 19, 2012.

Best, Wallace D. *Passionately Human, No Less Divine: Religion and Culture in Black Chicago, 1915–1952*. Princeton, NJ: Princeton University Press, 2007.

Betteridge, Anne H. "To Veil or Not to Veil: A Matter of Protest or Policy." In *Women and Revolution in Iran*, edited by Guity Nashat, 109–128. Boulder, CO: Westview Press, 1983.

Billingsley, A., and B. Morrison-Rodriguez. "The Black Family in the 21st Century and the Church as an Action System: A Macro-perspective." *Journal of Human Behavior in the Social Environment* 1, nos. 2–3 (1998): 31–47.

Booker, James. "Lawson Hits Press; Defends His Role." *New York Amsterdam News*, November 21, 1959.

Breitman, George, ed. *Malcolm X Speaks: Selcted Speeches and Statements*. New York: Merit Publishers, 1965.

Brooks, Geraldine. *Nine Parts of Desire: The Hidden World of Islamic Women*. New York: Anchor Books, 1995.

Clegg, Claude Andrew. *An Original Man: The Life and Times of Elijah Muhammad*. New York: St. Martin's Press, 1998.

Collins, Patricia Hill. *Black Feminist Thought: Knowledge, Consciousness, and the Politics of Empowerment*. 2nd ed. New York: Routledge, 2000.

———. "Learning to Think for Ourselves: Malcolm X's Black Nationalism Reconsidered." In *Malcolm X: In Our Own Image*, edited by Joe Wood, 59–86. New York: St. Martin's Press, 1992.

———. "What's in a Name? Womanism, Black Feminism, and Beyond." *Black Scholar* 26, no. 1 (2001): 9–17.

Combahee River Collective. "A Black Feminist Statement." In *This Bridge Called My Back: Writings by Radical Women of Color*, edited by Cherríe Moraga and Gloria Anzaldúa, 234–244. Berkeley: Third Woman Press, 2002. Earlier published in *Capitalist Patriarchy and the Case for Social Feminism*, edited by Zillah Eisenstein. New York: Monthly Review Press, 1978.

cooke, miriam. "Multiple Critique: Islamic Feminist Rhetorical Strategies." *Nepantla: Views from South* 1, no. 1 (2000): 91–110.

Corber, Robert J. *Homosexuality in Cold War America: Resistance and the Crisis of Masculinity*. Durham, NC: Duke University Press, 1997.

Cottee, Simon, and Mia Bloom. "The Myth of the ISIS Female Suicide Bomber." *Atlantic*, September 2017. www.theatlantic.com.

Crenshaw, Kimberlé. "Mapping the Margins: Intersectionality, Identity Politics, and Violence against Women of Color." *Stanford Law Review* 43, no. 6 (1991): 1241–1299.

Cummings, Judith. "Demonstrators in City Back Iranian Women's Rights." *New York Times*, March 16, 1979.

Cuordileone, K. A. "'Politics in an Age of Anxiety': Cold War Political Culture and the Crisis in American Masculinity, 1949–1960." *Journal of American History* 87, no. 2 (2000): 515–545.

Curtis, Edward E., IV. *Black Muslim Religion in the Nation of Islam, 1960–1975*. Chapel Hill: University of North Carolina Press, 2006.

———. *Islam in Black America*. Albany: State University of New York Press, 2002.

———. *Muslims in America: A Short History*. Religion in American Life. Oxford: Oxford University Press, 2009.

Curwood, Anastasia C. *Stormy Weather: Middle-Class African American Marriages between the Two World Wars*. Chapel Hill: University of North Carolina Press, 2010.

Dannin, Robert. *Black Pilgrimage to Islam*. New York: Oxford University Press, 2005.

Daulatzai, Sohail. *Black Star, Crescent Moon: The Muslim International and Black Freedom beyond America*. Minneapolis: University of Minnesota Press, 2012.

Davis, Angela Y. *Blues Legacies and Black Feminism: Gertrude "Ma" Rainey, Bessie Smith, and Billie Holiday*. New York: Vintage Books, 1998.

Day, Iyko. *Alien Capital: Asian Racialization and the Logic of Settler Colonial Capitalism*. Durham, NC: Duke University Press, 2016.

DeCaro, Louis, Jr. *On the Side of My People: The Religious Life of Malcolm X*. New York: New York University Press, 1995.

Deutsch, Nathaniel. "The Asiatic Black Man: An African American Orientalism?" *Journal of Asian American Studies* 4, no. 3 (2001): 193–208.

Didier, Roger. "Those Who're Missionaries to Christians." *Chicago Defender*, August 19, 1922.

Domosh, Mona. "A 'Civilized' Commerce: Gender, 'Race', and Empire at the 1893 Chicago Exposition." *Cultural Geographies* 9 (2002): 181–201.

Donadey, Anne, and Huma Ahmed-Ghosh. "Why Americans Love Azar Nafisi's *Reading Lolita in Tehran*." *Signs: Journal of Women in Culture and Society* 33, no. 3 (2008): 623–646.

Dorman, William, and Mansour Farhang. *The U.S. Press and Iran*. Berkeley: University of California Press, 1988.

DuBois, W. E. B. *The Souls of Black Folk*. New York: Penguin Books, 1903.

Dudziak, Mary. *Cold War Civil Rights: Race and the Image of American Democracy*. Princeton, NJ: Princeton University Press, 2000.

Dyson, Michael Eric. *Making Malcolm: The Myth and Meaning of Malcolm X*. Oxford: Oxford University Press, 1996.

Editorial. "Iran's Women Talk Back." *San Francisco Chronicle*, March 9, 1979.

———. "Who Will Follow the Chador?" *Chicago Tribune*, March 19, 1979.

Ellicot City. "Civil War." Ellicott City, Maryland, website, n.d. www.ellicottcity.net.

Elsayed, Nourhan. "Feeling Muslim." *Chronicle* (Duke University), February 16, 2015.

Evanzz, Karl. *The Judas Facto: The Plot to Kill Malcolm X*. New York: Thunder's Mouth Press, 1992.

———. *The Messenger: The Rise and Fall of Elijah Muhammad*. New York: Vintage Books, 1999.

Faludi, Susan. *Backlash: The Undeclared War against American Women*. New York: Crown, 1991.

Federal Bureau of Investigation. "COINTELPRO." *FBI Records: The Vault*, n.d. www .fbi.gov.

Feldman, Keith. *A Shadow over Palestine: The Imperial Life of Race in America*. Minneapolis: University of Minnesota Press, 2015.

Fernea, Elizabeth Warnock. *In Search of Islamic Feminism: One Woman's Global Journey*. New York: Doubleday, 1998.

Field, Douglas. "Baldwin's FBI Files as Political Biography." In *The Cambridge Companion to James Baldwin*, edited by Michele Elan, 194–210. Cambridge: Cambridge University Press, 2015.

———. "Introduction." In *American Cold War Culture*, edited by Douglas Field, 1–16. Edinburgh: Edinburgh University Press, 2005.

Frazier, E. Franklin. *The Negro Family in the United States*. Chicago: University of Chicago Press, 1939.

Freeman, Elizabeth. "Marriage." In *Keywords for American Cultural Studies*, edited by Bruce Burgett and Glenn Hendler, 162–164. New York: New York University Press, 2007.

Friedan, Betty. *The Feminine Mystique*. New York: Norton, 1963.

Friedwald, Will. *A Biographical Guide to the Great Jazz and Pop Singers*. New York: Pantheon, 2010.

Gardell, Mattias. *In the Name of Elijah Muhammad: Louis Farrakhan and the Nation of Islam*. Durham, NC: Duke University Press, 1996.

Gibson, Dawn-Marie, and Jamillah Karim. *Women of the Nation: Between Black Protest and Sunni Islam*. New York: New York University Press, 2014.

Gillespie, Dizzy, and Al Fraser. *To Be, or Not . . . to Bop*. Minneapolis: University of Minnesota Press, 1979.

Goldschmidt, Henry, and Elizabeth McAlister, eds. *Race, Nation, and Religion in the Americas*. Oxford: Oxford University Press, 2004.

Gomez, Michael A. *Black Crescent: The Experience and Legacy of African Muslims in the Americas*. Cambridge: Cambridge University Press, 2005.

Goodell, William. *The American Slave Code in Theory and Practice*. 1853; reprint, London: Forgotten Press, 2015.

Goodwin, Jan. *Price of Honor: Muslim Women Lift the Veil of Silence on the Islamic World*. New York: Plume, 1994.

Goring, Darlene. "The History of Slave Marriage in the United States." *John Marshall Law Review* 39 (2006): 299–347.

Graham, Alfredo. "Dakota Staton Sues Muhammad: Asks Ban on Use of Muslim." *New Pittsburgh Courier*, June 16, 1962.

———. "Suit against Muhammad Ridiculous; Is a Publicity Stunt, Says Malcolm X." *Pittsburgh Courier*, June 23, 1962.

Grewal, Inderpal, and Caren Kaplan. "Global Identities: Theorizing Transnational Studies of Sexuality." *GLQ: A Journal of Lesbian and Gay Studies* 7, no. 4 (2001): 663–679.

Grewal, Zareena. *Islam Is a Foreign Country: American Muslims and the Global Crisis of Authority.* New York: New York University Press, 2014.

Griffin, Farah Jasmine. "'Ironies of the Saint': Malcolm X, Black Women, and the Price of Protection." In *Sisters in the Struggle: African American Women in the Civil Rights–Black Power Movement,* edited by Bettye Collier-Thomas and V. P. Franklin, 214–229. New York: New York University Press, 2001.

Haddad, Yvonne Yazbeck, Jane I. Smith, and Kathleen M. Moore. *Muslim Women in America: The Challenge of Islamic Identity Today.* Oxford: Oxford University Press, 2006.

Hall, David D., ed. *Lived Religion in America: Toward a History of Practice.* Princeton, NJ: Princeton University Press, 1997.

Hall, Stuart. "New Ethnicities." In *Stuart Hall: Critical Dialogues in Cultural Studies,* edited by David Morley and Kuan-Hsing Chen, 441–449. London: Routledge, 1996.

Hammer, Juliane. *American Muslim Women, Religious Authority, and Activism: More than a Prayer.* Austin: University of Texas Press, 2013.

———. "Marriage in American Muslim Communities." *Religious Compass* 9, no. 2 (2015): 35–44.

Hammer, Juliane, and Omid Safi, eds. *The Cambridge Companion to American Islam.* Cambridge: Cambridge University Press, 2013.

Hassan, Riffat. "Marriage: Islamic Discourses." In *Encyclopedia of Women and Islamic Cultures,* edited by Suad Joseph. Leiden: Brill Online, 2009. www.brill.com.

Helminski, Camille Adams. *Women of Sufism: A Hidden Treasure.* Boston: Shambhala, 2003.

Hidayatullah, Aysha A. *Feminist Edges of the Quran.* Oxford: Oxford University Press, 2014.

Higginbotham, Evelyn Brooks. *Righteous Discontent: The Women's Movement in the Black Baptist Church, 1880–1920.* Cambridge, MA: Harvard University Press, 1993.

Hirschkind, Charles, and Saba Mahmood. "Feminism, the Taliban, and the Politics of Counterinsurgency." *Anthropological Quarterly* 75, no. 2 (2002): 339–354.

Hoffman, Paul. "However Slight, an Opposition Does Exist in Iran." *New York Times,* April 2, 1978.

Hoodfar, Homa. "The Veil in Their Minds and on Our Heads: Veiling Practices and Muslim Women." In *The Politics of Culture in the Shadow of Capital,* edited by Lisa Lowe and David Lloyd, 249–279. Durham, NC: Duke University Press, 1997.

hooks, bell. *Feminist Theory from Margin to Center.* Cambridge, MA: South End Press, 1984.

Howell, Sally. *Old Islam in Detroit: Rediscovering the Muslim American Past.* Oxford: Oxford University Press, 2014.

Huntington, Samuel P. *The Clash of Civilizations and the Remaking of World Order.* New York: Simon & Schuster, 1996.

Ibrahim, Youssef M. "Iran's 'New' Women Rebel at Returning to the Veil." *New York Times,* March 11, 1979.

Jackson, Sherman A. *Islam and the Blackamerican*. Oxford: Oxford University Press, 2005.

Jaynes, Gregory. "Iranian Women: Looking beyond the Chador." *New York Times Magazine*, April 22, 1979.

——. "Iran Women March against Restraints on Dress and Rights." *New York Times*, March 11, 1979.

Jeffries, Bayyinah. *A Nation Can Rise No Higher than Its Women: African American Muslim Women in the Movement for Black Self-Determination, 1950–1975*. Lanham, MD: Lexington Books, 2014.

Jones, Jacqueline. *Labor of Love, Labor of Sorrow: Black Women, Work, and the Family, from Slavery to Present*. 1985; rev. and updated ed., New York: Basic Books, 2010.

Jordan, June. "To Be Black and Female." *New York Times Book Review*, March 18, 1979.

Kahf, Mohja. *The Girl in the Tangerine Scarf*. New York: Caroll & Graf, 2006.

——. "The Marvelous Women." In *E-mails from Scheherazad*. Gainesville: University Press of Florida, 2003.

——. *Western Representations of Muslim Women: From Termagant to Odalisque*. Austin: University of Texas Press, 1999.

Kaplan, Amy. "Manifest Domesticity." *American Literature* 70, no. 3 (1998): 581–606.

KARAMAH: Muslim Women Lawyers for Human Rights. "About," n.d. http://karamah.org.

Karim, Jamillah. *American Muslim Women: Negotiating Race, Class, and Gender within the Ummah*. New York: New York University Press, 2009.

Kazi, Seema. *Muslim Women in India*. London: Minority Rights Group International, 1999.

Kelber, Mim. "Iran: Five Days in March." *Ms.* magazine, June 1979.

Kelley, Robin D. G. *Freedom Dreams: The Black Radical Imagination*. Boston: Beacon Press, 2002.

Khabeer, Su'ad Abdul. *Muslim Cool: Race, Religion, and Hip Hop in the United States*. New York: New York University Press, 2016.

Kidd, Thomas S. *American Christians and Islam: Evangelical Culture and Muslims from the Colonial Period to the Age of Terrorism*. Princeton, NJ: Princeton University Press, 2009.

Kifner, John. "Iran's Women Fought, Won, and Dispersed." *New York Times*, March 16, 1979.

Latifa, My Forbidden Face: Growing Up under the Taliban—a Young Woman's Story. New York: Hyperion, 2003.

Leak, Jeffrey B. "Malcolm X and Black Masculinity in Progress." In *The Cambridge Companion to Malcolm X*, edited by Robert E. Terrill. Cambridge: Cambridge University Press, 2010.

Lincoln, C. Eric. *The Black Muslims in America*. 3rd ed. Grand Rapids, MI: William B. Eerdmans Publishing Co., 1994.

Lindsey, Ben B., and Wainwright Evans. *The Companionate Marriage*. New York: Garden City Publishing, 1929. Available at the *Internet Archive*. https://archive.org.

Lipsitz, George. *The Possessive Investment in Whiteness: How White People Profit from Identity Politics*. Philadelphia: Temple University Press, 1998.

Lye, Colleen. *America's Asia: Racial Form and American Literature, 1893–1945*. Princeton, NJ: Princeton University Press, 2004.

Mahmood, Saba. *Politics of Piety: The Islamic Revival and the Feminist Subject*. 2005; reprint, Princeton, NJ: Princeton University Press, 2011.

Mahmoody, Betty. *Not without My Daughter*. With William Hoffer. New York: St. Martin's Press, 1987.

Majeed, Debra. *Polygyny: What It Means When African American Women Share Their Husbands*. Gainesville: University Press of Florida, 2015.

Mamiya, Lawrence H. "African-American Muslims." In *Encyclopedia of Muslim-American History*, edited by Edward E. Curtis IV, 12–18. New York: Facts On File, 2012.

Marable, Manning. *Malcolm X: A Life of Reinvention*. New York: Penguin Books, 2011.

May, Elaine Tyler. *Homeward Bound: American Families in the Cold War Era*. New York: Basic Books, 2008.

McCloud, Aminah Beverly. *African American Islam*. New York: Routledge, 1995.

McGuire, Meredith. *Lived Religion: Faith and Practice in Everyday Life*. Oxford: Oxford University Press, 2008.

Mernissi, Fatima. *Beyond the Veil: Male-Female Dynamics in Modern Muslim Society*. 1975; 2nd ed., Bloomington: Indiana University Press, 1987.

———. *The Veil and the Male Elite: A Feminist Interpretation of Women's Rights in Islam*. New York: Basic Books, 1992.

The Message of the Qur'an, translated and edited by Muhammad Asad. Gibraltar: Dar Al Andalus, 1980.

Millett, Kate. *Going to Iran*. New York: Coward, McCann, & Geoghegan, 1982.

———. *Sexual Politics*. New York: Doubleday, 1970.

Mitchem, Stephanie Y. "Womanist Theology: Looking to the Future." *New Theology Review* 21, no. 1 (February 2008): 52–56.

Moallem, Minoo. *Between Warrior Brother and Veiled Sister: Islamic Fundamentalism and the Politics of Patriarchy in Iran*. Berkeley: University of California Press, 2005.

Moraga, Cherríe, and Gloria Anzaldúa. *This Bridge Called My Back: Writings by Radical Women of Color*. Berkeley, CA: Third Woman Press, 2002.

Morrison, Toni. *Playing in the Dark: Whiteness and the Literary Imagination*. New York: Random House, 1992.

———. *Sula*. New York: Penguin Books, 1973.

———. "Toni Morrison on Cinderella's Stepsisters," *Ms.* magazine. September 1979.

Muhammad, Elijah. *Message to the Blackman in America*. Philadelphia: House of Knowledge Publications, 1965.

Murray, Rolland. *Our Living Manhood: Literature, Black Power, and Masculine Ideology*. Philadelphia: University of Pennsylvania Press, 2007.

Nafisi, Azar. *Reading Lolita in Tehran: A Memoir in Books*. New York: Random House, 2003.

Nashat, Guity, ed. *Women and Revolution in Iran*. Boulder, CO: Westview Press, 1983.

O'Leary, Kevin. "The Legacy of Proposition 13." *Time* magazine, June 27, 2009. http://time.com.

Omi, Michael, and Howard Winant. *Racial Formation in the United States: From the 1960s to the 1990s*. 2nd ed. New York: Routledge, 1994.

Orsi, Robert. *Between Heaven and Earth: The Religious Worlds People Make and the Scholars Who Study Them*. Princeton, NJ: Princeton University Press, 2006.

———. "Everyday Miracles: The Study of Lived Religions." In *Lived Religion in America: Toward a History of Practice*, edited by David D. Hall, 3–21. Princeton, NJ: Princeton University Press, 1997.

Pabst, Naomi. "Iran Expulsion Terrifying, Says Kate Millett." *Los Angeles Times*, March 19, 1979.

Padgett, Tim. "Why So Many Latinos Are Becoming Muslims." *WLRN Miami*, October 9, 2013. wlrn.org.

Parks, Gordon. "'What Their Cry Means to Me'—a Negro's Own Evaluation." *Life* magazine, May 31, 1963.

Pennock, Pamela E. *The Rise of the Arab American Left: Activist, Allies, and Their Fight against Imperialism and Racism, 1960s–1980s*. Chapel Hill: University of North Carolina Press, 2017.

Perry, Bruce, ed. *Malcolm X: The Last Speeches*. New York: Pathfinder Press, 1989.

Pinckney, Darryl. "The Magic of James Baldwin." *New York Review of Books*, November 19, 1998.

Pew Research Center. "A Demographic Portrait of Muslim Americans." Section 1 of *Muslim Americans: No Signs of Growth in Alienation or Support for Extremism*. Washington, DC: Pew Research Center, August 30, 2011. www.people-press.org.

Powers, Charles T. "Veiled Warning: Modern Iran Women Cool to Holy Edicts." *Los Angeles Times*, March 9, 1979.

Pratt, Mary Louise. "Arts of the Contact Zone." *Profession*, 1991, 33–40.

Prentiss, Craig R., ed. *Religion and the Creation of Race and Ethnicity*. New York: New York Univeristy Press, 2003.

Prial, Frank J. "Feminist Philosopher: Katherine Murray Millett." *New York Times*, August 27, 1970.

Quraishi, Asifa. "Understanding Sharia in an American Context." Policy brief. Washington, DC: Institute for Social Policy and Understanding. July 26, 2011. www.ispu.org.

Radford-Hill, Sheila. "Womanizing Malcolm X." In *The Cambridge Companion to Malcolm X*, edited by Robert E. Terrill. Cambridge: Cambridge University Press, 2010.

Rana, Junaid. "The Story of Islamophobia." *Souls* 9, no. 2 (2007): 148–161.

———. *Terrifying Muslims: Race and Labor in the South Asian Diaspora*. Durham, NC: Duke University Press, 2011.

Randal, Jonathan C. "Militant Women Demonstrators Attack Khomeini Aide Who Heads Iran Radio." *Washington Post*, March 12, 1979.

———. "Sexual Politics in Iran: Kate Millett Finds Tehran's Feminists Are Not United." *Washington Post*, March 12, 1979.

———. "Women Protest in Iran, Shout 'Down with Khomeini.'" *Washington Post*, March 9, 1979.

Reuters. "U.S. Feminist Calls Khomeini 'Chauvinist.'" *San Francisco Chronicle*, March 12, 1979.

Rickford, Russell J. *Betty Shabazz, Surviving Malcom X: A Journey of Strength from Wife to Widow to Heroine*. Naperville, IL: Sourcebooks, 2003.

Rivera, Nancy. "Feminist Fears for Iran Women Leaders." *Los Angeles Times*, April 10, 1979.

Robinson, Major. "New York Beat." *Jet* magazine, November 28, 1957.

Ross, Rosetta E. *Witnessing and Testifying: Black Women, Religion, and Civil Rights*. Minneapolis: Fortress Press, 2003.

Rouse, Carolyn Moxley. *Engaged Surrender: African American Women and Islam*. Berkeley: University of California Press, 2004.

Sadiq, Mufti Muhammad. "Brief Report of the Work in America." *Moslem Sunrise*, July 1922.

———. "Brief Report of the Work in America." *Moslem Sunrise*, January 1923.

———. "If Jesus Comes to America." *Moslem Sunrise*, April 1922.

———. "My Advice to the Muhammedans in America." *Moslem Sunrise*, October 1921.

———. "One Year's Moslem Missionary Work in America." *Moslem Sunrise*, July 1921.

———. "The Only Solution of Color Prejudice." *Moslem Sunrise*, October 1921.

———. "A Verse from the Holy Book—AL-QURAN." *Moslem Sunrise*, July 1921.

Said, Edward. *Orientalism*. New York: Vintage Books, 1978.

Sanchez, Sonia. *A Blues Book for Blue Black Magical Women*. Detroit, MI: Broadside Press, 1974.

———. Interview, conducted by Blackside. Transcript for *Eyes on the Prize II Interviews*, PBS series, March 7, 1989. St. Louis, MO: Washington University Libraries, Film and Media Archive, Henry Hampton Collection. https://library .wustl.edu.

———. "We Are Muslim Women." Poem. *Black World* magazine, January 1974.

Sasson, Jean. *The Princess Trilogy*. 1992–1999; reprinted, Marietta, GA: Windsor-Brooke Books, 2001–2002.

Schlesinger, Arthur. "The Crisis of American Masculinity." *Esquire* magazine, November 1958, 63–65.

Shabazz, Betty. "The Legacy of My Husband, Malcolm X." *Ebony*, June 1969, 172–182.

Shabazz, Ilyasah. *Growing up X: A Memoir by the Daughter of Malcolm X*. New York: One World Books, 2002.

Shah, Idries. *The Sufis*. New York: Doubleday, 1964.

Shaikh, Yasmine. "We Have a Marriage Crisis." *Huffington Post*, December 27, 2014. www.huffingtonpost.com.

Sherman, Robert. "MUSIC; Ending a Recital Year with a Commencement." *New York Times*, May 24, 1998.

Shulman, George. "Baldwin, Prophecy, and Politics." In *James Baldwin: America and Beyond*, edited by Cora Kaplan and Bill Schwartz, 106–125. Ann Arbor: University of Michigan Press, 2011.

Siddiqui, Samana. "Divorce among American Muslims: Statistics, Challenges, and Solutions." *Sound Vision*, October 2009. www.soundvision.com.

Simmons, Gwendolyn Zoharah. "Are We Up to the Challenge? The Need for a Radical Re-ordering of the Islamic Discourse on Women." In *Progressive Muslims: On Justice, Gender, and Pluralism*, edited by Omid Safi, 235–248. Oxford: Oneworld Publications, 2003.

Simons, Margaret A. "Racism and Feminism: A Schism in the Sisterhood." *Feminist Studies* 5, no. 2 (Summer 1979): 384–401.

Smith, Barbara. "Racism and Women's Studies." In "National Women's Studies Association: Selected Conference Proceedings, 1979," special issue, *Frontiers: A Journal of Women's Studies* 5, no. 1 (1980): 48–49.

Sokolsky, George E. "These Days: The Nation of Islam." *Washington Post*, June 4, 1962.

Spear, Allan H. *Black Chicago: The Making of a Negro Ghetto, 1890–1920*. Chicago: University of Chicago Press, 1967.

Steinem, Gloria. "The Way We Were—and Will Be." *Ms.* magazine, December 1979.

Still, Larry. "Why Singer Believes in Four Wives: Dakota Staton Reveals Why She Is Polygamy Supporter." *Jet* magazine, April 19, 1962, 18–20.

Tabari, Azar. "The Enigma of Veiled Iranian Women." *Feminist Review* 5 (1980): 19–31.

———. "The Women's Movement in Iran: A Hopeful Prognosis." *Feminist Studies* 12, no. 2 (1986): 342–360.

Talbot, Margaret. "The Story of a Hate Crime." *New Yorker*, June 22, 2015.

Tate, Sonsyrea. *Little X: Growing Up in the Nation of Islam*. San Francisco: HarperSanFrancisco, 1997.

Taylor, Ula. "As-Salaam Alaikum, My Sister, Peace Be unto You: The Honorable Elijah Muhammad and the Women Who Followed Him." *Race and Society* 1, no. 2 (1998): 177–196.

———. "Elijah Muhammad's Nation of Islam: Separatism, Regendering, and a Secular Approach to Black Power after Malcolm X (1965–1975)." In *Freedom North: Black Freedom Struggles outside the South, 1940–1980*, edited by Jeanne Theoharis and Komozi Woodard. New York: Palgrave Macmillan, 2003.

Tchen, John Kuo Wei. *New York before Chinatown: Orientalism and the Shaping of American Culture, 1776–1882*. Baltimore: Johns Hopkins University Press, 1999.

Thaha, Mrs. Mustapha [Rahatullah]. "Islam My Savior." *Moslem Sunrise*, October 1922.

Tribune Wire Service. "Millett, Friend Arrested, Told to Leave Iran." *Chicago Tribune*, March 19, 1979.

———. "Mob of Men Attacks Women Protesting Loss of Rights in Iran." *Chicago Tribune*, March 11, 1979.

Tucker, Judith E. *Women, Family, and Gender in Islamic Law*. Cambridge: Cambridge Univeristy Press, 2008.

Tulloch, Carol. *The Birth of Cool: Style Narratives of the African Diaspora*. London: Bloomsbury, 2016.

Turman, Eboni Marshall. "'The Greatest Tool of the Devil': Mamie, Malcolm X, and PolitiX of the Black Madonna in Black Churches and the Nation of Islam in the United States." *Journal of Africana Religions* 3, no. 1 (2015): 130–150.

Turner, Richard Brent. *Islam in the African American Experience*. Bloomington: Indiana University Press, 1997.

Viner, Katharine. "Feminism as Imperialism." *Guardian*, September 21, 2002.

Wadud, Amina. "American Muslim Identity: Race and Ethnicity in Progressive Islam." In *Progressive Muslims: On Justice, Gender, and Pluralism*, edited by Omid Safi, 270–285. Oxford: Oneworld Publications, 2003.

———. *Inside the Gender Jihad: Women's Reform in Islam*. Oxford: Oneworld Publications, 2006.

———. *Qur'an and Woman: Rereading the Sacred Text from a Woman's Perspective*. 1992; reprint, Oxford: Oxford University Press, 1999.

Walker, Alice. "One Child of One's Own—a Chapter on Creativity," *Ms.* magazine, August 1979.

———. "Coming Apart." In *The Womanist Reader*, edited by Layli Phillips. 1979; reprint, New York: Routledge, 2006.

———. *In Search of Our Mothers' Gardens: Womanist Prose*. San Diego, CA: Harcourt Brace Jovanovich, 1983.

Wallace, Michele. *Black Macho and the Myth of the Superwoman*. New York: Dial Press, 1978.

Wallace, Mike. Interview, conducted by Blackside. Transcript for *Eyes on the Prize II Interviews*, PBS series, October 12, 1988. St. Louis, MO: Washington University Libraries, Film and Media Archive, Henry Hampton Collection. https://library .wustl.edu.

Wallace, Mike, and Louis Lomax, producers. *The Hate That Hate Produced*. Documentary, *CBS News*. Newark, NJ: WNTA-TV, 1959.

Wolcott, Victoria W. *Remaking Respectability: African American Women in Interwar Detroit*. Gender and American Culture, edited by Thadious M. Davis and Linda K. Kerber. Chapel Hill: University of North Carolina Press, 2001.

Women in Islam. "Dr. Betty Shabazz Award Ceremony," [2010]. www.womeninislam.org.

WTTW. "From Riots to Renaissance: Bronzeville: The Black Metropolis." *DuSable to Obama: Chicago's Black Metropolis*. Website. PBS affiliate station. May 26, 2016. www.wttw.com.

X, Malcolm, and Alex Haley. *The Autobiography of Malcolm X*. 1965; reprint, New York: Ballantine, 1992.

X, Marvin, and Faruk. "Islam and Black Art: An Interview with LeRoi Jones." In *Conversations with Amiri Baraka*, edited by Charlie Reilly, 51–61. Jackson: University of Mississippi Press, 1994.

Yuenger, James. "New Revolt in Iran: Feminism." *Chicago Tribune*, March 11, 1979.

Zinn, Maxine Baca, and Bonnie Thornton Dill. "Theorizing Difference from Multiracial Feminism." *Feminist Studies* 22, no. 2 (1996): 321–331.

Zuberi, Hena. "The Muslim Marriage Crisis." *Muslim Matters*, September 27, 2013. www.muslimmatters.org.

INDEX

Abdul-Jabbar, Kareem, 22
Abu-Lughod, Lila, 25
Abu-Salah, Razan, 12–13, 228n13
Abu-Salah, Yusor, 12–13, 228nn13–14
affective insurgency: as againstness, 15–16; of Betty Shabazz, 119; of Black Muslim women's bodies, 23–24; of Black U.S. women, 5–6, 23–24, 43–44; defined, 15–16; of Islam, 10, 186, 219–20; Muslim-ness as, 13, 23; of U.S. Muslim feminism, 211–12; of U.S. Muslim women, 23–24, 106, 211–12, 220
affirmative action, 171, 245n61
African American Women's Clubs, 55–56, 114
againstness, 15–16, 228n18; affective insurgency as, 15–16; of U.S. Muslim women, 211
Ahmad, Hazrat Mirza Ghulam, 67–68, 231n7, 233n33; as heretic, 234n45; on "jihad of words," 72; teachings of, 64, 73
Ahmadi Muslims: as *kafirs*, 45, 231n7; persecution of, 45, 231n8; and Sunni Muslims, 45, 235n49. *See also* Ahmadiyya Movement in Islam; "Four American Moslem Ladies"; Watts, Florence
Ahmadiyya Movement in Islam (AMI), 33, 34–35, 37, 39; American converts in, 41–42; and anti-Black racism, 63; Black Americans, appeal to, 62–63, 65–66, 231n3; Black women in, 41–42, 220; Chicago mosque, 60 fig. 1.3, 64–65; as community space, 56; gender in, 66–68; gender roles in, 115, 150; as

heretical movement, 64; jazz musicians in, 140, 141–42; and kinship, 56; marginalization of, 45; marriage in, 115–16; and Muslim Brotherhood of America, 111; publicity efforts of, 63, 65, 66; racial caste system of, 235n49; and racial equality, 66, 231n3; reading materials of, 72–73; as space of safety, 45; universalism of, 235n49; white converts to, 68. *See also* Ahmadi Muslims; "Four American Moslem Ladies"; Watts, Florence
Ahmed, Leila, 153–54, 197, 201; on colonial feminism, 25
Ahmed, Sarah, 228n18
Aisha (wife of Muhammad), 193
al-'Adawiya, Rabi'a, 193
Al-Adawiya, Aisha, 186, 189–94, 190 fig. 5.1; Betty Shabazz, friendship with, 112, 119, 192; conversion to Islam, 191–93, 211; naming of, 193; and Nation of Islam, 191–92
al-Hibri, Azizah, 197
Ali, Maulana Muhammad, 73
Ali, Muhammad, 22
Ali, Najee, 153, 157
Ali, Noble Drew (Timothy Drew), 57, 233n38; and masculinity, 45
Allen, Harvey, 157
Al-Marayati, Laila, 186, 187, 197, 199–203, 199 fig. 5.3; on "bully Islam," 203; on feminism, 203
AMILA (American Muslims Intent on Learning and Activism), 194

ABOUT THE AUTHOR

Sylvia Chan-Malik is Assistant Professor in the Departments of American and Women's and Gender Studies at Rutgers University–New Brunswick.